Lecture Notes in Computer Science 10475

Commenced Publication in 1973
Founding and Former Series Editors:
Gerhard Goos, Juris Hartmanis, and Jan van Leeuwen

Antónia Lopes · Rogério de Lemos (Eds.)

Software Architecture

11th European Conference, ECSA 2017
Canterbury, UK, September 11–15, 2017
Proceedings

 Springer

Editors
Antónia Lopes
Universidade de Lisboa
Lisbon
Portugal

Rogério de Lemos
University of Kent
Canterbury
UK

ISSN 0302-9743   ISSN 1611-3349   (electronic)
Lecture Notes in Computer Science
ISBN 978-3-319-65830-8   ISBN 978-3-319-65831-5   (eBook)
DOI 10.1007/978-3-319-65831-5

Library of Congress Control Number: 2017948645

LNCS Sublibrary: SL2 – Programming and Software Engineering

Printed on acid-free paper

This Springer imprint is published by Springer Nature
The registered company is Springer International Publishing AG
The registered company address is: Gewerbestrasse 11, 6330 Cham, Switzerland

Preface

This volume contains the proceedings of the 11th European Conference on Software Architecture (ECSA 2017), held during September 11–15, 2017, at the University of Kent at Canterbury, UK.

The goal of the European Conference on Software Architecture is to provide researchers, practitioners, and educators with a platform to present and discuss the most recent, innovative, and significant findings and experiences in the field of software architecture research and practice. ECSA 2017 has continued the tradition of attracting a varied type of submissions ranging from fundamental research to applied work in industrial context, focused on different types of systems and challenges raised by new developments.

The technical program included a main research track of accepted papers, keynote talks, a doctoral symposium track, a poster track, and a tool demonstration track. In addition, we also offered several workshops on diverse topics related to the software architecture discipline.

These proceedings contain nine regular and six short papers. They were selected by the Program Committee (PC) among 54 submissions. Each submission was assigned to at least three PC members for reviewing and was discussed afterwards during a 10-day electronic meeting. We sincerely thank the PC members and the 25 external reviewers for their work in preparing the 164 reviews and the effort taking in discussing the submissions.

The selected papers constitute a very interesting program and address topics including software architecture analysis and verification, software architecture evolution, architectural decisions, and software architecture practice. In addition to the selected papers, we were quite fortunate to have two excellent invited talks: Paola Inverardi of the University of Aquila, Italy on "Software Architectures: How Components Can Go Politely Social," and Peter Eeles from IBM on "How to Architect Anything."

We are grateful to the University of Kent for hosting ECSA 2017, the Organizing Committee for their excellent job, and the ECSA Steering Committee for their guidance. We thank also the providers of EasyChair Conference Management System that was a great help in organizing the submission and reviewing process and in the preparation of the proceedings. We would also like to acknowledge the prompt and professional support from Springer, who published these proceedings in printed and electronic volumes as part of the *Lecture Notes in Computer Science* series.

Finally, we would like to thank the authors of all the ECSA 2017 submissions and the attendees of the conference for their participation and we look forward to seeing you in Madrid for ECSA 2018.

September 2017

Antónia Lopes
Rogério de Lemos

Organization

General Chair

Rogério de Lemos   University of Kent, UK

Program Committee

Muhammad Ali Babar	University of Adelaide, Australia
Jesper Andersson	Linnaeus University, Sweden
Paris Avgeriou	University of Groningen, The Netherlands
Rami Bahsoon	University of Birmingham, UK
Luciano Baresi	Politecnico di Milano, Italy
Thais Batista	Federal University of Rio Grande do Norte, Brazil
Stefan Biffl	TU Wien, Austria
Jan Bosch	Chalmers University of Technology, Sweden
Tomas Bures	Charles University, Czech Republic
Rafael Capilla	Universidad Rey Juan Carlos, Madrid, Spain
Michel Chaudron	Chalmers, Gothenborg University, Sweden
Vittorio Cortellessa	Università dell'Aquila, Italy
Ivica Crnkovic	Chalmers University of Technology, Sweden
Carlos E. Cuesta	Universidad Rey Juan Carlos, Madrid, Spain
Elisabetta Di Nitto	Politecnico di Milano, Italy
Khalil Drira	LAAS-CNRS, France
Laurence Duchien	University of Lille, France
Matthias Galster	University of Canterbury, New Zealand
David Garlan	Carnegie Mellon University, USA
Ian Gorton	Northeastern University, Seattle, USA
Volker Gruhn	Universität Duisburg-Essen, Germany
Rich Hilliard	IEEE Computer Society, USA
Paola Inverardi	Università dell'Aquila, Italy
Pooyan Jamshidi	Carnegie Mellon University, USA
Anton Jansen	Philips Innovation Services, The Netherlands
Patricia Lago	Vrije Universiteit Amsterdam, The Netherlands
Antónia Lopes (Chair)	Universidade de Lisboa, Portugal
Sam Malek	University of California, Irvine, USA
Raffaela Mirandola	Politecnico di Milano, Italy
Henry Muccini	Università dell'Aquila, Italy
Tomi Männistö	University of Helsinki, Finland
Elisa Nakagawa	University of Sao Paulo, Brazil
Elena Navarro	University of Castilla-La Mancha, Spain
Flavio Oquendo	Université Bretagne-Sud, France
Claus Pahl	Dublin City University, Ireland

Cesare Pautasso	University of Lugano, Switzerland
Jennifer Perez	Technical University of Madrid, Spain
Ralf Reussner	Karlsruhe Institute of Technology, Germany
Riccardo Scandariato	Chalmers, University of Gothenburg, Sweden
Clemens Szyperski	Microsoft Research, USA
Bedir Tekinerdogan	Wageningen University, The Netherlands
Rainer Weinreich	Johannes Kepler University Linz, Austria
Danny Weyns	Linnaeus University, Sweden
Eoin Woods	Artechra, USA
Uwe Zdun	University of Vienna, Austria
Liming Zhu	Data61, CSIRO, Australia
Olaf Zimmermann	HSR FHO, Switzerland

Additional Reviewers

Fahimeh A. Moghaddam	Milena Guessi	Reinhold Plösch
Ana Paula Allian	Mahmoud Hammad	Clément Quinton
Hugo Andrade	Robert Heinrich	Paul Rimba
Lucas B. Oliveira	Sebastian D. Krach	Daniel Romero
Sofia Charalampidou	Max E. Kramer	Misha Strittmatter
Daniel Feitosa	Ivano Malavolta	Smrithi Rekha
Joshua Garcia	Christian Manteuffel	Hang Yin
Federico Giaimo	Jürgen Musil	
Iris Groher	Brauner Oliveira	

Software Architectures:
How Components Can Go Politely Social
(Invited Talk)

Paola Inverardi

Università dell'Aquila, L'Aquila, Italy

Software architectures (SA) serve many purposes. One of the most interesting characteristics of SA is their glue/connectivity nature that allows subsystems/components to interact, correctly. I will discuss this behavioral facet of SA in a historical perspective by also crossing the software engineering boundaries. Recent approaches in which SAs are instrumental to synthesize correct systems in an open world setting characterized by partial knowledge of the final system components provide a fresher interpretation of their role in the design of future software systems.

Contents

Software Architecture Practice

Software Architecture Analysis and Verification

Synthesis and Quantitative Verification of Tradeoff Spaces for Families of Software Systems

Javier Cámara[✉], David Garlan, and Bradley Schmerl

Carnegie Mellon University, Pittsburgh, PA 15213, USA
{jcmoreno,garlan,schmerl}@cs.cmu.edu

Abstract. Designing software subject to *uncertainty* in a way that provides guarantees about its run-time behavior while achieving an acceptable balance between multiple extra-functional properties is still an open problem. Tools and techniques to inform engineers about poorly-understood design spaces in the presence of uncertainty are needed. To tackle this problem, we propose an approach that combines synthesis of spaces of system design alternatives from formal specifications of architectural styles with probabilistic formal verification. The main contribution of this paper is a formal framework for specification-driven synthesis and analysis of design spaces that provides formal guarantees about the correctness of system behaviors and satisfies quantitative properties (e.g., defined over system qualities) subject to uncertainty, which is factored as a first-class entity.

Keywords: Tradeoff analysis · Uncertainty · Architectural style · Architecture synthesis · Formal guarantees · Quantitative verification · Probabilistic model checking

1 Introduction

Engineering modern software-intensive systems requires engineers to explore design spaces that are often poorly understood due to their complexity and different kinds of *uncertainty* about the behavior of their constituent components [8] (e.g., faults, network delays). Achieving a good design with behavioral guarantees and a balance between extra-functional concerns is challenging – especially when the context that the system will run in contains unknown attributes that are hard to predict. Designing for this context is as often a matter of luck as it is principled engineering.

Design decisions frequently involve the selection and composition of loosely-coupled, pre-existing components or services with different levels of quality (e.g., of reliability, performance) that may be offered by independent providers. For instance, modern robotic software systems consist of a set of processes running in components, potentially on a number of different hosts, connected at run time in a peer-to-peer topology [22]. Different implementations of these components

© Springer International Publishing AG 2017
A. Lopes and R. de Lemos (Eds.): ECSA 2017, LNCS 10475, pp. 3–21, 2017.
DOI: 10.1007/978-3-319-65831-5_1

(e.g., for navigation, planning) offer different levels of energy consumption, reliability, or accuracy. Similarly, service-based systems are built by composing third-party services with different levels of availability, performance, and cost [18]. Quality attributes of constituent components in such systems are often subject to *uncertainties* introduced by nondeterministic behaviors of individual components (e.g., derived from the lack of control over system components in the cloud, humans-in-the-loop, or physical interactions in cyber-physical systems) that can be captured in the form of probability distributions (e.g., over the response time of a Web service, fault occurrence). For a designer, *it is difficult to envisage how these uncertainties will affect overall system behavior and qualities, despite the fact that they can sometimes have a remarkable impact on them.*

Often, design spaces are also constrained by the need to design systems within certain patterns or constraints that comprise an architectural style. Architectural styles [23] characterize the design space of families of software systems in terms of patterns of structural organization, defining a *vocabulary* of component and connector types, as well as a set of *constraints* on how they can be combined. Styles help designers constrain design space exploration to within a set of legal structures that the system must conform to. However, while the structure of a system may be constrained by some style, there is still considerable design flexibility left for exploring the tradeoffs on many of the qualities that a system must achieve.

Formal characterization of architectural styles combined with formal methods like Alloy [11] have proved to be a valuable tool to aid designers in exploring rich solution spaces, by synthesizing possible system configurations that satisfy the constraints imposed by a given architectural style [3,7,19]. However, these solutions tend to focus on structural properties, and when available, analysis of system behaviors and qualities are performed separately. So, these approaches are limited in their ability to consider interactions between behavioral properties and qualities (e.g., impact of failure in serving a request and a subsequent retry on overall system performance). Moreover, the approaches that explore non-structural properties tend to be based either on dynamic analysis or simulations. Such approaches *cannot exhaustively explore the state space of design alternatives or provide formal guarantees* that encompass both their behavior and qualities (both in general, and in particular, in the presence of *uncertainties*).

Architects need tools and techniques that can help them explore this complex design space and guide them to good designs. Providing such tool support demands investigating questions such as: (i) how to integrate formal descriptions of structural, behavioral, and quality aspects of design alternatives to enable integrated reasoning about all these aspects, and (ii) how to effectively streamline the exploration of the solution space while providing formal guarantees about solutions in the presence of uncertainty (e.g., with respect to correctness of behaviors, or quantitative and structural constraints).

This paper explores these questions by introducing a formal framework that enables the: (i) exhaustive *exploration of a rich space of design alternatives* by automatically synthesizing architecture configurations that satisfy the constraints imposed by an architectural style, and (ii) provision of *formal guarantees with respect to the functional behaviors and qualities* (i.e., extra-functional properties) of configurations by analyzing exhaustively the state space of each configuration's behavior. Our framework explicitly considers *interactions between functional behaviors and extra-functional properties* while factoring in *uncertainty* as a first-class entity.

The framework is grounded on two related formalisms: (i) predicate logic and sets capture the structural aspects of system configurations, and (ii) probabilistic automata and formal quantitative verification (e.g., probabilistic model checking [15]) capture behavior and qualities.

The key novelty of our approach *is that it is the first, to the best of our knowledge, that combines automatic synthesis of design alternatives with quantitative formal verification that factors in uncertainty as a first-class entity.* This combination is enabled by the seamless integration of different types of models by means of common abstractions that enable reasoning about different types of properties in a combined manner. More specifically: (i) interaction points (e.g., ports) on the component-and-connector view of configurations correspond to synchronization points of component and connector behaviors, (ii) uncertainties are captured as probabilities in the behavior models of components and connectors, and (iii) reward structures built on behaviors enable reasoning about quantitative aspects of system behaviors (e.g., qualities). We implemented our approach in a prototype tool that uses a back-end based on Alloy and the PRISM probabilistic model checker [16]. We illustrate the approach on a Tele Assistance System (TAS) [25] for the validation of service compositions.

The rest of this paper is organized as follows: Sect. 2 provides an overview of our approach. Section 3 describes the TAS exemplar. Next, Sect. 4 describes the formalization of models employed by our approach. Section 5 details our approach, Sect. 6 presents results, and Sect. 7 overviews related work. Finally, Sect. 8 presents some conclusions and future work.

2   Overview of the Approach

Finding system configurations in an architectural style that satisfy a set of formal guarantees with respect to their behavior and qualities requires appropriate models and mechanisms to: (i) systematically generate configurations in the style, and (ii) formally verify their behavior and qualities. To achieve this goal, we propose a formalization of architectural style extended with

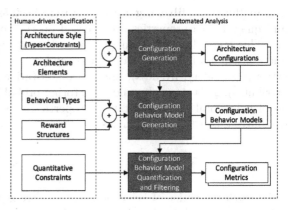

Fig. 1. Overview of the approach.

behavioral types that specify the abstract behavior of components and connectors, as well as quantitative aspects via reward structures built on their behavioral descriptions (described in Sect. 4).

Based on our formalization, our approach for design space exploration consists of three stages (Fig. 1):

Configuration generation (Sect. 5.1), during which a set of configurations that satisfy a set of structural constraints is generated. This process takes as input the description of an architectural style formalized as a set of constraints in predicate logic defined over abstract types (e.g., those imposed by the style, such as *a component of type X can only be connected to a component of type Y*) and a set of concrete architectural element definitions (i.e., the different instances of candidate components and connectors that can be employed to realize the architecture). The output is the collection of system configurations that satisfy the style constraints.

Configuration behavior model generation (Sect. 5.2), during which a set of behavioral models that refine the configurations obtained in (1) is generated. This process takes as input: (i) the set of concrete architecture element definitions, (ii) the configurations generated in (1), and (iii) the set of *behavioral types*[1] that capture the behavior of each abstract type in the architectural style. For every configuration, the behavior of each concrete component and connector is instantiated using the behavioral types of their corresponding abstract types. To realize the binding among components and connectors in the behavioral model (via synchronization actions), we employ the topological information of the graph from the system configuration. Note that, while the behavioral type is shared among all component (or connector) instances of the same type, their actual behavior can differ due to the specific attributes of the instance that parameterize its behavior (e.g., response time for a service, or number of retries after a failed service invocation). The behavioral model of a configuration is constructed as the parallel composition of the behavior of all the instances in the configuration.

Quantification, filtering and ranking (Sect. 5.3), during which behavioral and quantitative properties are checked on the configuration behavioral models. This step filters out configurations that do not meet a set of properties and constraints imposed by designers, which may include: (i) behavioral properties (e.g., safety, liveness), and (ii) quantitative constraints (e.g., on quality attributes). This stage also allows factoring probabilistic aspects into the analysis of behavioral and quantitative properties, as well as solution selection that optimizes quantitative properties.

---

[1] Although the notion of behavioral type is more general [21], we employ the term to refer to an abstract state machine specification capturing the behavior of an architectural abstract type.

3 Motivating Scenario

We illustrate our approach the TAS exemplar system [25], whose goal is tracking a patient's vital parameters to adapt drug type or dose when needed, and taking actions in case of emergency. The system combines three service types in a workflow (Fig. 2).

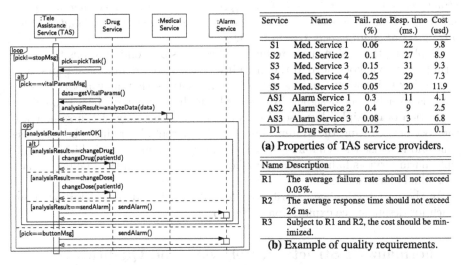

Service	Name	Fail. rate (%)	Resp. time (ms.)	Cost (usd)
S1	Med. Service 1	0.06	22	9.8
S2	Med. Service 2	0.1	27	8.9
S3	Med. Service 3	0.15	31	9.3
S4	Med. Service 4	0.25	29	7.3
S5	Med. Service 5	0.05	20	11.9
AS1	Alarm Service 1	0.3	11	4.1
AS2	Alarm Service 2	0.4	9	2.5
AS3	Alarm Service 3	0.08	3	6.8
D1	Drug Service	0.12	1	0.1

(a) Properties of TAS service providers.

Name	Description
R1	The average failure rate should not exceed 0.03%.
R2	The average response time should not exceed 26 ms.
R3	Subject to R1 and R2, the cost should be minimized.

(b) Example of quality requirements.

Fig. 2. Tele assistance service workflow, service provider properties, and quality requirements.

When TAS receives a request that includes the vital parameters of a patient, its *Medical Service* analyzes the data and replies with instructions to: (i) change the patient's drug type, (ii) change the drug dose, or (iii) trigger an alarm for first responders in case of emergency. When changing the drug type or dose, TAS notifies a local pharmacy using a *Drug Service*, whereas first responders are notified via an *Alarm Service*.

The functionality of each service type can be implemented by a number of providers that offer the service with different levels of performance, reliability, and cost (Fig. 2a). The metrics employed for the different quality attributes in TAS are the percentage of service failures for reliability, and service response time for performance.

In this context, finding an adequate design for the system entails understanding the tradeoff space by finding the set of system configurations that satisfy: (i) structural constraints imposed by the style (e.g., the *Drug Service* should not be connected to an *Alarm Service*), (ii) behavioral correctness properties (e.g., the system is eventually going to provide a response – either by dispatching an

ambulance or notifying the pharmacy about a change), and (iii) quality requirements, which can be formulated as a combination of quantitative constraints and
optimizations (Fig. 2b).

Generalizing from this scenario, the problem to solve is: *"Given an architectural style* A, *a set of concrete architecture elements* E, *a specification of correct
behaviors* B, *and a set of quality requirements* Q, *find the set of system configurations combining elements of* E *that: (i) conform to style* A *(i.e., satisfy its
structural constraints), (ii) satisfy the specification of correct behaviors* B *(i.e.,
safety and liveness properties), and (iii) maintain the desired level and/or optimize a set of quality goals specified by* Q.*"*

Exploring the design space to find the best possible configurations that conform to the style goes beyond the mere instantiation of architectural types, and
entails flexibility when envisaging design alternatives that may not always be
obvious to a human designer. An example in the context of TAS is allowing
invocation of multiple alarm services concurrently. This may of course increase
the cost of operating the system, but can also potentially reduce the response
time and increase the reliability of the system (the combined probability of multiple alarm services failing is much smaller than the probability of failure of each
individual alarm service).

In the next section we describe our formal model, and then detail our approach for design space exploration in Sect. 5.

4   Formalizing Structure, Behavior, and Qualities

4.1   Architectural Style, Configurations, and States

We characterize the possible structures of a family of systems that are related by
shared structural and semantic properties employing an *architectural style* [23].

Definition 1 (Architectural Style). *Formally, we characterize an architectural style as a tuple* $(\Sigma, \mathcal{C}_S)$, *where:*

- $\Sigma = (CompT, ConnT, \Pi, \Lambda)$ *is an architectural signature, such that:*
  - *CompT and ConnT are disjoint sets of component and connector types.*
  - $\Pi : (CompT \cup ConnT) \rightarrow 2^{\mathcal{D}}$ *is a function that assigns sets of symbols typed
    by datatypes in a fixed set* $\mathcal{D}$ *to architectural types* $\kappa \in CompT \cup ConnT$.
    $\Pi(\kappa)$ *represents the properties associated with type* κ. *To refer to a property*
    $p \in \Pi(\kappa)$, *we simply write* $\kappa.p$. *To denote its datatype, we write* $dtype(\kappa.p)$.
  - $\Lambda : CompT \cup ConnT \rightarrow 2^{\mathcal{P}} \cup 2^{\mathcal{R}}$ *is a function that assigns a set of sym-
    bols typed by a fixed set* $\mathcal{P}$ *to components* $\kappa \in CompT$. *This function also
    assigns a set of symbols in a fixed set* $\mathcal{R}$ *to connectors* $\kappa \in ConnT$. $\Lambda(\kappa)$ *rep-
    resents the ports of a component (conversely, the roles if* κ *is a connector),
    which define logical points of interaction with* κ*'s environment. To denote a
    port/role* $q \in \Lambda(\kappa)$, *we write* $\kappa :: q$.

- $\mathcal{C}_S$ *is a set of structural constraints expressed in a constraint language based on first-order predicate logic in the style of Acme* [9] *or OCL* [24] *constraints (e.g.,* ∀ t:AssistanceServiceT •∃ a:AlarmServiceT • connected(t,a) *– "every tele assistance service must be connected at least to one alarm service").*

For the remainder of this section, we assume a fixed universe $\mathcal{A}_\Sigma$ of architectural elements, i.e., a finite set of components and connectors for Σ typed by $ConnT \cup CompT$. For a given architectural element $c \in \mathcal{A}_\Sigma$, we denote its type as $type(c)$.

A *configuration* is a graph that captures the topology of a feasible structure of the system in the style.

Definition 2 (Configuration). *A configuration in an architectural style* $(\Sigma, \mathcal{C}_S)$, *given a fixed universe of architectural elements* $\mathcal{A}_\Sigma$, *is a graph* $\mathcal{G} = (\mathcal{N}, \mathcal{E})$ *satisfying the constraints imposed by* $\mathcal{C}_S$, *where:* $\mathcal{N}$ *is a set of nodes, such that* $\mathcal{N} \subseteq \mathcal{A}_\Sigma$, *and* $\mathcal{E}$ *is a set of pairs typed by* $\mathcal{P} \times \mathcal{R}$ *that represent attachments between ports and roles.*

A *system state* is the combination of a system configuration, along with an assignment of values for the properties of the nodes in the configuration graph.

Definition 3 (Σ-system State). *A Σ-system state s is a pair $(\mathcal{G}, \lambda)$, where $\mathcal{G}$ is a system configuration, and λ is a function that assigns a value $[\![c.p]\!]^s$ in the domain of $dtype(\kappa.p)$ to every pair $c.p$, such that c is a node of $\mathcal{G}$, $\kappa = type(c)$, and $p \in \Pi(\kappa)$. The set of all Σ-system states is denoted by $\mathcal{S}_\Sigma$.*

Example 1. We can characterize the family of TAS systems by a style with the following architectural signature:

CompT = {MedicalServiceT, DrugServiceT, AlarmServiceT, AssistanceServiceT}
ConnT = {HttpConnT}
Π = {(MedicalServiceT, {FailRate, RespTime, Cost}), ...}
Λ = { (MedicalServiceT, {analyzeDataPS}), (HttpConnT, {CallerR, CalleeR}),
(AssistanceServiceT, {changeDrugPTS, changeDosePTS, sendAlarmPTS, analyzeDataPTS}),
(DrugServiceT, {changeDrugPD, changeDosePD}), (AlarmServiceT, {sendAlarmPAS}) }

Employing the elements of that signature, we can specify a set of structural constraints that the style imposes on valid configurations (c.f. Listing 1.1).

Figure 3 depicts a sample TAS configuration with service instances TAS1, S1, D1, and AS2 (c.f. Fig. 2a). The connectors are instances of the http connector type (HttpConnT) for each of the operations that are invoked by the assistance service TAS1 to change drug type or dose in D1, invoke an alarm in AS2, and analyze patient data on S1, connecting the corresponding ports on the component instances.

4.2 Behavior

To extend our formalization of
architectural style with behaviors, we introduce the notion
of *behavioral type*, characterized
as a state machine that captures the abstract behavior of
an architectural type in a given
style.

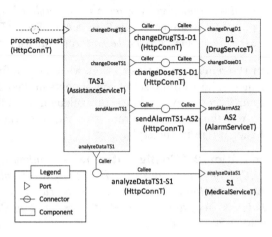

Our instantiation of behavioral type is inspired by discrete-
time Markov chains (DTMC),
although it can be easily adapted
to other formalisms like Markov
decision processes (MDP) or
probabilistic timed automata
(PTA) to capture aspects such
as fully nondeterministic choices
or continuous time.

Fig. 3. Sample TAS configuration.

Definition 4 (Behavioral Type). *The behavioral type of an architectural type*
$\kappa \in CompT \cup ConnT$ *is a tuple* $(S_\kappa, s_i, P_\Lambda)$, *where* S_κ *is* κ'*s state space, characterized by the set of all possible value assignments for properties* $\Pi(\kappa)$, $s_i \in S_\kappa$
is an initial state, and $P_\Lambda : S_\kappa \times S_\kappa \rightarrow [0,1] \times (\Lambda(\kappa) \cup \{\bot\})$ *is a transition
probability matrix extended with ports (if* κ *is a component) or roles (when* κ *is
a connector).*

In the definition above, each element $P_\Lambda(s, s')$ yields: (i) the probability of making a transition from state s to state s', and (ii) the port/role (if any) on which
the architectural element typed by κ interacts with its environment when the
transition between s and s' occurs. From a behavioral standpoint, ports and roles
define potential synchronization points for the interaction of different architectural elements in a configuration. We denote the behavioral type of an architecture element $c \in \mathcal{A}_\Sigma$ as $btype(c)$.

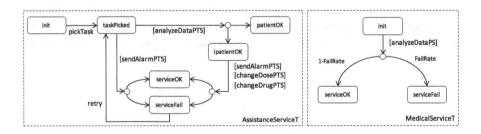

Fig. 4. AssistanceServiceT and MedicalServiceT behavioral types.

Example 2. Figure 4 depicts the abstract behavior specification of the Assistance-ServiceT and MedicalServiceT architectural types. Transition labels represent internal actions, which can be internal to the component (e.g., pickTask after the initial state in the assistance service), whereas transition labels between brackets denote potential interactions with the environment. Branching transitions (denoted by a circle) indicate a probabilistic choice, where each branch is labeled by a probability (e.g., the medical service captures the probability of the service invocation failing with a branching transition parameterized by the value of property MedicalServiceT.FailRate and its complementary). Unlabeled branching transitions implicitly specify a uniform probability distribution. Non-branching transitions indicate probability 1.

The behavior model of a configuration is obtained by instantiating the behavioral type all architecture elements in the configuration (c.f. Sect. 5.2), and performing the parallel composition (with synchronization on shared actions) of the resulting processes.

Definition 5 (Configuration Behavior Model). *Given an architecture configuration $\mathcal{G} = (\mathcal{N} = \{n_1, \ldots, n_n\}, \mathcal{E})$, we define its behavior model as the parallel composition $(bn_1 \| \ldots \| bn_n)$, where $bn_{i \in \{1..|\mathcal{N}|\}}$ is an instance of the behavioral type $btype(n_i)$.*

4.3 Qualities

In addition to structure and behavior, we also need to capture quantitative aspects of systems to enable the analysis of their qualities. To achieve this goal, we employ *reward structures* to quantify information that emerges from the combined behavior of the different elements in the system and is not explicitly captured by properties in architectural elements. Two examples are the overall number of lost requests, and average end-to-end response time of a system, which could be employed to analyze run-time quality attributes such as reliability and performance, respectively.

Definition 6 (Reward Structure). *A reward structure for a system with architectural signature Σ is a pair (ρ, ι), where $\rho : \mathcal{S}_\Sigma \to \mathbb{R}_{\geq 0}$ is a function that assigns rewards to system state, and $\iota : \mathcal{S}_\Sigma \times \mathcal{S}_\Sigma \to \mathbb{R}_{\geq 0}$ is a function assigning rewards to transitions.*

State reward $\rho(s)$ is acquired in state $s \in \mathcal{S}_\Sigma$ per time step, i.e., each time that the system spends one time step in s, the reward accrues $\rho(s)$. In contrast, $\iota(s, s')$ is the reward acquired every time that a transition between s and s' occurs. Our approach is agnostic with respect to the way in which reward structures are defined. However, in this paper we assume that rewards over states are defined as sets of pairs (pd, r), where pd is a predicate over states $\mathcal{S}_\Sigma$, and $r \in \mathbb{R}_{\geq 0}$ is the accrued reward when $s \in \mathcal{S}_\Sigma \models pd$. We consider transition rewards as sets of pairs (p, r), in which $p \in \mathcal{P}$ is a port type, and reward $r \in \mathbb{R}_{\geq 0}$ is accrued when an interaction over a port of type p occurs.

Example 3. To compute the cost of operating a TAS configuration, we define a reward structure that accrues the cost of invoking each of the services in a configuration as: $(\rho, \iota) = (\emptyset, \{(\text{DrugServiceT} :: \text{changeDrugPD}, \text{DrugServiceT.Cost}), (\text{DrugServiceT} :: \text{change-DosePD}, \text{DrugServiceT.Cost}), (\text{AlarmServiceT} :: \text{sendAlarmPAS}, \text{AlarmServiceT.Cost}), (\text{MedicalServiceT} :: \text{analyzeDataPS}, \text{MedicalServiceT.Cost})\})$.

5   Exploring the Design Space

5.1   Configuration Generation

Generating structurally correct configurations entails: (i) formalizing a set of structural style constraints that all configurations must respect, (ii) instantiating the constraints for a specific set of architecture entities into a concrete relational model, and (iii) synthesizing the configurations that satisfy the constraints in the relational model.

Formalizing Structural Constraints. This is a manual process that can be carried out by producing a specification in an ADL like Acme, and then translated automatically to an Alloy specification [14], or directly producing a specification in the latter. Listing 1.1 shows an excerpt of the encoding of the TAS architectural style in Alloy. Lines 1–4 encode the definitions of abstract architectural elements that belong to the architectural signature like components or connectors, whereas lines 6–8 show a part of the encoding of general constraints of the architecture (e.g., a component cannot be connected to itself). The service types in TAS are encoded as signatures that extend the base signature Component defined in line 1. For instance, the AssistanceServiceT component type definition (lines 16–20) includes constraints indicating that it must contain at least one port for invoking every possible operation type on other services (lines 17–18), and that those invocation port types can only belong to that type of component (lines 19–20).

Instantiating Constraints. Once the set of structural constraints of the style is formalized, we can instantiate a full relational model that will enable us to apply these constraints to a set of concrete instances that realize concrete configurations. Listing 1.2 presents an excerpt of concrete components in TAS that correspond to alternative implementations of services available from various providers. This specification includes the name of the concrete service implementation, along with its type, which matches one of the abstract types in the specification of structural constraints in Listing 1.1, and information related to its quality attributes (Fig. 2a).

```
1   abstract sig Component {ports: set Port} // Component and Connector abstract definition
2   abstract sig Connector {roles: set Role}
3   sig Port {component: Component}
4   sig Role {connector: Connector, attachment: one Port}
5   // General constraints of the architecture
6   fact { all p:Port | one r:Role | p in r.attachment } // A port is connected to only one role
7   pred conn[c: Component, c':Component] { some r,r':Role | r!=r' and r.attachment.component=c and
        r'.attachment.component=c' and r.connector=r'.connector } // Two components are connected
8   fact { all c,c':Component | c=c' => not conn[c,c'] } // A component must not be connected to itself
9   ... // TAS−specific definitions
10  pred invokes[p:Port, p':Port] { one r:Caller,r':Callee | r.attachment=p and r'.attachment=p' and
        r.connector=r'.connector } // A port (p) carries out invocations on another one (p')
11  pred invokesOnly[p:Port, p':Port] { invokes[p,p'] and all p'':Port−p' | not invokes[p,p''] } // A port
        carries out invocations ∗only∗ on another specific port
12  abstract sig HttpConnT extends Connector {} // *** HTTP Connector ***
13  abstract sig Caller, Callee extends Role{} // An http connector has a caller and a callee role
14  fact { all c:HttpConnT | one r:Caller, r':Callee | r in c.roles and r' in c.roles }
15  fact { all c:HttpConnT | #c.roles=2 } // Every http connector has ∗exactly∗ two roles
16  one abstract sig AssistanceServiceT extends Component{} // *** Tele Assistance Service ***
17  { changeDrugPTS & ports != none and changeDosePTS & ports != none and sendAlarmPTS & ports
        != none and analyzeDataPTS & ports != none} // A TAS has one port for every possible
        operation
18  abstract sig changeDrugPTS, changeDosePTS, sendAlarmPTS, analyzeDataPTS extends Port{}
19  fact { all p:changeDrugPTS+changeDosePTS+sendAlarmPTS+analyzeDataPTS | p.component in
        AssistanceServiceT }
20  fact { all c:AssistanceServiceT | c.ports in
        changeDrugPTS+changeDosePTS+sendAlarmPTS+analyzeDataPTS }
21  abstract sig DrugServiceT extends Component{ } // *** Drug Service ***
22  { changeDrugPD & ports != none and changeDosePD & ports != none and #ports=2 }
23  abstract sig changeDrugPD, changeDosePD extends Port{}
24  fact { all p:changeDrugPD+changeDosePD | p.component in DrugServiceT }
25  fact { all c:DrugServiceT | c.ports in changeDrugPD+changeDosePD }
26  ... // General structure (allowed invocations among ports in different components)
27  fact { all pt:analyzeDataPTS | one ps:analyzeDataPS | invokesOnly[pt,ps] }
28  fact { all pt:changeDrugPTS | one pd:changeDrugPD | invokesOnly[pt,pd] }
29  ...
30  fact { all t:AssistanceServiceT | one d:DrugServiceT | conn[t,d] } // A TAS connects to ∗only one∗ DS
```

Listing 1.1. TAS architecture style constraint specification in Alloy (excerpt).

Entity definitions are employed to automatically extend the constraints into a full relational model that includes concrete instances of the different entities in the system. Listing 1.3 shows the Alloy code generated to complement the specification in Listing 1.1. Every instance is encoded into a signature that extends its corresponding abstract type. The definition of every signature is preceded by a lone quantifier, indicating that the presence of a specific instance in a valid system configuration is optional. Quality attribute information is not used to analyze structural aspects of the system, and hence is abstracted in the Alloy specification. These are used later for behavioral configuration model generation (Sect. 5.2).

```
S1 [type: MedicalServiceT, failureRate: 0.06, responseTime: 22, cost: 9.8];
AS1 [type: AlarmServiceT, failureRate: 0.3, responseTime: 11, cost: 4.1];
```

Listing 1.2. Concrete service implementation definitions for TAS (excerpt).

```
lone sig D1 extends DrugServiceT{}
lone sig S1, S2, S3, S4, S5 extends MedicalServiceT{}
lone sig AS1, AS2, AS3 extends AlarmServiceT{}
lone sig TAS1 extends AssistanceServiceT{}
```

Listing 1.3. Concrete service implementation definitions for TAS in Alloy.

Configuration Synthesis. Once a model instantiating the style constraints is available, we use the Alloy analyzer to find all relational models that describe configurations satisfying the constraints imposed by the style and employ a set of concrete architecture elements (e.g., TAS service implementations).

To do that, we invoke the run command and impose a constraint on the cardinality of the different sets of entities (determined by the maximum available number of components of each type) using an additional predicate (Listing 1.4). As an example, we run the predicate TAS for a maximum number of 10 instances of each signature in the model, and impose a restriction of one implementation per type of service, except for AlarmServiceT, for which we impose a maximum of 2 instances.

```
pred TAS {#DrugServiceT=1 and #AlarmServiceT=2 and #MedicalServiceT=1}
run TAS for 10
```

Listing 1.4. Synthesizing TAS configurations in Alloy.

Figure 5 shows two TAS configurations, generated from the Alloy model described in this section. The structure on the left is analogous to the one depicted in Fig. 3, in which TAS is able to invoke a service of each type. However, the structure on the right describes a configuration in which TAS can invoke alarm services AS2 and AS3, potentially increasing reliability and performance when an alarm is raised, but probably at the expense of a higher cost. This second configuration results from the flexibility in the cardinality constraints imposed by Listing 1.4, line 1, which allows more than one alarm service to be employed in a configuration.

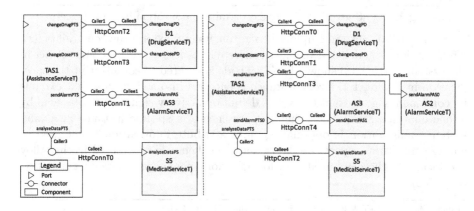

Fig. 5. Graphical representation for two TAS configurations synthesized using Alloy.

At this point, we can generate alternative configurations for a system in a given style, employing a set of concrete elements as building blocks for the configuration. However, if we want to be able to determine which configurations satisfy some criteria defined over the behavior or the qualities of the solution, we need to include additional specifications that go beyond structure. In the next section, we describe how to expand structures into behavioral models that are amenable to analysis that takes into consideration behavioral and quantitative aspects of system configurations.

5.2   Configuration Behavior Model Generation

The behavior model of a configuration can be obtained by instantiating the behavioral type of each of the architecture elements in the configuration, and performing the parallel composition of the resulting processes. Algorithm 5.2 receives as input the configuration of the system $\mathcal{G} = (\mathcal{N}, \mathcal{E})$ and the set of behavioral types for the different architecture elements β, and returns the configuration behavior model for $\mathcal{G}$.

The algorithm starts with an empty set of behaviors B (line 1), and incrementally adds the behavior of each node in the configuration graph, which is instanced by: **(1)** Determining the set of transitions P_Λ^* of the behavioral type that interact with the environment (line 4). Function ip returns the interaction

Algorithm 1. Configuration behavior model generation

```
1: B := ∅
2: for all n ∈ 𝒩 do
3:     Pᵥ := ∅
4:     P*_Λ := {t ∈ P_Λ | btype(n) = (S_κ, s_i, P_Λ) ∧ ip(t) ≠ ⊥}
5:     for all t ∈ P*_Λ do
6:         A_t := {(p, r) ∈ ℰ | (parent(p) = n ∨ parent(r) = n) ∧ iptype(p) = ip(t)}
7:         for all a_t ∈ A_t do
8:             Pᵥ := Pᵥ ∪ {states(t) ↦ (prob(t)/|A_t|, label(a_t))}
9:         end for
10:    end for
11:    B := B ∪ {(S_κ, s_i, (P_Λ\P*_Λ) ∪ Pᵥ)}
12: end for
13: return (b₁|| ... ||bₙ) • b_{i∈{1..|𝒩|}} ∈ B
```

point (port or role type) associated with every element of P_Λ in the behavioral type. $btype$ returns the behavioral type of an architecture element. **(2)** For each transition identified in (1), creating an instance of the transition for every other node to which the current one is attached in the configuration (lines 6–9). In line 6, the set of attachments in the configuration graph for the current node is identified. Here, interaction point type function $iptype$ identifies the type of a port or role, whereas $parent$ returns the node that a port or role belongs to. Line 8 adds new transition instances, adjusting the probability contribution of the transition according to the number of instances created for a given transition in P_Λ^*.[2] Function $states$ return the pair of source and target state for a transition, whereas $prob$ returns its associated probability. Function $label$ generates a unique label for an attachment, defined as a pair port-role. **(3)** Creating a new behavior instance incorporating the original elements of $btype(n)$ (line 11). This

---

[2] The semantics of behavioral types are inspired by discrete-time Markov chains, so the original probability of the transition $prob(t)$ is divided equally among transition instances.

process describes the behavior of graph node n, in which transitions identified in (1) are substituted by the new set of transition instances P_ν identified in (2). The algorithm finishes returning the parallel composition of the processes in B.

5.3   Quantification, Filtering and Ranking

After obtaining the behavioral models for the possible configurations of the system, we can assess behavioral, as well as quantitative constraints and properties on them. This analysis might also include probabilistic aspects in the behavioral and quantitative properties (e.g., reliability of services on which TAS relies), so we propose to employ probabilistic temporal logics to capture them. We illustrate formalization using PCTL [15], although these specifications can be adapted to other types of probabilistic temporal logic for behavioral descriptions inspired by other formalisms (e.g., continuous-time Markov chains, probabilistic timed automata).

This step identifies configurations that do not meet a set of properties and constraints imposed by designers, which may include: (i) behavioral properties (e.g., safety, liveness), and (ii) quantitative constraints (e.g., on quality attributes).

Example 4. We want to assess the overall response time, reliability, and cost of configurations in TAS. We define serviceOK $\triangleq$ changeDoseOK$\lor$ changeDrugOK $\lor$ sendAlarmOK as a predicate indicating that TAS provided some of the possible service types correctly. Moreover, we assume the predicate timeout captures failed service invocation.

Based on these predicates, we define properties $R_{rt=?}$[F (serviceOK $\lor$ timeout)] and $R_{cost=?}$[F (serviceOK $\lor$ timeout)] that employ the reward quantifier of PCTL to quantify the expected response time and cost of a configuration by accruing the response time and cost rewards rt and cost, respectively. Property $1 - P_{=?}$[F serviceOK] quantifies the overall reliability of a configuration (i.e., that the system will fail to provide correct service) by employing the probabilistic quantifier of PCTL.

6   Results

We present in this section our experimental results. To test our proposal, we ran a prototype implementation of our approach that employed Alloy 4.2 for synthesizing configurations and PRISM 4.3.1 for behavioral and quantitative analysis. The experiment was run on an Intel Core i7 2.8 GHz with 16 GB RAM. We ran our analysis to compute the set of feasible solutions for TAS that meet the set of structural constraints described in Listing 1.1, using the set of service implementations described in Fig. 2a.

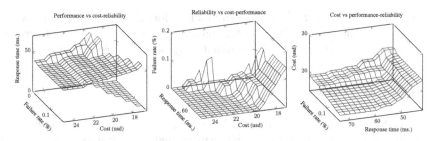

Fig. 6. TAS configurations constrained by: (a) cost and reliability (left), (b) cost and performance (center), and (c) performance and reliability (right). (Color figure online)

Space size and computation time. Table 1 shows that the overall computation time for generating and analyzing the solution space was approximately 9 seconds, out of which 15% was used to generate 90 configurations (Alloy) and 270 behavioral configuration models (90×3 possible values for the parameter that specifies number of retries after a failed service invocation). Checking deadlock freeness and the three quantitative properties defined in Example 4 took approximately 85% of the time.

Analysis results. The plot on the left of Fig. 6 shows the best response time

Table 1. Problem instance size and computation time.

# Configurations	90
# Configuration behavioral models	270
Configuration behavior model generation time	1.361 s (15.1 %)
Configuration behavioral model checking time (PRISM)	7.66 s (84.9 %)
Total computation time	**9.021 s**

that can be achieved in a system configuration when the cost and failure rate are constrained to the thresholds on the horizontal axes. As expected, we observe that lower response times and failure rates incur higher cost. This is consistent with the properties of service providers (better response times and reliability are more expensive), and the fact that having the flexibity to add redundant services (e.g., alarm service) to increase reliability and reduce response time increases cost. Our technique enables us to identify the thresholds in cost and failure rate for which there are no system configurations satisfying style constraints (in the range ≤ 19 usd – the red squares on the bottom plane).

The plot in the center shows how failure rate of configurations increases noticeably with lower costs, whereas with high cost, it is fairly stable and does not vary much with overall response time, except for very low values.

Finally, the plot on the right shows the overall cost of configurations for different levels of response time and reliability. As expected, we can observe how higher response times and failure rates correspond to lower costs, whereas peaks in cost are reached with lowest failure rates and response times.

An architect can take these results and make informed design decisions based, for instance, on the available budget for the project and legal constraints on the level of reliability and timeliness demanded of systems for first-aid response.

7   Related Work

Work related to our proposal can be categorized into: (i) formalization of architectural styles, and (ii) architecture-based quantitative analysis and optimization.

(1) Formalization of architectural styles: Formalization of styles has been explored to define formal semantics of modeling languages. Kim and Garlan [14] propose an automatic translation from Acme into Alloy relational models on which they verify properties implied by the style. Wong et al. [26] also employ Alloy to check the consistency of rules among multiple styles that might be combined in complex systems. In addition to property verification, other approaches also explore constraint solving for synthesizing architectures [3,19]. Bagheri and Sullivan [3] employ architecture synthesis for generating architectural models from architecture-independent application models, emphasizing the separation of style choices from application description. In contrast, Maoz et al. [19] propose an approach that employs synthesis to merge different partial component-and-connector views. All the aforementioned approaches focus on structural properties and differ from ours in that they do not consider behavioral, quantitative, or probabilistic aspects of system descriptions, being unable to systematically analyze nondeterministic system behaviors and their effects on quality attributes.

(2) Architecture-based quantitative analysis and optimization: Other approaches focus on analyzing and optimizing quantitative aspects of architectures using mechanisms that include stochastic search and/or Pareto analysis [1,5,20]. *PerOpteryx* [20] takes as input an architectural model described using the Palladio component model and tries to automatically improve it by searching for pareto-optimal solutions employing a genetic algorithm. *ArcheOpterix* [1] uses an evolutionary algorithm for optimizing the architecture of embedded systems. *DeepCompass* [5] is a framework that analyzes different architectural alternatives along the dimensions of performance and cost to find pareto-optimal solutions. While these and other approaches in systems engineering (e.g., [17]) can give estimates and optimize quantitative aspects of designs, they do not support synthesis of configurations (which have to be manually specified), and do not provide any formal guarantees concerning the behavior or quantitative properties of the variants.

Other approaches [4,7] have recently combined architecture synthesis with simulation and dynamic analysis to provide estimates of quantitative properties of system variants. *TradeMaker* [4] synthesizes design spaces for object-relational database mappings, in which individual designs are subject to static and dynamic analysis to extract performance metrics. Dwivedi et al. [7] propose using architectural models coupled with automated design space generation for making fidelity and timeliness tradeoffs. These approaches share with ours the idea of synthesizing a solution space from a set of constraints and analyzing individual solutions independently. However, they do not explore exhaustively the state space of individual solutions and hence are unable to provide guarantees about solution behaviors or their interaction with system qualities.

8 Conclusions and Future Work

We have presented an approach to help architects explore the design space of families of software systems, giving them a tool to make informed design decisions by providing insight into the formal guarantees of solutions and tradeoffs among their qualities. Our approach enables the analysis of behavioral (i.e., safety, liveness) and quality properties (e.g., quantitative constraints, optimality) of solutions, considering interactions among them, as well as uncertainties captured via probabilities in models.

Concerning generality, the current embodiment of the approach is inspired by a specific model of formal architectural description (Acme) and behavioral formalism (DTMC). However, most constructs employed to formalize the architectural style are fairly standard and the approach for synthesis of configurations is adaptable to other languages and underlying models. In terms of behavior descriptions, DTMCs constrain the analysis to a discrete time model and average case of probabilities/rewards, although straightforward adaptations can be carried out to adapt behavioral analysis to other probabilistic behavior descriptions such as MDPs (for worst-case scenario analysis) or PTAs for finer-grained time analysis. We will explore these areas in future work.

Moreover, although in this paper we have focused on spaces in which design decisions are dominated by the selection and composition of pre-existing components, design spaces in which a non-trivial part of the system components have to be built from scratch have been left out of scope. We plan on extending our approach for such systems by exploring probabilistic parametric model checking techniques [10] to automatically find the ranges for quality attribute values that components to be implemented would have to provide to satisfy global system constraints on qualities.

A third direction for future work concerns scalability. The degree of formal assurance on configurations provided by the approach is computationally expensive, and entails risks on the computation cost of configuration synthesis (derived from the cost of finding instances of configurations in a rich configuration space) and configuration behavior analysis (derived from exploring potentially large state spaces of individual configuration behavior). These risks can be mitigated by exploiting the hierarchical structure and relations that are naturally present in complex architectures in which components interact in a structured way. Hence, synthesis of different subsystems with local constraints can be done independently and then composed, reducing the cost of configuration synthesis. This approach has been successfully used in other works that exploit mappings between specifications defined at different levels of abstraction [13], or incremental analysis techniques [2]. This mitigation also allows exploiting parallelism in the analysis, during which the behavior of configurations of subsystems can be independently analyzed using assume-guarantee compositional quantitative verification [12]. In this case, the computation time for the analysis would be dominated by the largest subsystem that can be independently analyzed (prior experience with PRISM suggest times under 10 s for configurations of 250+ components, including probabilistic behavior [6]).

Acknowledgments. This material is based on research sponsored by AFRL and DARPA under agreement number FA8750-16-2-0042. The U.S. Government is authorized to reproduce and distribute reprints for Governmental purposes notwithstanding any copyright notation thereon. The views and conclusions contained herein are those of the authors and should not be interpreted as necessarily representing the official policies or endorsements, either expressed or implied, of the AFRL, DARPA or the U.S. Government.

References

1. Aleti, A., Bjornander, S., Grunske, L., Meedeniya, I.: Archeopterix: an extendable tool for architecture optimization of AADL models. In: ICSE Workshop on Model-Based Methodologies for Pervasive and Embedded Software, MOMPES 2009 (2009)
2. Bagheri, H., Malek, S.: Titanium: efficient analysis of evolving alloy specifications. In: Proceedings of the 24th Symposium on Foundations of Software Engineering, FSE 2016 (2016)
3. Bagheri, H., Sullivan, K.J.: Model-driven synthesis of formally precise, stylized software architectures. Formal Asp. Comput. **28**(3), 441–467 (2016)
4. Bagheri, H., Tang, C., Sullivan, K.J.: Trademaker: automated dynamic analysis of synthesized tradespaces. In: 36th International Conference on Software Engineering. ACM (2014)
5. Bondarev, E., Chaudron, M.R.V., de Kock, E.A.: Exploring performance trade-offs of a jpeg decoder using the deepcompass framework. In: 6th WS on Software and Performance, WOSP. ACM (2007)
6. Cámara, J., Garlan, D., Schmerl, B., Pandey, A.: Optimal planning for architecture-based self-adaptation via model checking of stochastic games. In: 30th ACM Symposium on Applied Computing (SAC) (2015)
7. Dwivedi, V., Garlan, D., Pfeffer, J., Schmerl, B.: Model-based assistance for making time/fidelity trade-offs in component compositions. In: 11th International Conference on Information Technology: New Generations, ITNG 2014. IEEE CS (2014)
8. Garlan, D.: Software engineering in an uncertain world. In: Proceedings of the Workshop on Future of Software Engineering Research, FoSER (2010)
9. Garlan, D., Monroe, R.T., Wile, D.: Acme: an architecture description interchange language. In: Proceedings of the 1997 Conference of the Centre for Advanced Studies on Collaborative Research, Toronto, Ontario, Canada, 10–13 November 1997. IBM (1997)
10. Hahn, E.M., Hermanns, H., Wachter, B., Zhang, L.: PARAM: a model checker for parametric markov models. In: Touili, T., Cook, B., Jackson, P. (eds.) CAV 2010. LNCS, vol. 6174, pp. 660–664. Springer, Heidelberg (2010). doi:10.1007/978-3-642-14295-6_56

11. Jackson, D.: Alloy: a lightweight object modelling notation. ACM Trans. Softw. Eng. Methodol. **11**(2), 256–290 (2002)
12. Johnson, K., Calinescu, R., Kikuchi, S.: An incremental verification framework for component-based software systems. In: Proceedings of the 16th International ACM SIGSOFT Symposium on Component-based Software Engineering, CBSE 2013. ACM (2013)
13. Kang, E., Milicevic, A., Jackson, D.: Multi-representational security analysis. In: Proceedings of the 24th Symposium on Foundations of Software Engineering, FSE (2016)
14. Kim, J., Garlan, D.: Analyzing architectural styles. J. Syst. Softw. **83**(7), 1216–1235 (2010)
15. Kwiatkowska, M., Norman, G., Parker, D.: Stochastic model checking. In: Bernardo, M., Hillston, J. (eds.) SFM 2007. LNCS, vol. 4486, pp. 220–270. Springer, Heidelberg (2007). doi:10.1007/978-3-540-72522-0_6
16. Kwiatkowska, M., Norman, G., Parker, D.: PRISM 4.0: verification of probabilistic real-time systems. In: Gopalakrishnan, G., Qadeer, S. (eds.) CAV 2011. LNCS, vol. 6806, pp. 585–591. Springer, Heidelberg (2011). doi:10.1007/978-3-642-22110-1_47
17. MacCalman, A.D., Beery, P.T., Paulo, E.P.: A systems design exploration approach that illuminates tradespaces using statistical experimental designs. Syst. Eng. **19**(5), 409–421 (2016)
18. Mahdavi-Hezavehi, S., Galster, M., Avgeriou, P.: Variability in quality attributes of service-based software systems: a systematic literature review. Inf. Softw. Technol. **55**(2), 320–343 (2013)
19. Maoz, S., Ringert, J.O., Rumpe, B.: Synthesis of component and connector models from crosscutting structural views. In: European Software Engineering Conference and Symposium on the Foundations of Software Engineering, ESEC/FSE 2013. ACM (2013)
20. Martens, A., Koziolek, H., Becker, S., Reussner, R.: Automatically improve software architecture models for performance, reliability, and cost using evolutionary algorithms. In: International Conference on Performance Engineering, WOSP/SIPEW. ACM (2010)
21. Maydl, W., Grunske, L.: Behavioral types for embedded software – a survey. In: Atkinson, C., Bunse, C., Gross, H.-G., Peper, C. (eds.) Component-Based Software Development for Embedded Systems. LNCS, vol. 3778, pp. 82–106. Springer, Heidelberg (2005). doi:10.1007/11591962_5
22. Quigley, M., Conley, K., Gerkey, B.P., Faust, J., Foote, T., Leibs, J., Wheeler, R., Ng, A.Y.: Ros: an open-source robot operating system. In: ICRA WS on Open Source Software (2009)
23. Shaw, M., Garlan, D.: Software Architecture - Perspectives on an Emerging Discipline. Prentice Hall, Upper Saddle River (1996)
24. Warmer, J., Kleppe, A.: The Object Constraint Language: Getting Your Models Ready for MDA. Addison-Wesley, Reading (2003)
25. Weyns, D., Calinescu, R.: Tele assistance: a self-adaptive service-based system exemplar. In: 10th IEEE/ACM International Symposium on Software Engineering for Adaptive and Self-Managing Systems, SEAMS 2015. IEEE Computer Society (2015)
26. Wong, S., Sun, J., Warren, I., Sun, J.: A scalable approach to multi-style architectural modeling and verification. In: 13th IEEE International Conference on Engineering of Complex Computer Systems (ICECCS 2008) (2008)

PARAD Repository: On the Capitalization of the Performance Analysis Process for AADL Designs

Thanh Dat Nguyen, Yassine Ouhammou(✉), and Emmanuel Grolleau

LIAS Laboratory, ISAE-ENSMA and University of Poitiers, Futuroscope, France
{thanh-dat.nguyen,yassine.ouhammou,grolleau}@ensma.fr
https://www.lias-lab.fr

Abstract. In this paper, we focus on RTES (real-time embedded systems) designs expressed in AADL (Architecture and Analysis Design Language) and we propose a model-based approach to improve the way that designers check and analyze the performance of their system designs by capitalizing the analysis process. Our approach is based on proposing customized repositories of models using formal AADL-compliant query and constraint languages in order to orient designers to choose the most suitable analysis models and tests. Furthermore, this work is also dedicated to research teams to share their researches and prototypes, in order to enhance the (re-)usability of the real-time performance analysis tests.

1 Introduction

Critical real-time embedded systems (RTES) are used in many domains (such as avionics, nuclear and automotive) where the development life-cycle takes months up to several years. Hence, RTES designs need to be analyzed at an early phase of the life-cycle in order to check if all the requirements are met, including temporal requirements (e.g. deadlines, end-to-end delays, etc.). For that, numerous analysis tests have been proposed, based on the scheduling theory, dedicated to different system behaviours and architectures. However, one of the main difficulties that system designers face is to choose the suitable analysis test helping to validate and/or to dimension their designs properly. Also, improving reuse in complex systems like real-time systems is increasingly recognized as primordial as it contributes to paring down costs for the engineering and shortening the development time. In order to analyze the temporal behavior of a critical RTES and to ensure its correctness, a set of quantitative performance tests (e.g., schedulability tests) has to be applied to analysis models by using algebraic methods.

1.1 Context

RTES are composed of a set of interacting tasks sharing communication resources, generating several messages, executing on a set of hardware components and are arbitrated by scheduling algorithms and network protocols.

© Springer International Publishing AG 2017
A. Lopes and R. de Lemos (Eds.): ECSA 2017, LNCS 10475, pp. 22–39, 2017.
DOI: 10.1007/978-3-319-65831-5_2

To study the temporal correctness of a system, a schedulability test takes into account all of these elements. Architectures of RTES have been sharply impacted by the technology evolution in terms of hardware and software components (mutli-core processors, cache memories, avionics networks, hierarchical processes, mixed criticality, etc.) [11,22,25,28]. The performance analysis community follows actively this evolution by proposing numerous tests that match the variety of RTES architectures due to the critical aspect of RTES. The result of a performance analysis test can never be reliable unless the system's architecture fits accurately with the analysis model of the applied test. That is, choosing a non-suitable test may conduct to a wrong optimistic result (e.g. the calculated response-time of a task can be less than the time required for its execution in practical cases), or it can lead to a very pessimistic result generating a system over-sizing (usage of non-required processors and wires).

Once upon a time, the design (modeling and performance analysis) of RTES was several come-and-go flows between designers and analysts. Nowadays, Model-Driven Engineering (MDE) [24] gains in terms of popularity and becomes used during the design process of RTES. Thanks to MDE settings (modeling, transformation, code generation) the design of RTES becomes a model-based process tool-chain integrating both modeling and performance analysis phases and shortening the time-to-market. Indeed, a set of design languages have been proposed like UML-MARTE [16] and AADL [4] to help designers to get a pivot centric-model that can support several kinds of functional and non-functional analyses (energy, time, safety, etc.). The timing performance analysis community has also taken benefits from the MDE facilities. Hence, numerous implementations of analysis tests and models have been produced as commercial and academic analysis tools (such as Rt-Druid [23], MAST [17]). Each tool supports one or several kinds of RTES architectures, and provides a set of analysis tests in order to help designers to conclude about the schedulability of the system under design.

1.2   Problem Statement

Nowadays, we witness a gap between the real-time scheduling research theory and its utilization in the industry [20]. Performing analysis tests, as it is currently used, is still driven by the real-time designers experience. Therefore, determining what type of analysis tests to use for a given architecture may be difficult. This is due to several reasons. (i) By analyzing the literature[1], we realized the presence of a "jungle" of analysis tests whose analysis models are sometimes well defined in the scientific papers, but sometimes they are drowned in paper discussions, or even left implicit. For example, the survey presented in [28] enumerates a dozen of analysis models, which are only dedicated to simple systems with independent tasks, uni-processor architecture and fixed priority scheduling algorithms. Therefore, to know if a performance analysis test of a specific system

---

[1] We have analyzed papers published in the main real-time system conferences like: RTSS (rtss.org), ECRTS (ecrts.eit.uni-kl.de) and RTAS (rtas.org).

architecture exists is time-consuming. (ii) Moreover, the existing analysis tools are more dedicated to automatize the test calculation than orienting designers to the right tests that match their needs, and the analysis models of the computed tests are often explicit and need a deep knowledge of both modeling and scheduling theory, which is uncommon.

In the light of these mentioned problems, the current situation is penalizing in terms of reusing and finding easily appropriate analysis tests. It also deepens the gap between the tests presented by the researches community and their utilization in the industry.

1.3 Paper Contribution

In this research, we are interested on RTES designs based on AADL standard design language. We propose a collaborative framework called PARAD (Performance Analysis Repository for AADL Designs)[2]. This framework is dedicated to construct performance analysis repositories playing the role of "decision supports". Thanks to our proposition, designers can be helped during the analysis phase in order (i) to detect the analysis situation corresponding to the system design and (ii) to choose the most suitable analysis tests. Our proposition also aims at enhancing the applicability of the real-time performance analysis theory. Indeed, this work can be used as showcase and teaching-aid allowing the research teams to show their results (e.g. analysis models, tests, prototypes) and to share them with other teams among the RTES community.

1.4 Paper Outline

The remainder of the paper is organized as follows. Section 2 introduces real-time advances in terms of tests, tools and design languages, and presents a running example which will be used to motivate our contribution and to highlight its relevance. Section 3 is devoted to present formally the concepts of PARAD. Section 4 shows the proof of concept through a case study. Finally, Sect. 5 summarizes and concludes this article.

2 Background and Work Positioning

The development life-cycle of RTES can span over years. Indeed, any wrong choice during the design phase can impact sharply the time-to-market. Therefore, the analysis should be carried out at an early-stage of the design phase. In practice, a RTES design has to satisfy many constraints, including the temporal ones. That means, threads have to respect their deadlines, the execution order, end-to-end delays, etc. To ensure the satisfaction of these constraints in a system design, we use temporal performance tests.

---

[2] https://forge.lias-lab.fr/projects/parad.

2.1   Real-Time Concerns

The RTES analysis research community is very active and has been offering various analysis tests since the 1970's (like worst-case response time analysis, time demand analysis, simulation, etc.) [8,25,28]. The provided analyses are not only schedulability tests (which allow to conclude if the system is schedulable or not) but they also address other aspects such as the dimensioning, the sensitivity analysis and the quality of service, etc. The inputs of each test represent an analysis model (a.k.a. workload model) which is an abstract representation of the system being under design. Moreover, each test is characterized as a sufficient test, a necessary test, or both of them (i.e., exact test). A test is defined to be *sufficient* if all of the task-sets that are deemed schedulable according to the test are in fact schedulable. A test can also be referred to as *necessary* if failure of the test will indeed lead to a deadline miss at some points during the execution of the system. Schedulability test that is both *sufficient* and *necessary* is labeled as *exact*, then it is in some sense optimal. The result provided by each test can help to conclude about the temporal satisfaction of the RTES.

Actually, during the progress from the modeling phase to the analysis phase, designers should choose between two main pathways to analyze their designs. (i) The first one is related to the use of analysis tools that are already integrated to a model-based tool chain. In other words, a "push-button" action can be enough to analyze the design. However, the designer cannot know if the chosen test perfectly matches the design characteristics. That is, since a "push-button" action is enough to analyze the design, the analysis result may be optimistic (which means wrong because of the criticality of RTES) or oversized (thus, it can be costly in terms of equipments and wiring). Moreover, in case of analysis failures, designers may not be informed about the failure reasons. Hence, designers could not know if the problem is due to a wrong choice of the analysis techniques or due to the analysis tool itself which may not support the architecture and the specificities of the system under design. (ii) The second pathway is to ask an expert. This pathway is safer but also more expensive. During the development process, an expert has to repetitively examine architectures provided by designers till finding out the configuration that meets the temporal requirements. Unfortunately, this work-flow is not capitalized, hence the idea behind this paper.

2.2   Motivating and Running Example

In this section, we present a toy example for initiating the discussion. We consider a software architecture of a RTES consisting of four periodic independent tasks. Each task is characterized by a set of temporal properties (See Table 1): the worst-case execution time (WCET), the deadline, the period, the release-time and the priority.

The four tasks are preemptive and scheduled referring to their priorities. They are executed on a uni-processor hardware architecture. Task1's priority is higher than Task2's priority, which is higher than Task3's priority, which is higher than Task4's priority. After launching the analysis process through two

Table 1. Example of the task-set configuration of a RTES

Task	WCET	Deadline	Period	Release time	Priority
Task1	3 ms	15 ms	20 ms	2 ms	4
Task2	4 ms	8 ms	23 ms	0 ms	3
Task3	5 ms	13 ms	23 ms	5 ms	2
Task4	9 ms	23 ms	23 ms	7 ms	1

Table 2. Worst-case response times (WCRT) provided by the tools

Task	WCRT (SimSo)	WCRT (Rt-Druid)
Task1	3 ms	3 ms
Task2	7 ms	7 ms
Task3	8 ms	12 ms
Task4	14 ms	33 ms

different analysis tools (Rt-Druid [23] and Simso [27]), we have obtained two different results for the same input architecture as shown in Table 2.

Discussion: The difference is not related to a wrong implementation of the analysis methods, but to the choice of the analysis models. The result in the second column of Table 2 is carried out as a simulation by Simso [27] so that the tasks release-times are taken into consideration. Whereas, the analysis model chosen via Rt-Druid (whose result is presented in the third column) ignores the release-times and considers that all tasks are released at the same time [14]. Figure 1 presents differences of behaviors related to the analysis models considered by Simso and RT-Druid. Indeed, the result provided by Rt-Druid are not wrong,

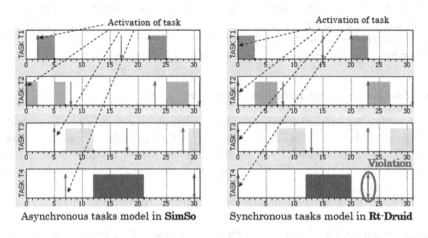

Asynchronous tasks model in **SimSo**   Synchronous tasks model in **Rt-Druid**

Fig. 1. Analysis models of SimSo and RT-Druid

but the analysis model used via the Rt-Druid tool represents the worst-case behavior that can never be produced by the system under-analysis. Consequently, the test that corresponds to this analysis model leads to pessimistic results that are not close to the practical case of the system under analysis.

2.3 AADL in a Nutshell

Although the approach that we propose in this paper can be generalized to be used with any prescriptive design language, in this paper, we focus on AADL designs. Then, we propose a brief presentation of the language to have a self-content paper. AADL (**A**rchitecture **A**nalysis and **D**esign **L**anguage) [4] is a domain specific language dedicated to design software and hardware architectures of real-time embedded systems. AADL provides components helping to define hardware (such as processors and buses) and software concerns (such as threads and data). Interactions between components are expressed through their interfaces (i.e., ports, bus access, etc.). In addition, AADL provides a set of properties which can be easily extended. These properties make AADL designs become pivot model-centric since they enable to apply different analyses and settings (e.g., formal methods, schedulability analysis, energy consumption).

Modeling the example with AADL. Figure 2 represents the AADL design that corresponds to the running example (presented previously in Sect. 2.2). To ease

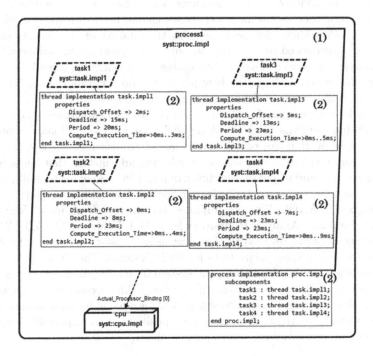

Fig. 2. Running example expressed in AADL language

the understanding and to give sufficient details we have mixed graphical and textual syntaxes. While Parts (1) give an overview of the architecture thanks to the graphical syntax, Parts (2) give more temporal details thanks to the AADL textual syntax.

2.4   Related Work

Recently, several works have coped with the problem of helping designers to analyze the temporal performance of their AADL architectures. Peres et al. [21] have proposed the usage of techniques based on model checking. This approach requires the transformation of AADL designs to another formalism (e.g., petrinets or timed automata). Moreover, the utilization of this technique seems to be complex since it suffers from the problem of the combination explosion. Gaudel et al. [12] implemented through Cheddar tool [2] an extraction of information from AADL models. That requires a set of ad-hoc information as design patterns that must be mentioned to support the analysis of AADL models and which is recognized only by the Cheddar tool. In addition, the recognition of the design patterns is based only on the architectural model, so it does not consider the behavior of the modeled system. Ouhammou et al. [19] suggested an example of model transformation from AADL to *MoSaRT Language* dedicated to the schedulability analysis. However, this approach requires to be familiar with MoSaRT language. Moreover, the transformation is not always equivalent. There are some concepts in one language which cannot be described in others languages or there are some concepts which can be transformed to different concepts in other languages depending on the context of the transformation. Brau et al. [9] proposed to construct an analysis repository to deduce all feasible pathways (a sequence of successive analyses) for achieving a predefined goal. However, authors do not focus on how pertinent and accurate the application of an analysis to a system, while it is an important factor.

Generally, we can classify all these works into two categories. Those which use the design patterns (piece of design-solution for conventional problem in design) and those that are based on the model transformation. However both categories contains hard-coded solutions. Also the information that helps designers to understand and to justify the choice of a test instead of others still implicit.

In this article, we adapt the solution proposed in [19] to support the systems designed in AADL. We have implemented this approach into a framework named **P**erformance **A**nalysis **R**epository for **A**ADL **D**esigns (PARAD). We propose two usages of our framework. The first usage consists in helping the AADL designers to choose appropriate tests for their systems. The choice is accompanied by sufficient explanation about the system under design and how it matches characteristics of the proposed test (if it exists). The second usage consists in helping analysts and researchers to share their knowledge by proposing repositories with relevant information making the repository users (especially designers) sufficiently autonomous during the analysis phase.

3   PARAD Approach and Its Fundamentals

This section is devoted to present our model-based contribution. The PARAD framework is mainly based on a description language allowing to instantiate repositories with contents based on analysis models, analysis tests and their characteristics. First, we present an overview of PARAD framework approach by highlighting briefly different capabilities. Secondly, we present the relevant foundation elements of PARAD and their roles. Our contribution is based on the facilities of model-driven engineering settings.

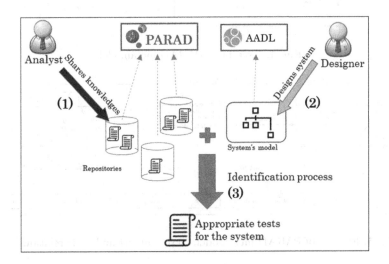

Fig. 3. Overview of Parad's utilization

3.1   PARAD Overview

Figure 3 shows an overview of the PARAD framework. PARAD offers two mechanisms. (i) The first one consists in creating analysis repositories, it is dedicated to analysts and researchers (process (1) in Fig. 3). An analysis repository can be made by one or many analysts. It represents the knowledge and expertise that analysts would like to share with other collaborators. (ii) The second mechanism is the identification process, dedicated to designers (process (3) in Fig. 3). Indeed, designers can apply their systems architectures, expressed in AADL (process (2) in Fig. 3), to a chosen analysis repository (provided by an expert analyst) in order to be assisted during the analysis phase. In the sequel, we will detail those two mechanisms.

3.2   Core Concepts of PARAD

The approach behind PARAD is based on a set of concepts related to the performance analysis theory. Figure 4 shows the principal excerpt of PARAD's metamodel. In the following we present the relevant concepts of PARAD.

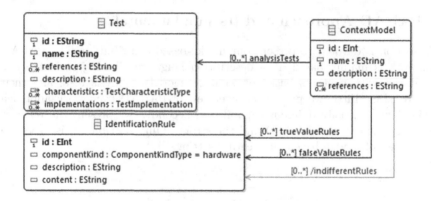

Fig. 4. Excerpt of PARAD metamodel

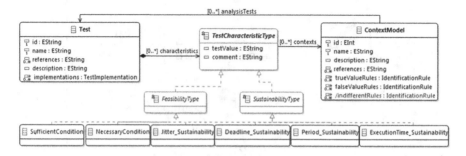

Fig. 5. Excerpt of PARAD metamodel: *Test, Context* and their relationship

- The *IdentificationRule* is the cornerstone notion of PARAD. An *Identifica-tionRule* represents an assumption on the system (e.g., 'System has only periodic tasks', 'System has mono-processor architecture', etc.). The value of each *IdentificationRule* is not always true or false but depends on the studied system. Due to evaluated values of these *IdentificationRules* on a system, we can determine the analysis situation of this system.

- *ContextModel* (or *Context* in short) represents the analysis situation of system, that let us know about the analysis model simulating the system and what analyses can be applied. In fact, a *ContextModel* is a set of hypotheses on the system. For example, Liu&Layland context [15] is based on these following hypotheses: 'System has mono-processor architecture', 'All tasks are independent', 'All tasks are characterised by worst-case execution time and period', etc. The hypotheses that constitute *ContextModel* are modelled by *IdentificationRule* with an expected value on the system: *trueValueRule*, *falseValueRule* and *indifferentValueRule*. *trueValueRule* represents the *Iden-tificationRule* that the system have to satisfy, *falseValueRule* represents the *IdentificationRule* that the system must not satisfy. It sometimes happens that a *ContextModel* can match a system whether the system satisfies an

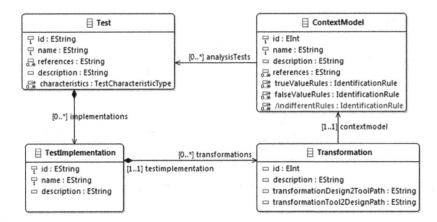

Fig. 6. Excerpt of PARAD metamodel: *TestImplementation* and *Transformation*

IdentificationRule or not, for example: Liu&Layland context [15] does not care whether system's tasks are concrete or not. We qualify this type of *IdentificationRule* as *indifferentValueRule*.

- *Test* represents the analysis technique which allows to conclude about the schedulability of systems. Since *ContextModel* represents the analysis situation of systems, in it, a number of *Tests* is applicable. To a specific *ContextModel*, a *Test* may be exact or sufficient or necessary (as we have already explained in Sect. 2.1). Tests are also characterised by the sustainability aspect [6]. In fact, analysis tests often consider the worst-case values (e.g. worst-case execution time, minimal period, maximal release jitter). During the execution of the system, the task parameters are always better than those considered in analysis, so the validity of analysis should retain. It is an important quality of an analysis. An analysis test with respect to a system is called sustainable, if the system, deemed valid by the test, remains valid even after changing tasks parameters: (Fig. 5) decreasing execution time (ExecutionTime_Sustainability), increasing period or inter-arrival times (Period_Sustainability), decreasing jitter (Jitter_Sustainability) and increasing relative deadline (Deadline_Sustainability).

- *TestImplementation* (Fig. 6) represents implementation of an analysis technique in a tool allowing to perform this test. *Transformation* represents a technique of assimilating concepts between the studied model and the input formalism of the associated tool. Each instance of *Transformation* enables to define the location of a program (executable files, call of web services,...) which can be used to automatize the transformation process.

Since we aim at examining AADL designs to detect the corresponding analysis contexts by evaluating *IdentificationRules*, they have to be based on a formalism. Therefore, we have opted for OCL and LUTE as languages to express these rules. Users can choose the language that they are more familiar with.

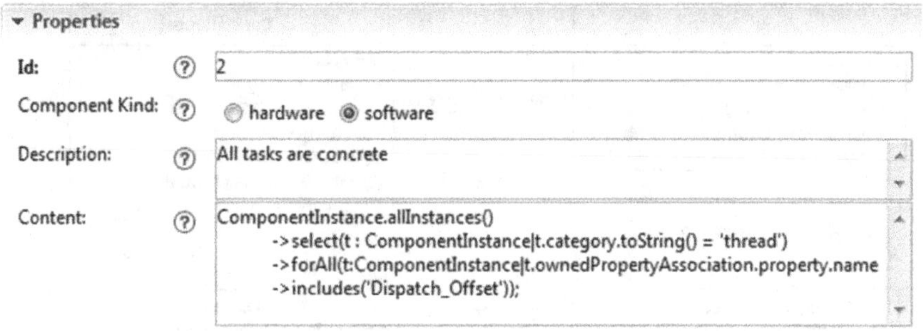

Fig. 7. Identification rule: "All tasks must have the Offset property" in OCL's syntax

- OCL (**O**bject **C**onstraint **L**anguage [18]) is Ecore-compliant. While the AADL metamodel conforms to Ecore [1], the content of *IdentificationRules* can be written in OCL's syntax. Thanks to OCL's checker, these rules can be evaluated. Figure 7 presents an identification rule expressed in OCL.
- LUTE is a constraint language that allows to query AADL models and therefore helps designers to check model structures and system requirements. It is composed of different functions to query the components hierarchy as well as their features (ports, connections, etc.) and properties [3]. The following listing shows an example of LUTE query which represents the same identification rule as the one of Fig. 7.

```
1     theorem Offset_Defined
2         foreach t in Thread_Set do
3             check Property_Exists(t,"Dispatch_Offset");
4     end;
```

Listing 1.1. An identification rule expressed in LUTE's syntax

3.3 PARAD Identification Process

The *Identification Process* is the way PARAD repositories seek the context of a system. It is composed of 2 steps: The first one is to evaluate all Identification rules (of the chosen repository) on the system and the second one compares results obtained in step 1 with the expected values of contexts of the repository to find out the appropriate contexts. Figure 8 presents an example sketching the identification process. We notice that the context model that corresponds to the system is the one which is defined by the same way as the evaluation result (obtained in step 1). In other words, the corresponding context is the one whose *trueValueRules* must be all evaluated as true on the system and whose *falseValueRules* must be evaluated as false on the system. Note that, a system can match more than one context. Moreover, the identification process can be called several times throughout an iterative design process.

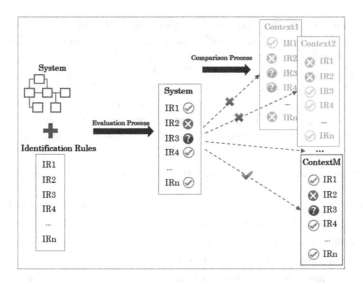

Fig. 8. Steps of Identification process

4   Proof of Concept

We introduce a simple case study to highlight the utilization of PARAD for choosing appropriate analyses for RTES and to demonstrate the possibility of combining several tests. We prepared a sample analysis repository, which is fulfilled with a list of conventional analysis tests. Thanks to the analysis repository, we can find the appropriate tests for a given system. Also, the results produced by an analysis test for a system make possible to apply other tests for the system. That enables to combine a number of test into a an incremental analysis-chain. The detail is presented hereafter.

4.1   PARAD Repository

We propose an *Analysis Repository* - instance of PARAD with the following schedulability analysis tests: *Response Time Analysis - RTA* [14], *Holistic Analysis* [29], *Request Bound Function - RBF* [7,13], *Rate Monotonic schedulability test* [26], *Audsley Priorities Assignment - OPA* [5]. These tests are already implemented in many academic and industrial third-party tools.

We also defined 4 contexts for tests: (Ctx1) Liu&Layland for tasks with pre-assigned priority - constrained deadline - fixed priority scheduler, (Ctx2) Periodic tasks model with arbitrary deadline in distributed system, (Ctx3) Liu&Layland for tasks with constrained deadline - EDF (Earliest Deadline First) scheduler, (Ctx4) Liu&Layland for tasks with offset - arbitrary deadline - fixed priority scheduler. The *Response Time Analysis* is sufficient, sustainable in Ctx1. Although the *Holistic Analysis* is a generic test, it can be applied in both Ctx1 and Ctx2. The application of *Holistic Analysis* in Ctx1 is identical to *Response*

Time Analysis, so we only added it to Ctx2 to deal with distributed system architecture. *Holistic Analysis* is sufficient and sustainable in Ctx2. The *Request Bound Function* is exact and non-sustainable in Ctx3. *Rate Monotonic schedulability test* is sufficient test in Ctx1 and Ctx4. And last *Audsley Priorities Assignment* is exact, non-sustainable in both Ctx1 and Ctx4. We introduce several *IdentificationRules* to identify these contexts. The content of each rule and its expected evaluation result in each context are presented in Table 3. To simplify the comprehension, we only choose 20 relevant rules for each context.

Table 3. Description of *ContextModel* in term of *IdentificationRule*

Contexts	Ctx1	Ctx2	Ctx3	Ctx4
IR1: All tasks must have predefined offset	U	U	U	✓
IR2: All tasks must have predefined execution time	✓	✓	✓	✓
IR3: All tasks must have predefined deadline	✓	✓	✓	✓
IR4: All tasks must have predefined period	✓	✓	✓	✓
IR5: All tasks must have predefined priority	✓	✓	U	U
IR6: All tasks must have predefined scheduling protocol	✓	✓	✓	✓
IR7: Mono-processor architecture	✓	✗	✓	✓
IR8: Earliest deadline first policy	✗	✗	✓	✗
IR9: Deadline monotonic policy	U	✓	✗	✗
IR10: Rate monotonic policy	U	✓	✗	✗
IR11: No predefined scheduling policy	U	U	U	U
IR12: All tasks must be concrete	U	U	U	✓
IR13: Tasks must be non-concrete	U	U	U	✗
IR14: All tasks must be periodic	✓	✓	✓	✓
IR15: All tasks must be synchronously activated	U	U	U	U
IR16: All tasks must be asynchronously activated	U	U	U	U
IR17: All tasks must be independent	✓	U	✓	✓
IR18: Deadline of all tasks must be implicit	U	U	U	U
IR19: Deadline of all tasks must be constrained	✓	U	✓	U
IR20: Deadline of all tasks must be arbitrary	✗	✓	✗	U

– ✓: rule whose evaluated value should be true in the context.
– ✗: rule whose evaluated value should be false in the context.
– U: regarding to the context, evaluation value of this rule is not important so it can be true or false.

4.2　Analysis Process Using PARAD as a Decision Support

System's description: we consider the same system presented in the motivating example (Sect. 2.2), but without any preassigned priority.

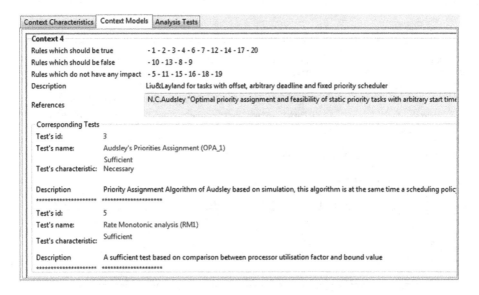

Fig. 9. Appropriate found contexts

We applied the constructed PARAD repository to the system expressed in AADL to find out the appropriate tests. The result is presented in Fig. 9. We notice that two contexts match the studied system, hence we have two tests are available at this stage: Audsley's Priorities Assignment (OPA) and the Rate Monotonic schedulability test (RM1). RM1 is <u>sufficient</u> in this context and OPA is <u>exact</u> in this context, so we choose OPA for the first analysis. The result of OPA is not only schedulability of system but also priority of tasks under which the system is schedulable (if the test is succeed). Part (1) in Fig. 11 sketches the obtained result of OPA. The system is schedulable by the calculated task's priority configuration. We assign the calculated priorities to tasks in the system and retry detection process. Due to priorities assigned, Response Time Analysis (RTA1) is also available (Fig. 10). Once again we apply RTA1 and get the result displayed in part (2) of Fig. 11. The provided result shows the worst-case response time of each task of the studied system. All tasks respect their deadlines except the last one. Note that RTA is a sufficient test in this context so the system remains schedulable under the priorities calculated by OPA.

4.3   Learned Lessons and Discussion

The case study has stressed usefulness of our approach to find appropriate analyses for a system model. Our approach has been used in two industrial projects with avionics partners [10, 30]. Therefore, we have realized some points to improve:

Context Characteristics	Context Models	Analysis Tests

Context 1

Rules which should be true	- 2 - 3 - 4 - 5 - 6 - 7 - 14 - 17 - 19
Rules which should be false	- 20 - 8
Rules which do not have any impact	- 1 - 11 - 12 - 13 - 18 - 9 - 10
Description	Liu&Layland for tasks with pre-assigned priority, constrained deadline, fixed priority
References	K. Tindell, "An Extendible Approache for Analysing Fixed Priority Hard Real-Time Ta

Corresponding Tests

Test's id:	3
Test's name:	Audsley's Priorities Assignment (OPA_1)
Test's characteristic:	Sufficient Necessary
Description	Priority Assignment Algorithm of Audsley based on simulation, this algorithm is at the same time

*********************   *********************

Test's id:	4
Test's name:	Response Time Analysis (RTA_1)
Test's characteristic:	Sufficient
Description	Calculate the response time of independent tasks deadline constrained with priority pre-assigned

*********************   *********************

Test's id:	5
Test's name:	Rate Monotonic analysis (RM1)

Fig. 10. Detection result

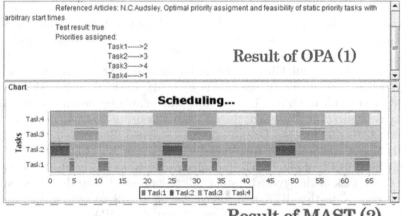

Referenced Articles: N.C.Audsley, Optimal priority assigment and feasibility of static priority tasks with arbitrary start times
Test result: true
Priorities assigned:
Task1----->2
Task2----->3
Task3----->4
Task4----->1

Result of OPA (1)

Chart

Scheduling...

Result of MAST (2)

Transaction	Event	Referenced Event	Worst Response	Hard Deadline
task1	deadline_monitor_task1	activator_task1	7.000	15.000
task2	deadline_monitor_task2	activator_task2	4.000	8.000
task3	deadline_monitor_task3	activator_task3	12.000	13.000
task4	deadline_monitor_task4	activator_task4	33.000	23.000

Fig. 11. Result of case study

1. The more *IdentificationRules* are defined, the more accurate is the context detection. Then, in practice, we provide a dozen of *IdentificationRules* to constitute analysis repositories.
2. Often, *IdentificationRules* are not independent. Their semantics are implicitly related. For example, the rule 'All tasks must be concrete' implies that 'All tasks must have Offset property'. So, we plan to explicit and model the relations between *IdentificationRules*.
3. In case of an existing repository with a huge number of *IdentificationRules*, the extension can be difficult since it can lead to some duplicates or semantic conflicts. We plan a verification process of the repository content by using formal methods.
4. Basically, all rules are inspired from the scheduling theory and are expressed in natural language. We interpret them using query languages (like OCL or LUTE), but the interpretation process is not easy and not reversible, we cannot retrieve easily the rule semantic from its interpretation in OCL or LUTE. Therefore, we plan to create a domain specific language which is close to natural language (humain-readable) and understandable by the machine to express the *IdentificationRules*.

5   Conclusion

The main difficulty that faces a RTES designer is the lack of an advisor during the performance analysis phase. The PARAD framework represents a solution for this problem by defining a way allowing a collaboration between analysts and designers thanks to the analysis repositories. Moreover, PARAD can be used to launch a set of detection processes to find out the most suitable performance tests for a system design. PARAD is not a hard-coded solution which eases its usage and extension. Through PARAD, we can automatize as much as possible the analysis. We are working on the relationships between analysis contexts to facilitate their instantiation in a repository, based on existing ones. We are also working on the relationships between identification rules to detect contradictory rules and complementary ones.

Acknowledgements. This work is co-funded through the Waruna project by the French Ministry of the Economy, Finances and Industry, and by the PIA CORAC Panda project.

References

1. Eclipse modeling framework. https://www.eclipse.org/modeling/emf/. Accessed 20 Feb 2017
2. The cheddar project: a GPL real-time scheduling analyzer (2015). http://beru.univ-brest.fr/~singhoff/cheddar/. Accessed 11 Feb 2015
3. Constraint language for AADL: LUTE (2016). http://www.aadl.info/aadl/osate/osate-doc/osate-plugins/lute.html

4. AADL. Architecture analysis and design language. http://www.aadl.info/
5. Audsley, N.C.: Optimal Priority Assignment and Feasibility of Static Priority Tasks with Arbitrary Start Times. Citeseer (1991)
6. Baruah, S., Burns, A.: Sustainable scheduling analysis. In: 27th IEEE International Real-Time Systems Symposium, RTSS 2006, pp. 159–168. IEEE (2006)
7. Baruah, S.K., Rosier, L.E., Howell, R.R.: Algorithms and complexity concerning the preemptive scheduling of periodic, real-time tasks on one processor. Real-Time Syst. 2(4), 301–324 (1990)
8. Bini, E., Di Natale, M., Buttazzo, G.: Sensitivity analysis for fixed-priority real-time systems. Real-Time Syst. 39(1–3), 5–30 (2008)
9. Brau, G., Hugues, J., Navet, N.: A contract-based approach to support goal-driven analysis. In: ISORC, pp. 236–243. IEEE (2015)
10. CORAC.Le conseil pour la recherche aéronautique civile. http://aerorecherchecorac.com/
11. Davis, R.I., Burns, A.: A survey of hard real-time scheduling for multiprocessor systems. ACM Comput. Surv. (CSUR) 43(4), 35 (2011)
12. Gaudel, V., Singhoff, F., Plantec, A., Rubini, S., Dissaux, P., Legrand, J.: An ada design pattern recognition tool for AADL performance analysis. In: SIGAda, pp. 61–68 (2011)
13. Jeffay, K., Stone, D.: Accounting for interrupt handling costs in dynamic priority task systems. In: 1993 Proceedings of the Real-Time Systems Symposium, pp. 212–221. IEEE (1993)
14. Joseph, M., Pandya, P.: Finding response times in a real-time system. Comput. J. 29(5), 390–395 (1986)
15. Liu, C.L., Layland, J.W.: Scheduling algorithms for multiprogramming in a hard-real-time environment. J. ACM (JACM) 20(1), 46–61 (1973)
16. MARTE. Modeling and analysis of real-time and embedded systems. http://www.omg.org/omgmarte/. Accessed 20 Feb 2017
17. MAST. Modeling and analysis suite for real-time applications. http://mast.unican.es/. Accessed 20 Feb 2017
18. Object constraint language proposed by object menagement group (omg). http://www.omg.org/spec/OCL/. Accessed 20 Feb 2017
19. Ouhammou, Y., Grolleau, E., Richard, M., Richard, P.: Towards a model-based approach guiding the scheduling analysis of real-time systems design. In: WATERS (2014)
20. Ouhammou, Y., Grolleau, E., Richard, P., Richard, M.: Reducing the gap between design and scheduling. In: 20th RTNS, pp. 21–30 (2012)
21. Peres, F., Hladik, P.-E., Vernadat, F.: Specification and verification of real-time systems using pola. Int. J. Crit. Comput.-Based Syst. 2(3–4), 332–351 (2011)
22. Rouhifar, M., Ravanmehr, R.: A survey on scheduling approaches for hard real-time systems. Int. J. Comput. Appl. 131(17), 41–48 (2015)
23. RT-Druid. http://www.evidence.eu.com/products/rt-druid.html
24. Schmidt, D.C.: Guest editor's introduction: model-driven engineering. IEEE Comput. 39(2), 25–31 (2006)
25. Sha, L., Abdelzaher, T., Årzén, K.-E., Cervin, A., Baker, T., Burns, A., Buttazzo, G., Caccamo, M., Lehoczky, J., Mok, A.K.: Real time scheduling theory: a historical perspective. Real-Time Syst. 28(2–3), 101–155 (2004)
26. Sha, L., Klein, M.H., Goodenough, J.B.: Rate monotonic analysis for real-time systems. In: van Tilborg, A.M., Koob, G.M. (eds.) Foundations of Real-Time Computing: Scheduling and Resource Management, pp. 129–155. Springer, New York (1991)

27. Simso.Simulation of multiprocessor scheduling with overheads. http://projects. laas.fr/simso/. Accessed 20 Feb 2017
28. Stigge, M., Yi, W.: Graph-based models for real-time workload: a survey. Real-Time Syst. **51**(5), 602–636 (2015)
29. Tindell, K., Clark, J.: Holistic schedulability analysis for distributed hard real-time systems. Microprocess. Microprogram. **40**(2–3), 117–134 (1994)
30. Waruna. Atelier de modélisation et de vérification de propriétés temporelles. http://www.waruna-projet.fr/

Continuous Rearchitecting of QoS Models: Collaborative Analysis for Uncertainty Reduction

Catia Trubiani[1(✉)] and Raffaela Mirandola[2]

[1] Gran Sasso Science Institute, L'Aquila, Italy
catia.trubiani@gssi.it
[2] Politecnico di Milano, Milano, Italy
raffaela.mirandola@polimi.it

Abstract. Architecting high quality software systems is not trivial, in fact to know whether a certain quality attribute has been achieved, it has to be continuously analysed. Reasoning about multiple quality attributes (e.g., performance, availability) of software systems is even more difficult since it is necessary to jointly analyze multiple and heterogeneous Quality-of-Service (QoS) models. The goal of this paper is to investigate the combined use of different QoS models and continuously re-architecting them since the acquired knowledge of a specific QoS model may affect another model, thus to put in place a collaborative analysis process that reduces the overall uncertainty. Starting from an example of interaction among two different QoS models, i.e., a Bayesian Network for availability and a Queueing Network for performance, we demonstrate that the collaborative analysis brings benefits to the overall process since the initial uncertainty is reduced. We identify the join/fork points within the analysis process to bring upfront the quality characteristics of software systems, thus to enable the rearchitecting of systems in case of quality flaws. In this way, the QoS analysis becomes an integrated activity in the whole software development life-cycle and quality characteristics are continuously exposed to system architects.

Keywords: Continuous rearchitecting · Collaborative QoS analysis · Uncertainty reduction · Bayesian Networks · Queueing Networks

1 Introduction

Early validation of Quality-of-Service (QoS) requirements has been assessed as fundamental in the software development process, in fact in [19] it has been demonstrated that the costs of fixing errors escalate in an exponential fashion as the project matures during the various phases of its life cycle. Interestingly, if the cost of fixing an error discovered during the requirements phase is defined to be 1 unit, the cost to fix that error if found during the design phase increases to 3–8 units; at the manufacturing/build phase, the cost to fix the error is 7–16 units;

A. Lopes and R. de Lemos (Eds.): ECSA 2017, LNCS 10475, pp. 40–48, 2017.
DOI: 10.1007/978-3-319-65831-5_3

at the integration and test phase, the cost to fix the error becomes 21–78 units, and at the operations phase, the cost to fix the requirements error ranged from 29 to more than 1500 units. This highly motivates the activities of evaluating software architectures that are the result of early design decisions [2].

In literature several methodologies emerged to perform the evaluation of software architectures [5], however the problem of integrating multiple formalisms [3] and supporting their heterogeneity [15] is indeed not trivial. The QoS evaluation of software architectures is even more difficult since it is necessary to jointly analyze multiple and heterogeneous QoS models, possibly pointing out different quality attributes (e.g., performance, availability). Some approaches recently emerged for multi-objective architecture optimization [1,11], however the problem of identifying the interactions between QoS models is still very critical.

In this paper we investigate the problem of bridging multiple and heterogeneous QoS models to support their collaborative analysis. The main difficulty in this context is to understand how to continuously rearchitect them due to the acquired knowledge of a specific QoS model that may affect another model. Consider for example a situation in which the availability of a certain software service may be conditioned by given threshold values of external factors (e.g., illumination, wind). Multiple copies of these services then could exist whose activation depends on these threshold values. The activation of these services will strongly affect the overall system performance in terms of latency and synchronisation overhead. In these situations, the uncertainty of the external factors, such as environmental conditions, affects the software system behavior and different models should be jointly analysed to derive its QoS characteristics.

We show through an illustrative case study, i.e., a wind generator system based on [18], this need of interaction among heterogeneous QoS models and how their collaborative analysis brings benefits to the overall process since the initial uncertainty is reduced. In particular, we focus on Bayesian Network (BN) to model the availability of services and Queueing Network (QN) models for system performance evaluation. The BN results are used to parametrize the QN models and possibly to change its structure adding or modifying some queueing centers to take into account the avalaibility/unavailability of certain software services. The QN models are then jointly analysed to derive QoS characteristics, such as the system response time. Besides, if QoS analysis results show flaws, then it is necessary to put in place further architectural modifications that aim to improve the results without affecting the system functionalities. The goal of the collaborative analysis is to identify the join/fork points within the analysis process to bring upfront the quality characteristics of software architectures, thus to reduce the overall uncertainty and overcome the QoS flaws. To this end, during the development of our illustrative example, we have identified three main challenges that need further investigations: (i) continuous rearchitecting, (ii) collaborative analysis, and (iii) uncertainty reduction.

The remaining of the paper is organised as follows. Section 2 presents related work; Sect. 3 motivates our investigation through an illustrative case study;

Sect. 4 discusses the main research challenges raised by the presented example and concludes the paper by outlining future research directions.

2 Related Work

In the following we group the related works while exposing the main contributions in the three research directions we are interested:

Continuous rearchitecting. The problem of continuous architecting has been recently discussed in [8] and its definition remains twofold: (i) continuous improvement due to new experiences gained by developers and architects; (ii) elimination of bottlenecks and bad practices to optimise the quality characteristics of architectures. We are interested to both definitions, the former goes in the direction of reducing the uncertainty, whereas the latter supports QoS-based reconfigurations. In [17] the practitioners' perspectives is reported, but the continuous deployment in practice is perceived as a struggling activity due to monolithic architectures. In [20] the removal of bad practices supports the fulfilment of performance requirements, but the continuous generation of architectural alternatives inevitably affects the efficiency of the evaluation process. These open issues need to be addressed by integrating stakeholders' knowledge with efficient optimisation techniques to achieve an agile continuous rearchitecting.

Collaborative analysis. Several works aim to optimise the QoS properties of software systems while considering multiple sources of information, e.g., in [13] QoS-optimised software architectures are reconfigured due to runtime variabilities, such as service binding and deploying coordination logic. Such variabilities can be explicitly expressed as features, however the development of feature-based configurable systems is usually infeasible due to features combinatorics [16], and it is still an open problem to determine an ideal set of samples that balances prediction accuracy and measurement effort. In [4] a framework for QoS management of self-adaptive service-based systems is proposed, however QoS models are analysed in isolation. These open issues need to be addressed by understanding the impact of variabilities across the heterogeneous QoS models to achieve a smart collaborative analysis.

Uncertainty reduction. In [6] the authors outline that existing architecture decision-making approaches do not provide a quantitative method for comparing different architectural alternatives that deal with uncertainty. Quantification for model-based performance and reliability evaluation of software architectures in presence of uncertainties is provided in [7,12], however no reduction of uncertainty is tackled. In [14] a methodology for managing uncertainties in software models is proposed, and software engineers are guided in the process of recognising the existence of uncertainty, but also this method does not support the reduction of uncertainty. These open issues need to be addressed by quantifying the impact of reducing the uncertainty across the heterogeneous QoS models to achieve an efficient model-based analysis.

Summarising, the novelty of our work with respect to the current state-of-the-art is that we aim to jointly consider these three aspects: the collaborative analysis between heterogeneous QoS models becomes of key relevance to smooth the continuous rearchitecting effort while targeting uncertainty reduction.

3   Wind Generator System

In this section we describe our idea of continuous rearchitecting through an illustrative example, i.e., a wind generator system (WGS), whose architecture is shown through a feature model in Fig. 1. The system consists of a wind turbine (WT) associated to a set of software services that are activated conditioned to the speed of the wind, i.e., light (L), moderate (M), or strong (S).

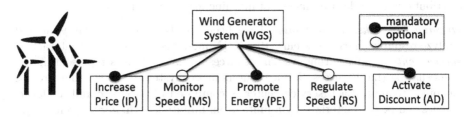

Fig. 1. Feature model for WGS.

If the wind is light, then two services are activated: (i) increasePrice (IP), i.e., the production of energy is reduced and it is necessary to increase the price to which the new users buy the energy under production; and monitorSpeed (MS), i.e., the speed of turbines needs to be monitored with a certain frequency. If the wind is moderate, then the monitorSpeed (MS) service keeps to be activated but the frequency associated to the monitoring is increased, and one further service is triggered: (ii) promoteEnergy (PE), i.e., the production of energy is augmented and it is necessary to promote it thus to attract new users with lower prices. If the wind is strong, then the promoteEnergy (PE) service keeps to be activated, and two further services are triggered: (i) regulateSpeed (RS), i.e., the turbines require to be regulated; (ii) activateDiscount (AD), i.e., the production of energy is largely increased, hence it is better to activate discounts to current users thus to incentive the consumption of energy.

3.1   WGS Modelling

Background. Hereafter, before showing the obtained system models, we provide some background information on the adopted QoS models, i.e., Bayesian Networks and Queuing Networks.

Bayesian Networks. These models have been recently applied to model beliefs in computational biology, bioinformatics, and also in financial and marketing informatics [9]. A BN model is a statistical model that represents a set of random variables and their conditional dependencies via a directed acyclic graph (DAG), where nodes represent random variables (i.e., they may be observable quantities, latent variables, unknown parameters or hypotheses) and edges represent conditional dependencies. Each node is associated with a probability function that takes, as input, a particular set of values for the node's parent variables, and gives (as output) the probability (or probability distribution, if applicable) of the variable represented by the node. Nodes that are not connected represent variables that are conditionally independent of each other. There are three main inference tasks for BNs, and efficient algorithms exist to perform such tasks. First, *inferring unobserved variables* performs the probabilistic inference by deriving the posterior distribution of all variables given the evidence of some of them. Second, *parameter learning* implies to specify for each node the probability distribution for that node conditional upon its parents. Third, *structure learning* implies to learn the network structure and the parameters of the local distributions from data by means of machine learning techniques.

Queuing Networks. These models have been widely applied to represent and analyze resource sharing systems [10]. A QN model is a collection of interacting *service centers* representing system resources and a set of *jobs* representing the users sharing the resources. Service centers model system resources that process customer request. Each service center is composed of a *Server* and a *Queue*. Queues can be characterized by a finite or an infinite length. Service centers are connected through *links* that form the network topology. Each server, contained in every service center, picks the next job from its queue (if not empty), processes it, and selects one link that routes the processed request to the queue of another service center. The time spent in every server by each request is modeled by exponential distributions. Jobs are generated by source nodes connected with links to the rest of the QN. Delay centers are nodes of the QN connected with links to the rest of the network exactly as service centers, but they do not have an associated queue. Delay centers are described only by a service time, with a continuous distribution, without an associated queue. In other words, QN representation is a direct graph whose nodes are service centers and their connections are represented by the graph edges. Jobs go through the graph's edge set on the basis of the behavior of customers' service requests.

QoS Models. Figure 2 illustrates the QoS models we have obtained for the WGS depicted in Fig. 1. In the left side we show the BN model, where the WT node is connected with the three nodes indicating the speed of the wind, i.e., light, moderate, and strong. In this model we make use of the inferring unobserved variables algorithm, in fact we introduce probabilistic inference rules to model the speed of the wind, and we derive the corresponding availability of the connected software services. In the right side we show the QN built to model the corresponding scenario, in particular a delay center node includes all the requests circulating in the system. Such requests are routed by means of probabilities related to the speed of the wind, and depending on these probabilities, then the corresponding connected services are activated, and we derive the system response time as indicator of its efficiency.

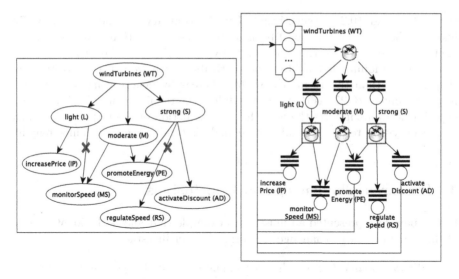

Fig. 2. Wind generator system modelled with BNs and QNs.

3.2 WGS Analysis

The QoS collaborative analysis of these two models is executed as follows. From the BN we are able to derive the software services activation probabilities since the initial uncertainty is reduced by means of inference rules that regulate the variations of the wind speed. Table 1 reports the BN analysis results of our illustrative case study while varying such inference rules; for example, when the wind is light (L), then the probability of invoking the increasePrice (IP) service is 0.89. In our experimentation whenever we get a service whose probability of being invoked is larger than 0.8 (see shaded entries of Table 1), then a copy of the corresponding service is added, i.e., the system is rearchitected, and it implies changes in the QN model.

Table 1. BN results.

	L	M	S
IP	0.89	0.18	0.18
MS	0.7	0.75	0.2
PE	0.2	0.8	0.55
RS	0.22	0.22	0.73
AD	0.31	0.31	0.86

Table 2 reports the QN analysis results that have been obtained by considering a workload of 100 requests/ms and the system response time (RT) is required to be not larger than 10 ms. In the first row of the table we can notice that the initial QN model shows a RT equal to 10.61 ms, i.e., larger than the requirement. Then, we considered to add additional copies for each of the services that has been identified in Table 1 and we solved the corresponding QN models. We can notice that the additional instances of IP and AD slightly improves the response time

Table 2. QN results.

		RT (ms)
	Initial	10.61
	IP	10.54
add	PE	9.14
	AD	10.29
delete	MS	9.91
	RS	10.27

(i.e., 10.54 and 10.29, respectively). On the contrary, the addition of a PE instance allows to get a RT of 9.14 ms that is lower than 10 ms. We also experimented the deletion of the optional software services, as shown in Fig. 1. In particular we found that if MS is not activated, then we get a RT of 9.91 ms that is lower than the 10 ms threshold, whereas by deactivating RS we get a response time of 10.27 ms that is not fulfilling the requirement. This illustrative experimentation supports the idea that the reduction of the initial uncertainty leads the system to put a collaborative analysis that triggers continuos rearchitecting.

4   Research Challenges and Conclusions

In this paper we presented an illustrative example that allows the identification of three main research challenges requiring further investigations:

- *continuous rearchitecting*: the continuous models' changes implies the need of designing a `controller` module that detects modifications in the analysis results of QoS models and highlights which refactorings lead to quality flaws;
- *collaborative analysis*: the presence of heterogeneous QoS models calls for the introduction of an `orchestrator` module that specifies in a principled manner how analysis results of QoS models are mutually affected;
- *uncertainty reduction*: the influence of non controllable external factors requires the design of a `tuner` module that extracts the ranges of these factors and transfers such knowledge to the involved QoS models.

The design of these three modules enables the possibility to conduct a collaborative analysis between heterogeneous QoS models and to smooth the continuous rearchitecting effort while targeting uncertainty reduction. We plan to support these activities by introducing an architectural description language aimed to bridge the heterogeneous QoS models and their analysis results through the identification of the join/fork points within the QoS analysis process. In particular, the `tuner` module includes the specification of uncertain parameters, their range of values, and the QoS model elements that are involved in such uncertainties. After the setup of parameters is completed, the `orchestrator` module comprises the specification of the relationships between the heterogeneous QoS models and their analysis results. Both the models and the results are then exploited by the `controller` module that is in charge of identifying quality flaws and rearchitecting the heterogeneous QoS models accordingly. The goal is to put in place a minimal set of architectural refactoring changes leading to the fulfilment of QoS requirements. The benefit of our architectural description language is that it jointly coordinates the heterogeneous QoS models and keeps under control the QoS analysis results.

These needs are further exacerbated when we consider software architectures that are embedded in dynamic contexts where requirements, environment assumptions, and usage profiles frequently change. Since these changes in the context happen in a way that is hard to predict when software systems are initially built, the outcome of the QoS models results to change quite frequently so to imply the need of (possibly) frequent changes in all the involved models. Besides this, the outcome of the model analysis may be subject to wider uncertainties because assumptions upon which they rely on are not verified. Recognising the presence of these uncertainties and managing them would minimise their influence and increase the level of trust in a given software architecture.

As future work, we plan to move along the research lines we have listed above thus to bring upfront the quality characteristics of software architectures and their rearchitecting in case of quality flaws. In this way, the QoS analysis becomes an integrated activity in the whole software development life-cycle and quality characteristics are continuously exposed to system architects.

References

1. Aleti, A., Buhnova, B., Grunske, L., Koziolek, A., Meedeniya, I.: Software architecture optimization methods: A systematic literature review. IEEE Trans. Softw. Eng. **39**(5), 658–683 (2013)
2. Bass, L.: Software Architecture in Practice, 3rd edn. Addison-Wesley Professional, Boston (2012)
3. Broman, D., Lee, E.A., Tripakis, S., Törngren, M.: Viewpoints, formalisms, languages, and tools for cyber-physical systems. In: Proceedings of the International Workshop on Multi-Paradigm Modeling, MPM@MoDELS, pp. 49–54 (2012)
4. Calinescu, R., Grunske, L., Kwiatkowska, M., Mirandola, R., Tamburrelli, G.: Dynamic qos management and optimization in service-based systems. IEEE Trans. Softw. Eng. **37**(3), 387–409 (2011)
5. Dobrica, L., Niemela, E.: A survey on software architecture analysis methods. IEEE Trans. Softw. Eng. **28**(7), 638–653 (2002)
6. Esfahani, N., Malek, S., Razavi, K.: Guidearch: guiding the exploration of architectural solution space under uncertainty. In: Proceedings of International Conference on Software Engineering, ICSE, pp. 43–52 (2013)
7. Etxeberria, L., Trubiani, C., Cortellessa, V., Sagardui, G.: Performance-based selection of software and hardware features under parameter uncertainty. In: International Conference on Quality of Software Architectures, QoSA, pp. 23–32 (2014)
8. Holmes, B., Nicolaescu, A.: Continuous architecting: Just another buzzword? Full-scale Software Engineering/The Art of Software Testing, p. 1 (2017)
9. Jensen, F.V.: An Introduction to Bayesian Networks. UCL press, London (1996)
10. Kleinrock, L.: Queueing Systems: Theory. Wiley, New York (1975)
11. Koziolek, A., Koziolek, H., Reussner, R.H.: Peropteryx: automated application of tactics in multi-objective software architecture optimization. In: International Conference on the Quality of Software Architectures, QoSA, pp. 33–42 (2011)
12. Meedeniya, I., Aleti, A., Grunske, L.: Architecture-driven reliability optimization with uncertain model parameters. JSS **85**(10), 2340–2355 (2012)
13. Menascé, D.A., Gomaa, H., Malek, S., Sousa, J.P.: SASSY: A framework for self-architecting service-oriented systems. IEEE Softw. **28**(6), 78–85 (2011)
14. Perez-Palacin, D., Mirandola, R.: Uncertainties in the modeling of self-adaptive systems: a taxonomy and an example of availability evaluation. In: International Conference on Performance Engineering, ICPE, pp. 3–14 (2014)

15. Rajhans, A., Bhave, A., Ruchkin, I., Krogh, B.H., Garlan, D., Platzer, A., Schmerl, B.R.: Supporting heterogeneity in cyber-physical systems architectures. IEEE Trans. Automat. Contr. **59**(12), 3178–3193 (2014)
16. Sarkar, A., Guo, J., Siegmund, N., Apel, S., Czarnecki, K.: Cost-efficient sampling for performance prediction of configurable systems. In: International Conference on Automated Software Engineering, ASE (2015)
17. Shahin, M., Babar, M.A., Zhu, L.: The intersection of continuous deployment and architecting process: practitioners' perspectives. In: ACM/IEEE International Symposium on Empirical Software Engineering and Measurement (2016)
18. Slootweg, J., De Haan, S., Polinder, H., Kling, W.: General model for representing variable speed wind turbines in power system dynamics simulations. IEEE Trans. Power Syst. **18**(1), 144–151 (2003)
19. Stecklein, J.M., Dabney, J., Dick, B., Haskins, B., Lovell, R., Moroney, G.: Error cost escalation through the project life cycle. NASA Technical report (2004)
20. Trubiani, C., Koziolek, A., Cortellessa, V., Reussner, R.H.: Guilt-based handling of software performance antipatterns in palladio architectural models. J. Syst. Softw. **95**, 141–165 (2014)

Software Architecture Evolution

The Evolution of Technical Debt in the Apache Ecosystem

Georgios Digkas[1]([✉]), Mircea Lungu[1], Alexander Chatzigeorgiou[2],
and Paris Avgeriou[1]

[1] Johann Bernoulli Institute for Mathematics and Computer Science,
University of Groningen, Nijenborgh 9, 9747 AG Groningen, The Netherlands
{g.digkas,m.f.lungu}@rug.nl, paris@cs.rug.nl
[2] Department of Applied Informatics, University of Macedonia,
Egnatia 156, 546 36 Thessaloniki, Greece
achat@uom.gr

Abstract. Software systems must evolve over time or become increasingly irrelevant says one of Lehman's laws of software evolution. Many studies have been presented in the literature that investigate the evolution of software systems but few have focused on the evolution of technical debt. In this paper we study sixty-six Java open-source software projects from the Apache ecosystem focusing on the evolution of technical debt. We analyze the evolution of these systems over the past five years at the temporal granularity level of weekly snapshots. We calculate the trends of the technical debt time series but we also investigate the lower-level constituent components of this technical debt. We aggregate some of the information to the ecosystem level.

Our findings show that the technical debt together with source code metrics increase for the majority of the systems. However, technical debt normalized to the size of the system actually decreases over time in the majority of the systems under investigation. Furthermore, we discover that some of the most frequent and time-consuming types of technical debt are related to improper exception handling and code duplication.

Keywords: Software evolution · Time series data mining · Technical debt · Mining software repositories · Empirical study

1 Introduction

The Technical Debt (TD) metaphor was coined by Ward Cunningham in 1992 as:
"Shipping first time code is like going into debt. A little debt speeds development so long as it is paid back promptly with a rewrite. Objects make the cost of this transaction tolerable. The danger occurs when the debt is not repaid. Every minute spent on not-quite-right code counts as interest on that debt. Entire engineering organizations can be brought to a stand-still under the debt load of an unconsolidated implementation, object-oriented or otherwise".

© Springer International Publishing AG 2017
A. Lopes and R. de Lemos (Eds.): ECSA 2017, LNCS 10475, pp. 51–66, 2017.
DOI: 10.1007/978-3-319-65831-5_4

Technical debt is present in both industrial software as well as in open-source projects. In industrial settings the tight deadlines are pushing the software engineers and the developers to compromise the quality of the system and take shortcuts in order to release a product as soon as possible. In open-source settings, the self-imposed deadlines of the developers working towards delivering their contributions to the community or the lack of processes regarding quality assurance might lead them to take similar shortcuts.

Taking all these shortcuts increases the change- and fault- proneness of the systems and aggravates long-term understandability, re-usability, reliability, efficiency, security, and maintainability. While it has been empirically proven that these shortcuts affect negatively the project's quality, completely eliminating technical debt from a system is undesirable as the investment to reduce TD would be extremely inefficient.

Although there has been extensive research with respect to technical debt [1] and there exists even a dedicated international forum for research on the topic (the MTD workshop) there is a lack of empirical evidence regarding the occurrence and evolution of technical debt in the open-source systems.

Moreover, technical debt has also not been studied before in software ecosystems. Software ecosystems are groups of software projects that are developed and co-evolve in the same environment [2,3]. Such projects can share code, they might depend on one another, and are often built on similar technologies and with similar processes.

In this paper we conduct an empirical study of sixty-six open-source software projects of the Apache ecosystem. We chose to analyze OSS projects of the Apache Software Foundation because it is one of the biggest communities which provide software products for the public good and its projects are highly appreciated and used.

Structure of the paper. The rest of the paper is organized as follows: Sect. 2 motivates our study through an analysis of an Apache project. Section 3 presents the methodology and the design of the study. Section 4 presents the results of our empirical study and Sect. 5 discusses the threats to its validity. Section 6 presents the related work and Sect. 7 concludes the paper.

2 A Motivating Example

Apache Sling[1], one of the most popular projects in the Apache ecosystem, is an open-source Web framework for the Java platform designed to create content-centric applications on top of a JSR-170-compliant content repository such as Apache Jackrabbit. The project represents a significant community effort: at the moment of writing this article, the system has more than a dozen contributors who have commit rights to the main repository; these committers have contributed more than twenty thousand commits over the years.

Imagine we are the developers of the Apache Sling. We decide to analyze it to learn about the evolution of its technical debt. To measure the technical debt and

---

[1] https://sling.apache.org/.

extract other metrics we decide to use an industrial strength tool. SonarQube [4] is an open-source tool for continuous inspection which features dashboards, rule-based defect analysis, and build integration. It supports various languages, including Java, C, C++, C#, PHP, and JavaScript.

SonarQube employs the SQALE [2] method for estimating the time required to fix the technical debt [5]. Technical debt evolution estimation using SonarQube is time consuming since when recomputing it for a new version of the system, no matter how small the difference between the two versions (even a single commit), the tool can not analyze only the differences, but instead, has to do the entire computation for the entire system again[3]. This means that the time necessary to analyze the history of a system is proportional to the number of versions of the system that are to be analyzed.

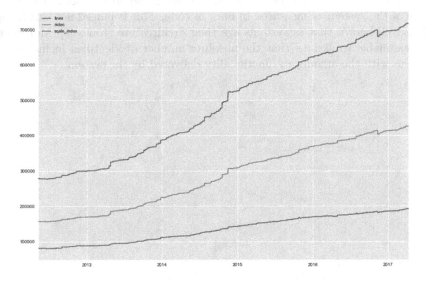

Fig. 1. The evolution of lines of code (blue, top), non commented lines of code (green, middle), and technical debt (red, bottom) in Apache Sling over the last 5 years. Technical debt represents effort to fix problems and is estimated in minutes. (Color figure online)

To drive this evolutionary analysis we do not use the graphical UI of the tool but rather we develop a program that interfaces with the API of the tool in order to compute the entire battery of analyses that SonarQube supports on that version, including technical debt related analysis.

---

[2] Software Quality Assessment based on Lifecycle Expectations.

[3] This problem is not exclusive to SonarQube. We are not aware of any analysis tools that perform complex, system-level analysis without re-analyzing the entire system when presented with a new version.

However, since analyzing all commits of the Sling project (which are more than twenty thousands) is not feasible as we explained earlier, we analyze snapshots of the system at one week intervals. More precisely we find the last commit in a given week, and we run the analysis on that version.

Figure 1 presents the evolution of the Apache Sling project over the last five years in terms of two metrics:

1. Lines of code (blue, topmost series) and non-comment lines of code (green, middle series)
2. SQALE Index which is the tool estimated technical debt (red, bottom series) in minutes

The most salient observation in the Fig. 1 is that the amount of measured technical debt as measured by the SQALE index grows in parallel to the magnitude of the system as measured in lines of code. This is indeed not surprising as it is well known that as systems age their architecture erodes [6]. Moreover, it is reasonable to assume that the absolute number of identified inefficiencies increases with the amount of functionality delivered by the system.

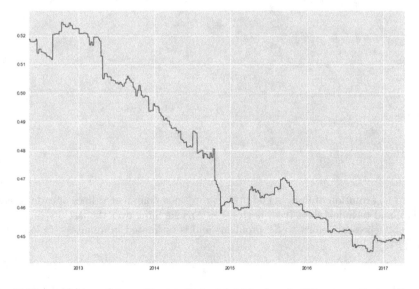

Fig. 2. The evolution of normalized technical debt in Apache Sling over the last 5 years shows a clear decreasing trend

To exclude the possibility that the growth of technical debt is correlated with the growth of the system, we compute the evolution of the *size-normalized technical debt* – that is, the technical debt normalized to the number of lines of code in the system. Figure 2 shows that the normalized technical debt is actually decreasing.

Open Questions. How this project compares with other similar ones? Is the growth of technical debt that our system exposes normal? Is the fact that the normalized technical debt decreases over time exceptional?

Table 1. The most frequently occurring types of issues in Apache Sling. The number in parenthesis is the percentage of the total violations detected

	Issue	Count	
1	The diamond operator ("<>") should be used	2,888	(10.75%)
2	String literals should not be duplicated	2,875	(10.70%)
3	Generic exceptions should never be thrown	1,856	(6.90%)
4	Control flow statements should not be nested too deeply	1,345	(5.00%)
5	Exception handlers should preserve the original exceptions	1,215	(4.50%)

The Components of Technical Debt. The technical debt estimation is based on what SonarQube calls "rule violations" or *issues*. The tool detects the violations of a large variety of rules for software quality. These issues are classified by the tool into three categories: bugs, violations, and code smells. The version 6.2 of the tool that we used distinguishes among 397 Java rules. It divides them in the following 3 types namely: Bug (150 rules), Vulnerability (31 rules), and Code Smell (216). Table 1 shows the top 5 most frequent issues that are being violated in the case-study system.

Table 2. The most costly to fix types of issues in Apache Sling. The starred issues did not appear in the previous table

	Issue	Time (minutes)	
1	String literals should not be duplicated	39,234	(13.8%)
2	Generic exceptions should never be thrown	37,120	(13.0%)
3	*Source files should not have any duplicated blocks	30,440	(10.7%)
4	*Cognitive complexity of methods should not be too high	16,061	(5.6%)
5	Control flow statements should not be nested too deeply	13,450	(4.7%)

Besides listing issues, SonarQube also estimates the time required to fix them. Table 2 shows the top 5 most time consuming issues as estimated by the tool.

The two tables show that the most frequent violations are not necessarily the most time consuming to fix: issue 1 in Table 2 was ranked lower in Table 1, and issues 3 and 4 did not even appear in that table. It is also interesting to see that some of the detected problems are quite low-level (e.g. string literal duplication) while others are relevant for the higher level architecture of the system (e.g. a seemingly absent exception policy, large scale code duplication).

Open Questions. Are the relative frequency and effort required to fix these issues are characteristic to the Apache Sling project or they are more generally characteristic to Java systems? Is this uneven distribution of effort towards some issues specific or generic?

3   Study Design

Inspired by the open questions presented in the previous section, the *goal* of our study is then, to analyze the evolution of OSS projects in the Apache ecosystem for the *purpose* of understanding and investigating the accumulation of TD and the evolution of source code metrics. More specifically, our study aims at addressing the following four research questions (RQs):

RQ$_1$: *How does the technical debt of the open-source systems in the Apache ecosystem evolve over time?*
The motivation for this question is to investigate the evolution of TD as it is generated by a widely acknowledged tool for a large set of OSS projects belonging to the same ecosystem.

RQ$_2$: *How does the normalized technical debt of the open-source systems in the Apache ecosystem evolve over time?*
Because the amount of TD might be related to the size of the code base this research question aims at investigating the evolution of TD when normalized over the size of each system.

RQ$_3$: *What are the most frequent types of technical debt in the studied ecosystem?*
The motivation for this question is to validate whether developers incur specific types of debt or not

RQ$_4$: *What are the most costly to fix types of technical debt in the studied ecosystem?*
Since the effort required to repay TD varies among violations the goal of this question to obtain an insight into the actual effort to eliminate the most frequent sources of TD.

It is for brevity, that in the research questions and the rest of the paper we talk about *technical debt* but we clearly mean *technical debt as estimated by SQALE method implemented in the SonarQube tool.* The evolutionary study of technical debt as measured and estimated with other tools falls outside of our intended scope for this study.

3.1   Project Selection

The context of the study is the evolution of the Java open-source software projects developed by the Apache Software Foundation. Since the analysis we perform is computationally intensive we limit our study to a sample of sixty-six

Table 3. The list of projects included in the study

Project	NCLOC	Classes	Project	NCLOC	Classes
sling	425, 831	6,058	opennlp	62, 141	998
zookeeper	74, 898	948	chukwa	42, 734	577
tomcat60	180, 766	1,676	tapestry-5	157, 911	3,266
jspwiki	57, 967	555	manifoldcf	209, 190	1,824
directory-shared	197, 377	1,611	crunch	52, 564	1,025
cayenne	232, 876	3,818	jena	444, 414	5,970
commons-collections	61, 637	741	oodt	128, 875	1,810
openjpa	431, 915	5,358	sis	205, 367	2,204
mina	23, 633	442	commons-csv	5, 197	35
poi	367, 828	3,907	commons-vfs	33, 315	427
nutch	51, 738	639	falcon	122, 277	1,015
commons-lang	74, 849	569	aurora	68, 894	1,156
commons-io	29, 267	271	jclouds	340, 647	6,950
httpclient	61, 657	685	helix	81, 729	1,060
wicket	211, 627	4,175	struts	152, 296	2,341
batik	191, 790	2,590	cxf	635, 020	8,295
roller	53, 540	603	knox	72, 188	1,177
maven	80, 161	1,061	stratos	119, 243	1,506
commons-cli	6, 859	54	phoenix	273, 435	2,134
wss4j	109, 259	782	commons-math	186, 584	1,685
pdfbox	136, 997	1,337	tomcat80	317, 555	3,425
aries	181, 779	2,710	nifi	354, 044	3,954
jmeter	124, 358	1,408	vxquery	45, 369	751
maven-surefire	58, 107	1248	zeppelin	81, 218	982
commons-validator	15, 930	159	polygene-java	159, 748	4,500
stanbol	160, 713	1,875	groovy	168, 705	2,099
sqoop	76, 273	837	apex-core	73, 029	1,086
flume	84, 882	1,000	apex-malhar	166, 972	2,682
rampart	24, 729	278	brooklyn-library	40, 387	629
kafka	120, 995	1,644	beam	199, 476	3,631
giraph	97, 952	1,870	tomcat85	306, 473	3,397
oozie	159, 043	1,325	incubator-hivemall	51, 984	666
tomcat	303, 901	3,428	qpid-proton-j	38, 055	613

randomly selected Java projects from the ecosystem[4]. These represent more than a quarter of the Java projects in Apache. Table 3 presents the analyzed systems together with statistics about their magnitude.

We used the Apache Software Foundation Index[5] in order to randomly select the projects that we analyzed. We used three inclusion criteria in order to decide whether we should analyze a project or not. We chose projects in which the main programming language is Java, have at least two years of evolution and are still active at the beginning of 2017. All the analyzed projects use git as version control system and they are hosted on GitHub, whence we cloned them.

The range in terms of weeks of evolution spans from 127 weeks to 767 weeks. We chose to analyze the last 5 years (260 weeks) of the evolution of the projects. The range of the number of classes for the first analyzed commit is from 0 to 7,040 and for the last analyzed commit from 35 - 8,295. At the same time the NCLOC for the first commit ranges from 0 to 450,186 and for the last commit from 5,197 to 635,020.

4   Results and Discussion

This section reports the analysis of the results achieved in our study and aims at answering the four research questions formulated in Sect. 3. A replication kit is available online at https://github.com/digeo/evolution-of-td-in-apache.

RQ$_1$: How does the technical debt of the open-source systems in the Apache ecosystem evolve over time? To answer RQ$_1$, for each project in the analyzed ones we created a weekly time series with the accumulation of technical debt. For each series we performed the Mann-Kendall test. The purpose of the Mann-Kendall (MK) test is to statistically assess if there is a monotonic upward or downward trend of the variable of interest over time. A monotonic upward (downward) trend means that the variable consistently increases (decreases) through time, but the trend may or may not be linear.

The null hypothesis (H$_0$) is that there is no monotonic trend and the alternative hypothesis (H$_a$) is that a monotonic trend is present. The value of the significance level (alpha error rate) is 0.01 (a = 0.01).

We run MK test for each one of the analyzed systems. Figure 3 visually summarizes the results by presenting the Z values for the analyzed systems. If the Z value is above (below) the horizontal grey line, it indicates that an increasing (decreasing) trend is present.

The Fig. 3 shows that in most of the projects, there is a monotonic upward trend of the technical debt over time.

RQ$_2$: How does the normalized technical debt of the open-source systems in the Apache ecosystem evolve over time? To address RQ$_2$ we

---

[4] The ecosystem contains projects written in more than 20 languages, but the majority of the projects is written in Java.

[5] https://projects.apache.org/projects.html?language#Java.

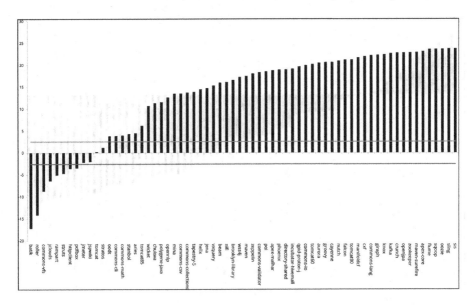

Fig. 3. Trend results for technical debt

extracted two series for each project. The first one contains data for the accumulation of technical debt and the second the number of the lines of code. Then, we divided the two series, namely: the technical debt series with the lines of code series to obtain what we call the *normalized technical debt* time series.

Finally, for each normalized technical debt series we performed again the Mann-Kendall test. Figure 4 presents the Z values for the analyzed systems using the same conventions as before. It shows that:

1. For seven systems (approx. 10%), there is no clear trend (values between the two grey lines)
2. For eleven systems (approx. 20%), the normalized technical debt increases with time (values above the top grey line)
3. for the majority of the systems, the normalized technical debt decreases over time (values below the low grey line)

We find the third result from above encouraging. Indeed, one possible explanation is that the developers of these systems are concerned with paying back the technical debt. This is plausible considering that the systems under analysis are some of the most successful open-source systems and are regarded as high quality projects by the open-source community.

However, another possible explanation could be related to the different phases through which a system evolves; as the system moves towards the maintenance phase, the changes to the system will tend to be smaller such as patches and bug fixes, and thus, less likely to introduce technical debt.

Based on the answer to this research question, we realize that Apache Sling, the system we discussed earlier, was not special in the fact that its normalized

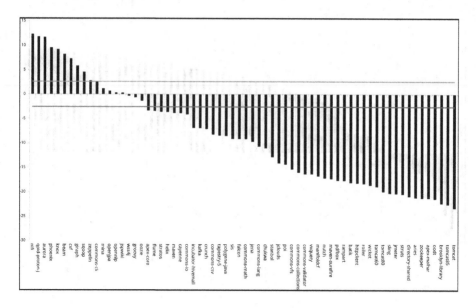

Fig. 4. Trend results for normalized technical debt

technical debt was decreasing. But this is not surprising now, since we see that this is the case with the majority of the systems in the ecosystem, and we have picked Sling at random.

RQ₃: What are the most frequent types of technical debt in the studied ecosystem? To answer this question we summed up all open issues from all the analyzed systems. We only look at the issues that are still open in the last analyzed commit.

To gather insight into the distribution of the various types of issues across the different systems, we use the Gini coefficient. The Gini coefficient is a statistical measure of the degree of variation or inequality represented in a set of values, used especially in analyzing income inequality. Its value is between 0 and 1. A low coefficient is indicative for a uniform distribution in the analyzed values, while a high coefficient is indicative of a very skewed distribution.

Since there are more than a hundred types of issues we do not to present all of them but we limit the presentation to the top ten most frequent ones. The replication kit available online contains the full table of issues in the ecosystem.

Table 4 shows the ten most frequent types of issues encountered in the projects that we analyzed. By analyzing the information in the table, we observe that:

- The top 10 most frequent rule violations account for more than 40% of the issues in the systems. This hints at the fact that, if automated tool support would be developed for these issues, that would make a big difference.
- The most frequent issue is also the most easily remedied, since all the modern IDEs provide an Extract Constant/Variable refactoring. In fact, a recent

study showed that Extract Constant/Variable is one of the most popular refactoring developers actually in practice [7]. This hints at the possibility that developers are not aware of the literal duplication and that future IDEs could auto-detect and suggest the removal of the problem.

- If we add up the two rules in the list that refer to exception handling, they are more frequent than the most frequent issue. This is a sign that exception handling in Java is still not being approached with sufficient discipline. Also this is a much higher-level abstraction than some of the other frequent issues.
- Code duplication, is another type of high-level, potentially architectural problem. It is not very frequent (2.4% of the issues pertain to it) but it has a very low Gini index, which means, it is very equally distributed among the analyzed systems.

Table 4. The ten most frequent types of technical debt in the Apache ecosystem

#	Issue	Count		Gini
1	String literals should not be duplicated	48,474	(7.0%)	.31
2	The members of an interface declaration or class should appear in a pre-defined order	38,756	(5.6%)	.43
3	Exception handlers should preserve the original exceptions	33,467	(4.8%)	.38
4	The diamond operator ("<>") should be used	30,659	(4.4%)	.55
5	Generic exceptions should never be thrown	29,393	(4.2%)	.47
6	Statements should be on separate lines	25,674	(3.7%)	.73
7	Control flow statements "if", "for", "while", "switch" and "try" should not be nested too deeply	24,513	(3.5%)	.34
8	Sections of code should not be "commented out"	22,039	(3.2%)	.52
9	Source files should not have any duplicated blocks	16,456	(2.4%)	.22
10	"@Override" should be used on overriding and implementing methods	16,291	(2.4%)	.64

RQ$_4$: What are the most costly to fix types of technical debt in the studied ecosystem? To answer this question we summed up all the open issues from all the analyzed systems but this time, we looked at the effort instead of the frequency. We are still only looking at the issues that are still open in the last analyzed commit.

Table 5 shows the ten most expensive in terms of effort types of issues in the analyzed projects. By analyzing the information in the table, we observe that:

- Code duplication, is the most expensive to fix in terms of the estimated required time. The function for estimating the time required to remove duplication estimates the effort linearly with the cardinality of the clone.

- Just as with the frequency, exception handling is again the most time-consuming problem to fix. The two types of issues regarding exceptions, account together for more than 13% of the estimated time for paying back the technical debt.
- Rule 3, is responsible in the ecosystem for 8.4% of the effort. Compared with the Apache Sling system presented in the Motivating Example section which had 13% this is much lower. This would probably be useful information for the developers of Sling.

Table 5. The ten most costly to fix types of technical debt in the Apache ecosystem

#	Issue	Effort in minutes		Gini
1	Source files should not have any duplicated blocks	967,490	(13.8%)	.33
2	String literals should not be duplicated	642,122	(9.2%)	.36
3	Generic exceptions should never be thrown	587,860	(8.4%)	.47
4	Cognitive Complexity of methods should not be too high	353,527	(5.0%)	.37
5	Exception handlers should preserve the original exceptions	334,670	(4.8%)	.39
6	Methods should not be too complex	257,213	(3.7%)	.34
7	Control flow statements "`if`", "`for`", "`while`", "`switch`" and "`try`" should not be nested too deeply	245,130	(3.5%)	.34
8	The members of an interface declaration or class should appear in a pre-defined order	193,780	(2.8%)	.43
9	Dead stores should be removed	165,990	(2.4%)	.42
10	Standard outputs should not be used directly to log anything	154,390	(2.2%)	.52

Since we cannot present all the 232 issues uniquely detected by the tool, we summarize their magnitude by computing again the Gini coefficient for the estimated effort per issue. Summing up the percentage of all the issues in Table 5 shows that 55.8% of all the estimated effort is due to these ten issues. We conjecture that if progress was made towards eradicating some of top problematic issues, the community would make considerable progress in avoiding much technical debt.

5   Threats to Validity

In this section, we present and discuss possible threats to the validity of our study.

Construct validity reflects how far the studied phenomenon is connected to the intended studied objectives. The main threats related to construct validity are due to possible inaccuracy in the identification of technical debt. Since we relied on the default SonarQube rules and the default threshold for each rule in order to detect the violations leading to technical debt, the results are subject to the SQALE model assumptions. This threat is partially mitigated by the fact that the analysis of technical debt evolution implies a relative rather than an absolute assessment of technical debt for the examined systems.

Since the Research Questions have been investigated through a case study, threats to the reliability should be examined. Reliability is linked to whether the experiment is conducted and presented in such a way that others can replicate it with the same results. We believe that the documentation of the adopted research process along with the online replication kit will facilitate any researcher who is interested in replicating this study.

Finally, as in any case study, external validity threats apply, limiting the ability to generalize the findings derived from sample to the entire population. However, the sixty-six systems that we analyzed have been randomly selected from the Apache ecosystem, and represent above a quarter and below a third of all contained Java projects. Moreover, we do not claim that the results on TD evolution or the types of TD hold for other Java systems or different ecosystems.

6   Related Work

This section reports the studies that are related to our work. Specifically, we report report empirical studies that study the Apache ecosystem, studies that deal with the introduction, evolution, and the survivability of the code smells on OSS projects and finally, studies that study the impact of code smells on the OSS projects.

Evolving code smells and software metrics. The evolution of code smells has been studied extensively. One of the first studies is by Olbrich et al. [8], who investigated the evolution of two code smells, namely God Class and Shotgun Surgery. They analyzed historical data of two large OSS projects from the Apache foundation: Apache Lucene and Apache Xerces 2 J, the results of their study report (i) that during the evolution of the projects there are phases that the number of these code smells decreases and phases that this number increases and (ii) the size of the system does not affect these changes.

Zazworka et al. [9] conducted a case study on the design debt. They analyzed two sample applications by a software development company and they investigated how God Classes affect the maintainability and the correctness of the projects. The results of their study show that God Classes have higher change-proneness when they are compared to the non-God Classes. Furthermore, they suggest that God Classes be seen as instances of technical debt and also they point that if the developers split the God Classes into multiple smaller classes that could lead to the generation of more problematic classes and that would have as result an increment to the number of the files that has to be edited.

Peters and Zaidman [10] also conducted a case study on the lifespan of the following code smells: God Class, Feature Envy, Data Class, Message Chain

Class, and Long Parameter List Class. They mined open-source projects and their main finding reports that the engineers are aware of the existence of the code smells in their systems but they do not worry for their impact and that has as result to perform very few refactoring activities. The main deference between our study and their that they analyzed only a small number of Java projects (only seven) and they focused their study only on five code smells. Furthermore, they did not measure how much effort is required in order to remove them.

Chatzigeorgiou and Manakos conducted a study on the evolution of code smells and they report that as the projects evolve over time the number of code smells increases [11]. Furthermore, the developers of the projects perform very few actions in order to remove the code smells from the projects.

All the previous studies focused on a limited number of types of smells and small number of systems. In contrast, Curtis et al. [12] performed a large-scale study on many business applications. They used more than 1200 rules of good architectural and coding practice and they reported the TD of 745 business applications. The main difference between their study and ours is the focus: we focused only on Java OSS projects by the Apache Foundation, they analyzed a big number of business applications that have been developed on many languages as diverse as COBOL, C++, .NET, ABAP, and Java. The similarity between their study and ours is that we also used a set of good architectural and coding practices.

Software Ecosystems. Software ecosystems have been studied in many contexts: their evolving size and developer activity [13,14], their evolving dependencies [15,16], their API evolution [17]. The very ecosystem that we study in this paper, Apache, has been studied from the perspective of sentiment analysis on the mailing lists [18] and the evolution of dependencies between the projects in an ecosystem [15].

One study on open-source systems that comes close to ours in its focus is the one of Tufano et al. [19] who contacted an empirical study on 200 OSS projects. They analyzed projects from three ecosystems namely Apache, Android, and Eclipse and they investigated questions about code smell life cycle. They found that the most code smells are introduced with the creation of the class or file when the developers implement new features or enhance already exist ones. They also report that the majority of the smells are not removed during the project's evolution and few are removed as a direct consequence of refactoring operations. Our study differs from their work in that we focus on the trends at the system level, and we also consider the estimated time that is required in order to resolve the issues of a project.

7   Conclusions and Future Work

In this paper we have studied sixty-six Java systems from the Apache ecosystem. We analyzed cumulatively more than 16,000 weekly commits and we mined 695,731 project issues as reported by SonarQube. From this data we have learned that in the majority of the systems that we studied, there is a significant increase trend on the size, number of issues, and on the complexity metrics of the project. On the other hand, the normalized technical debt decreases as the project evolves.

Some of the most frequently occurring issues regard low-level coding problems some of which could probably be decreased with good IDE support (e.g. duplicated strings). On the other hand, the most expensive types of technical debt that must be paid back in the ecosystem are actually higher-level problems: duplicated code and ad-hoc exception handling. Exception mis-handling is more unevenly distributed in the ecosystem than code duplication.

One of the reasons for which this study did not analyze the entire Apache ecosystem but rather a sample of it is the slowness of the analysis using Sonar-Qube for which the computation time required is linear with the number of versions. In order to allow the analysis of more systems and also a finer temporal granularity level than a week, in the future we will investigate approaches that would provide better scalability.

In the paper we also observed that a very small minority of problem types is responsible for the vast majority of estimated technical debt. We conjectured that if progress was possible towards *preventing* some of the top problematic issues the community could *avoid incurring* a large percentage of the technical debt in the first place. Even if for other communities the problem ranking would be different, we believe that the approach of aggregating the information from system level to the entire ecosystem will always provide valuable insights. Indeed we consider this to be one of the take-away messages of this study.

Finally, although larger than many earlier studies on the evolution of technical debt in open-source systems, our study is still limited to a random sample from one ecosystem. It would be valuable if these results would be replicated by other researchers in other open-source ecosystems, and maybe also in other languages.

References

1. Li, Z., Avgeriou, P., Liang, P.: A systematic mapping study on technical debt and its management. J. Syst. Softw. **101**(C), 193–220 (2015). http://dx.doi.org/10.1016/j.jss.2014.12.027
2. Manikas, K.: Revisiting software ecosystems research. J. Syst. Softw. **117**(C), 84–103 (2016). http://dx.doi.org/10.1016/j.jss.2016.02.003
3. Lungu, M.: Reverse engineering software ecosystems. Ph.D. dissertation, University of Lugano, November 2009. http://scg.unibe.ch/archive/papers/Lung09b.pdf
4. Campbell, G.A., Papapetrou, P.P.: SonarQube in Action, 1st edn. Manning Publications Co., Greenwich (2013)
5. Ilkiewicz, M., Letouzey, J.-L.: Managing technical debt with the sqale method. IEEE Softw. **29**, 44–51 (2012)
6. Perry, D.E., Wolf, A.L.: Foundations for the study of software architecture. SIGSOFT Softw. Eng. Notes **17**(4), 40–52 (1992)

7. Murphy-Hill, E., Parnin, C., Black, A.P.: How we refactor, and how we know it. In: Proceedings of the 31st International Conference on Software Engineering, ICSE 2009, pp. 287–297. IEEE Computer Society, Washington, DC (2009). http://dx.doi.org/10.1109/ICSE.2009.5070529

8. Olbrich, S., Cruzes, D.S., Basili, V., Zazworka, N.: The evolution and impact of code smells: a case study of two open source systems. In: 2009 3rd International Symposium on Empirical Software Engineering and Measurement, pp. 390–400, October 2009

9. Zazworka, N., Shaw, M.A., Shull, F., Seaman, C.: Investigating the impact of design debt on software quality. In: Proceedings of the 2nd Workshop on Managing Technical Debt, MTD 2011, pp. 17–23. ACM, New York (2011). http://doi.acm.org/10.1145/1985362.1985366

10. Peters, R., Zaidman, A.: Evaluating the lifespan of code smells using software repository mining. In: 2012 16th European Conference on Software Maintenance and Reengineering, pp. 411–416, March 2012

11. Chatzigeorgiou, A., Manakos, A.: Investigating the evolution of code smells in object-oriented systems. Innov. Syst. Softw. Eng. 10(1), 3–18 (2014). http://dx.doi.org/10.1007/s11334-013-0205-z

12. Curtis, B., Sappidi, J., Szynkarski, A.: Estimating the size, cost, and types of technical debt. In: Proceedings of the Third International Workshop on Managing Technical Debt, MTD 2012, pp. 49–53. IEEE Press, Piscataway (2012). http://dl.acm.org/citation.cfm?id=2666036.2666045

13. Vasilescu, B., Serebrenik, A., Goeminne, M., Mens, T.: On the variation and specialisation of workload - a case study of the gnome ecosystem community. Empirical Softw. Eng. 19(4), 955–1008 (2013)

14. Lungu, M., Malnati, J., Lanza, M.: Visualizing gnome with the small project observatory. In: Godfrey, M.W., Whitehead, J. (eds.) MSR, pp. 103–106. IEEE Computer Society (2009). http://dblp.uni-trier.de/db/conf/msr/msr2009.html#LunguML09

15. Bavota, G., Canfora, G., Penta, M.D., Oliveto, R., Panichella, S.: The evolution of project inter-dependencies in a software ecosystem: the case of apache. In: Proceedings of the 2013 IEEE International Conference on Software Maintenance, ICSM 2013, pp. 280–289. IEEE Computer Society, Washington, DC (2013). http://dx.doi.org/10.1109/ICSM.2013.39

16. Decan, A., Mens, T., Claes, M., Grosjean, P.: When github meets cran: an analysis of inter-repository package dependency problems. In: 2016 IEEE 23rd International Conference on Software Analysis, Evolution, and Reengineering (SANER), vol. 1, pp. 493–504, March 2016

17. Robbes, R., Lungu, M., Roethlisberger, D.: How do developers react to API deprecation? the case of a Smalltalk ecosystem. In: Proceedings of the 20th International Symposium on the Foundations of Software Engineering (FSE 2012), pp. 56:1–56:11 (2012)

18. Tourani, P., Jiang, Y., Adams, B.: Monitoring sentiment in open source mailing lists: exploratory study on the apache ecosystem. In: Proceedings of 24th Annual International Conference on Computer Science and Software Engineering, CASCON 2014, pp. 34–44 (2014)

19. Tufano, M., Palomba, F., Bavota, G., Oliveto, R., Di Penta, M., De Lucia, A., Poshyvanyk, D.: When and why your code starts to smell bad. In: Proceedings of the 37th International Conference on Software Engineering, ICSE 2015, vol. 1, pp. 403–414. IEEE Press, Piscataway (2015). http://dl.acm.org/citation.cfm?id=2818754.2818805

Preventing Erosion in Exception Handling Design Using Static-Architecture Conformance Checking

Juarez L.M. Filho[1], Lincoln Rocha[1(✉)], Rossana Andrade[1], and Ricardo Britto[2]

[1] Group of Computer Networks, Software Engineering, and Systems, Federal University of Ceará, Fortaleza, CE, Brazil
{juarezmeneses,lincoln,rossana}@great.ufc.br
[2] Blekinge Institute of Technology, 37179 Karlskrona, Sweden
ricardo.britto@bth.se

Abstract. Exception handling is a common error recovery technique employed to improve software robustness. However, studies have reported that exception handling is commonly neglected by developers and is the least understood and documented part of a software project. The lack of documentation and difficulty in understanding the exception handling design can lead developers to violate important design decisions, triggering an erosion process in the exception handling design. Architectural conformance checking provides means to control the architectural erosion by periodically checking if the actual architecture is consistent with the planned one. Nevertheless, available approaches do not provide a proper support for exception handling conformance checking. To fulfill this gap, we propose ArCatch: an architectural conformance checking solution to deal with the exception handling design erosion. ArCatch provides: (i) a declarative language for expressing design constraints regarding exception handling; and (ii) a design rule checker to automatically verify the exception handling conformance. To evaluate the usefulness and effectiveness of our approach, we conducted a case study, in which we evaluated an evolution scenario composed by 10 versions of an existing web-based Java system. Each version was checked against the same set of exception handling design rules. Based on the results and the feedback given by the system's architect, the ArCatch proved useful and effective in the identification of existing exception handling erosion problems and locating its causes in the source code.

Keywords: Exception handling design · Exception handling erosion · Architecture conformance checking

1 Introduction

Exception handling is a well-known error recovery approach to improve software robustness. An exception is an event or abnormal situation detected at runtime

© Springer International Publishing AG 2017
A. Lopes and R. de Lemos (Eds.): ECSA 2017, LNCS 10475, pp. 67–83, 2017.
DOI: 10.1007/978-3-319-65831-5_5

that disrupts the normal control flow of a program [10]. When this happens, the exception-handling mechanism deviates the normal control flow to the abnormal (exceptional) control flow to handle the exceptional situation. The exception handling mechanism structures the exceptional control flow by using proper constructs to indicate in the source code where exceptions can be raised and handled. Most of mainstream programming languages (e.g., Java, C++, and C#) provide built-in facilities to implement exception handling features [4].

Architecture erosion is a phenomenon that occurs when the implemented (concrete) architecture of a software system diverges from its intended (planned) architecture [20]. In fact, it is a side effect of a non-controlled software evolution process in which changes made in the source code lead to architecture design rules violations [12]. To cope with this problem, architecture conformance checking provides means to control the architectural erosion by automatically monitoring the compliance between the implemented architecture and the intended one [17]. This systematic control aims at guaranteeing that the architect's design decisions - and the quality attributes derived from it - are properly reflected in the system implementation [5]. Additionally, once the architecture conformance checking requires a design specification as input (e.g., architectural elements declaration, mapping between architectural and implementation elements, and design constrains), the knowledge about the architectural design decisions becomes better documented and easier to share.

Despite its importance, studies have reported that exception handling is commonly neglected by developers and is the least understood, documented, and tested part of a software system [6,13,19]. Additionally, to promote software maintainability, modern programming languages (e.g., C#, Ruby, and Python) have incorporated new maintenance-driven flexibilities in its built-in exception handling mechanism [3]. This make changes in the source code more agile by not forcing developers to follow the exception handling constraints (e.g., declare in each method interface a list of exceptions that might be signaled and, therefore, should be handled by caller methods). Nevertheless, this flexibility allows developers to postpone the implementation of some parts of exception handling, taking the risk of forgetting to return and implement the remaining exception handling features. All these issues may lead developers to violate the software architect's intention concerning the exception handling design during the development, maintenance and evolution phases. Such kind of violations are dangerous because it can lead to: (i) the exception handling mechanism to behave erroneously or improperly at runtime; and (ii) exception handling software faults [7]. We call this problem *exception handling erosion* (EHE).

The state of the art conformance checking solutions [5,8,11,15,22] do not provide a proper support for architecture conformance checking of exception handling design. Even a most recent solution [1], devoted to conformance checking of exception handling design, do not provide a full-fledged support to deal with the EHE problem. Therefore, we address this gap in this paper through answering the following research questions: **RQ1** - *How can the EHE problem be addressed in a systematic way?* **RQ1.1** - *How effective is the proposed approach* *in the identification of existing EHE problems?* and **RQ1.2** - *How useful is the proposed approach to identify EHE causes in the source code?*

To answer RQ1, we propose ArCatch, an architecture conformance checking solution that provides: (i) a declarative language (ArCatch.Rules) for expressing design constraints regarding exception handling; and (ii) a design rule checker (ArCatch.Checker) to automatically verify the exception handling conformance. The ArCatch is implemented as a Java internal DSL (Domain-Specific Language), easing its incorporation in a continuous integration environment by adopting the design test concept, a test-like program that automatically checks whether an implementation conforms to a specific design rule [2]. To answer RQ1.1 and RQ1.2, we conducted a case study [18].

The main contributions of this paper are: (i) a declarative DSL to specify and document design decisions about exception handling; (ii) an automatic verification tool to support the conformance check of exception handling design; and (iii) an automatic report generation to assist developers to find out which design rules are violated and locate in the source code the violation causes.

The remainder of this paper is organized as follows. Section 2 provides some background about exception handling design. The ArCatch solution is presented in Sect. 3 and the methodology, results and discussion of the case study are presented in Sect. 4. Finally, Sect. 5 discusses related work and Sect. 6 concludes the paper.

2 Exception Handling Design

In this section, we describe the exception handling concepts at the architecture level based on the IFTC (Idealized Fault-Tolerant Component) model (Sect. 2.1) and how design rules can be derived from it to express the exception handling design (Sect. 2.2).

2.1 Exceptions at the Architectural Level

At the software architecture level, exceptions and their control flow can be described using the IFTC model [14] (Fig. 1). It captures the essence behind the exception handling constructs of the mainstream object-oriented program languages [10], such as Java and C#. Each software component (callee) can receive service requests from other components (caller). The callee processes the request and sends back normal responses or exceptions.

Exceptions can be classified in three categories as depicted in Fig. 1: (i) interface exceptions - signaled when the request does not conform to the callee component service interface; (ii) failure exceptions - signaled to indicate that, for some reason, the callee component could not process the service request; and (iii) internal exceptions - raised and handled inside the callee component. The signaled exceptions are named external exceptions.

In the IFTC model, the component activity can be divided into normal and abnormal (exceptional) activities (Fig. 1). In the normal activity, the component processes service requests according to its specification. In the abnormal

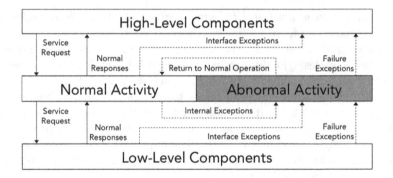

Fig. 1. Idealized Fault-Tolerant Component Model (adapted from [14]).

activity, the component performs contingency measures to deal with exceptions. Thus, a component can handle exceptions raised during its normal activity or exceptions signaled by low-level components (callees). However, exceptions that cannot be handled by a component are propagated to high-level components (callers) and so on. Moreover, before performing the exception propagation, a component can do either an exception re-raising or remapping. The exception re-raising occurs when the component captures the exception, performs some partial handling actions, and then re-raises it, forcing the exception propagation continuity. The remapping occurs when the component captures the exception, performs optionally some partial handling actions, and then raises another exception type, starting a new exception propagation.

At development time, the exception handling mechanism allows developers to define exceptions and structure the exception handling behavior by means of exception handlers. The exception handlers are component parts devoted to handle exceptions (gray parts in Fig. 1). At runtime, when an exception is raised, the exception handling mechanism deviates the normal control flow to the exceptional control flow, starting the search for an exception handler that can handle this exception. The search begins with the component in which the exception is raised and proceeds through all components in the service request chain in the reverse order in which they were called. When an appropriate handler is found, the exception handling mechanism passes the exception to the handler. After the exception is handled, the system may get back to its normal activity. Otherwise, if no handler is found, the system is forced to stop its execution.

2.2   Design Rules for Exception Handling

In the IFTC model, exceptions can be raised, signaled, handled, re-raised, and remapped by a system module and can flow through a list of several modules until be handled. These links can be expressed as different types of dependency relation between exceptions and modules at the architectural level. Based on such relations, dependency constraints can be derived to describe and to make explicit how exceptions and modules can be combined towards expressing design rules governing the architectural exception handling design.

A set of design rules for exception handling can be expressed by applying semantic modifiers (e.g., *"must"*, *"cannot"*, *"only... can"*, and *"can... only"*) to constrain dependency relations types between modules and exception. Design rules can be used to document and make explicit the architect/designer intention/decision regarding the exception handling and its control flow. They can make explicit: (i) which modules can, cannot, or must raise, re-raise signal, or handle a specific exception type; (ii) which modules can, cannot, or must re-map a specific exception type to another; and (iii) which exception types can, cannot, or must flow through a specific list of modules. In this paper, we provide a way to express this kind of design rules and use it to check the exception handling design conformance to avoid erosion problems.

3   The Proposed Approach

To address RQ1, we developed ArCatch, which aims at providing a way to document architectural design decisions about exception handling and uses it to check the source code conformance. It is composed by a specification language (ArCatch.Rules) to express exception handling design rules, and a design rule checker (ArCatch.Checker) to automatically perform the conformance checking.

The overall flow of the ArCatch is depicted in Fig. 2. First, ArCatch.Checker receives as input the software source code under evaluation and the exception handling design rules written in ArCatch.Rules. Next, it performs the conformance checking and outputs a report describing which design rules are violated.

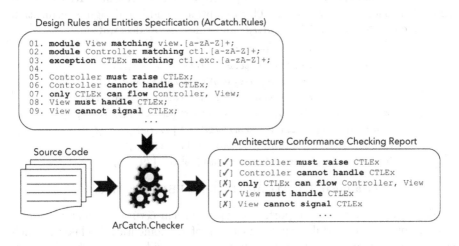

Fig. 2. The ArCatch Overview.

The architecture conformance checking report (at the bottom of Fig. 2) consists of a list of all specified design rules, which indicates the rules that passed and the ones that did not. Such a report is useful for identifying which parts of the source code do not conform to the specification. For example, as shown in Fig. 2, the design rules specified at lines 5, 6, and 8 are valid, while the design rules specified at lines 7 and 9 are violated. Additionally, for all violated rules, ArCatch.Checker generates a counter example pointing out which parts of the source code are breaking the rules (see Sect. 4). Furthermore, both the exception handling design rules specification and the conformance checking report can help software architects and developers to better document, refine, implement and evolve architectural design decisions regarding exception handling.

ArCatch is implemented in Java and its current version provides support for exception handling conformance checking of Java programs. The ArCatch source code can be found at GitHub[1] and be freely downloaded. We detailed ArCatch.Rules and ArCatch.Checker next.

3.1   ArCatch.Rules: The Syntax

In our approach, the knowledge of software architects and developers about the exception handling design is documented as design rules using ArCatch.Rules (e.g., lines 05–09 in Fig. 2). Knowledge about the source code is very helpful when mapping the architectural elements (modules and exceptions) to its respective implementation elements (regular classes and exception classes). This knowledge is also documented in the module/exception declarations using ArCatch.Rules (e.g., lines 01–03 in Fig. 2). Hence, the exception handling design rules' specification is a knowledge-sharing artifact which both software architects and developers can use to fulfill their tasks.

The Grammar 1.1 describes a simplified version of ArCatch.Rules EBNF (Extended Backus–Naur Form). The exception handling design specification ⟨spec⟩ is composed by entities ⟨entity⟩ and rules ⟨rule⟩ declaration.

⟨spec⟩	::=	(⟨entity⟩ | ⟨rule⟩))*
⟨entity⟩	::=	('module' | 'exception') ⟨id⟩ 'matching' ⟨regex⟩ ';'
⟨rule⟩	::=	(⟨only-can⟩ | ⟨can-only⟩ | ⟨cannot⟩ | ⟨must⟩)) ';'
⟨relation⟩	::=	'raise' | 'reraise' | 'signal' | 'handle' | 'remap' | 'flow'
⟨only-can⟩	::=	'only' ⟨id⟩ 'can' ⟨relation⟩ ⟨id⟩ ['to' ⟨id⟩ | (',' ⟨id⟩)⁺]
⟨can-only⟩	::=	⟨id⟩ 'can' ⟨relation⟩ 'only' ⟨id⟩ ['to' ⟨id⟩ | (',' ⟨id⟩)⁺]
⟨cannot⟩	::=	⟨id⟩ 'cannot' ⟨relation⟩ ⟨id⟩ ['to' ⟨id⟩ | (',' ⟨id⟩)⁺]
⟨must⟩	::=	⟨id⟩ 'must' ⟨relation⟩ ⟨id⟩ ['to' ⟨id⟩ | (',' ⟨id⟩)⁺]

Grammar 1.1. The ArCatch.Rules EBNF simplified.

The entity declaration supports two types of architectural elements: modules and exceptions. A module represents a set of implementation classes, which can be grouped or interact with each other to provide a well-defined system functionality. An exception represents a set of exception classes (types). The keywords 'module' and 'exception' are employed in the module and exception

---

[1] https://github.com/lincolnrocha/ArCatch.

entities declaration respectively. Both modules and exceptions have an identifier ⟨*id*⟩ (a string that must start with a letter) and a regular expression ⟨*regex*⟩ (a sequence of characters that define a search pattern) used to map it onto implementation elements (regular or exception classes).

The rule declaration ⟨*rule*⟩ describes how ArCatch.Rules expresses exception handling design rules as dependency constraints between exceptions and modules. Such dependencies can be expressed in terms of exception raising, re-raising, signaling, handling, remapping, and flow. The semantic modifiers *only... can, can... only, cannot*, and *must* are used to give a proper semantic to each rule.

All derived design rules follow the same syntactic structure, which includes: (i) a fixed part that comprises ... ⟨*id*⟩ ... ⟨*relation*⟩ ... ⟨*id*⟩; and (ii) an optional part that can be 'to'⟨*id*⟩ or $('$'⟨id⟩$)^+$. In both parts, fixed and optional, the identifier ⟨*id*⟩ can refer to an exception or a module identifier. The choice depends on the type of dependency relation ⟨*relation*⟩ being taken into account.

When the keyword 'raise', 'reraise', 'signal', or 'handle' is chosen, the first identifier in the fixed part refers to a module identifier and the second one refers to an exception identifier. In such cases, there is no optional part.

If the keyword 'remap' is chosen, the fixed part derivation is similar to the one for the other keywords, but the second identifier (the exception identifier) represents the exception type to be remapped. In the optional part 'to'⟨*id*⟩, the identifier refers to an exception identifier, which comprises the exception types that are targeted by the exception remapping process.

Finally, if the keyword 'flow' is chosen, the first identifier in the fixed part must refer to an exception identifier and the second one refers to a module identifier; the module where the exception type may be raised and signaled. In the optional part $('$'⟨id⟩$)^+$, each derived identifier refers to a module identifier. These identifiers are the list of modules in which the exception may flow through.

The ArCatch.Rules are implemented as a Java internal DSL, making it easy to incorporate it in a continuous integration environment by adopting the design tests concept [2], a programmatic approach to check the software source code against design rules via automated testing tools, such as JUnit.

3.2 ArCatch.Checker: The Semantics

The ArCatch.Checker is responsible for establishing a link between declared modules and exceptions to its implementing classes respectively, and checking the specified design rules against the software source code. Each entity (module or exception) has a regular expression associated with it. Every class name that matches the defined regular expression is linked to the corresponding entity.

ArCatch.Checker uses the following conventions about the exception handling dependency relations at the source code level: (i) $\mathtt{raise}(m,e)$ means method m raises exception e; (ii) $\mathtt{reraise}(m,e)$ means method m re-raises exception e; (iii) $\mathtt{signal}(m,e)$ means method m signals exception e; (iv) $\mathtt{handle}(m,e)$ means method m handle exception e; (v) $\mathtt{remap}(m,e,f)$ means method m remaps exception e to exception f; and (vi) $\mathtt{flow}(e,m_1,...,m_n)$ means exception e is signaled by method m_1 and flows through $m_2,...,m_{n-1}$ until be handled by method m_n.

In the following, we introduce some basic definitions and the exception handling design rules violation semantics.

Definition 1 (Implementation Class). *An implementation class is a 3-tuple $\langle n, t, \Phi \rangle$, where n is the class name, t is the class type, and Φ is the class methods.*

Definition 2 (Access Functions). *Let $c = \langle n, t, \Phi \rangle$ be an implementation class, (i) getName(c) returns the class name n, (ii) getType(c) returns the class type t, and (iii) getMethods(c) returns the set Φ of all class methods.*

Definition 3 (Architectural Element). *An architectural element $A = \langle n, t, \phi \rangle$ is a 3-tuple where n is the element name, $t \in \{M, E\}$ is the element type, which can be a module type (M) or an exception type (E), and ϕ is the regular expression used to map the implementation classes from source code.*

Definition 4 (The match Function). *Let ϕ be a regular expression and C be a set of implementation classes, the function match(ϕ, C) = $\{c \mid c \in C \wedge$ getName(c) $\in \omega(\phi)\}$ returns all classes whose names matches ϕ. $\omega(\phi)$ is all words described/matched by ϕ.*

Definition 5 (The map Function). *Let $A = \langle n, t, \phi \rangle$ be an architectural element, C be a set of implementation classes, ξ be the root type of the exception types hierarchy, and $<:$ be a subtype relation where C, ξ, and $<:$ are defined in compliance to the rules of the underlying programming language used to build the system. The function map(A, C) performs the mapping between an architectural element and its classes is defined as:*

$$\text{map}(A, C) = \begin{cases} t = M, & \{c \mid c \in \text{match}(\phi, C) \wedge \text{getType}(c) \not<: \xi\} \\ t = E, & \{c \mid c \in \text{match}(\phi, C) \wedge \text{getType}(c) <: \xi\} \end{cases}$$

Definition 6 (The methods Function). *Let $M = \langle n, M, \phi \rangle$ be a module and C be a set of implementation classes, the function methods(M, C) = $\{ m \mid \forall c \in \text{map}(M, C), m \in \text{getMethods}(c)\}$ returns all methods defined in each class of mapping map(M, C).*

Definition 7 (The call Function). *Let m and n be methods and C be a set of implementation classes, the function call(C, m, n) returns true if $\exists \, (c, d \in C \wedge m \in \text{getMethods}(c) \wedge n \in \text{getMethods}(d))$ s.t. "n calls m" and false otherwise.*

Definition 8 (The chains Function). *Let $M_1, \ldots, M_n$ be modules and C be a set of implementation classes, the function chains($C, M_1, \ldots, M_n$) = $\{(m_1, \ldots, m_n) \mid \forall i \in [1, n), m_i \in \text{methods}(M_i, C) \wedge m_{i+1} \in \text{methods}(M_{i+1}, C) \wedge \text{call}(C, m_i, m_{i+1})\}$ returns all method call chains of size n starting in M_1 and ending in M_n.*

Cannot Semantics: (Case 1) Let $E = \langle eid, E, \phi_E \rangle$ be an exception, $M = \langle mid, M, \phi_M \rangle$ be a module, $\oplus$ be a relation in $\{$raise, reraise, signal, handle$\}$, and S be a set of implementation classes. Rules of type "mid cannot $\oplus$ eid" are violated if $\exists\ (m \in \mathtt{methods}(M,S) \wedge e \in \mathtt{map}(E,S))$, such that $\oplus(m,e)$. (**Case 2**) Let $E = \langle eid, \mathtt{E}, \phi_E \rangle$ and $F = \langle fid, \mathtt{E}, \phi_F \rangle$ be exceptions, $M = \langle mid, \mathtt{M}, \phi_M \rangle$ be a module, and S be a set of implementation classes. Rules of type "*mid* `cannot remap` *eid* `to` *fid*" are violated if $\exists\ (m \in \mathtt{methods}(M,S) \wedge e \in \mathtt{map}(E,S) \wedge f \in \mathtt{map}(F,S))$, so that $\mathtt{remap}(m,e,f)$. (**Case 3**) Let $E = \langle eid, \mathtt{E}, \phi_E \rangle$ be an exception, $M_1 = \langle mid_1, \mathtt{M}, \phi_{M_1} \rangle, \ldots, M_n = \langle mid_n, \mathtt{M}, \phi_{M_n} \rangle$ be a list of n modules, and S be a set of implementation classes. Rules of type "*eid* `cannot flow` $mid_1, \ldots, mid_n$" are violated if $\exists\ (e \in \mathtt{map}(E,S) \wedge (m_1, \ldots, m_n) \in \mathtt{chains}(S, M_1, \ldots, M_n))$, so that $\mathtt{flow}(e, m_1, \ldots, m_n)$.

Must Semantics: (**Case 1**) Let $E = \langle eid, \mathtt{E}, \phi \rangle$ be an exception, $M = \langle mid, \mathtt{M}, \phi \rangle$ be a module, $\oplus$ be a relation in {`raise, reraise, signal, handle`}, and S be a set of implementation classes. Rules of type "*mid* `must` $\oplus$ *eid*" are violated if $\nexists\ (m \in \mathtt{methods}(M,S) \wedge e \in \mathtt{map}(E,S))$, such that $\oplus(m,e)$. (**Case 2**) Let $E = \langle eid, \mathtt{E}, \phi \rangle$ and $F = \langle fid, \mathtt{E}, \phi \rangle$ be exceptions, $M = \langle mid, \mathtt{M}, \phi \rangle$ be a module, and S be a set of implementation classes. Rules of type "*mid* `must remap` *eid* `to` *fid*" are violated if $\nexists\ (m \in \mathtt{methods}(M,S) \wedge e \in \mathtt{map}(E,S) \wedge f \in \mathtt{map}(F,S))$, so that $\mathtt{remap}(m,e,f)$. (**Case 3**) Let $E = \langle eid, \mathtt{E}, \phi \rangle$ be an exception, $M_1 = \langle mid_1, \mathtt{M}, \phi \rangle, \ldots, M_n = \langle mid_n, \mathtt{M}, \phi \rangle$ be a list of n modules, and S be a set of implementation classes. Rules of type "*eid* `must flow` $mid_1, \ldots, mid_n$" are violated if $\nexists\ (e \in \mathtt{map}(E,S) \wedge (m_1, \ldots, m_n) \in \mathtt{chains}(S, M_1, \ldots, M_n))$, so that $\mathtt{flows}(e, m_1, \ldots, m_n)$.

Only-Can Semantics: (**Case 1**) Let $E = \langle eid, \mathtt{E}, \phi \rangle$ be an exception, $M = \langle mid, \mathtt{M}, \phi \rangle$ be a module, $\oplus$ be a relation in {`raise, reraise, signal, handle`}, and S be a set of implementation classes. Rules of type "`only` *mid* `can` $\oplus$ *eid*" are violated if $\exists\ (c \in S \setminus \mathtt{map}(M,S) \wedge m \in \mathtt{getMethods}(c) \wedge e \in \mathtt{map}(E,S))$, such that $\oplus(m,e)$. (**Case 2**) Let $E = \langle eid, \mathtt{E}, \phi \rangle$ and $F = \langle fid, \mathtt{E}, \phi \rangle$ be exceptions, $M = \langle mid, \mathtt{M}, \phi \rangle$ be a module, and S be a set of implementation classes. Rules of type "`only` *mid* `can remap` *eid* `to` *fid*" are violated if $\exists\ (c \in S \setminus \mathtt{map}(M,S) \wedge m \in \mathtt{getMethods}(c) \wedge e \in \mathtt{map}(E,S) \wedge f \in \mathtt{map}(F,S))$, so that $\mathtt{remap}(m,e,f)$. (**Case 3**) Let $E = \langle eid, \mathtt{E}, \phi \rangle$ be an exception, $M_1 = \langle mid_1, \mathtt{M}, \phi \rangle, \ldots, M_n = \langle mid_n, \mathtt{M}, \phi \rangle$ be a list of n modules, and S be a set of implementation classes. Rules of type "`only` *eid* `can flow` $mid_1, \ldots, mid_n$" are violated if $\exists\ (e \in S \setminus \mathtt{map}(E,S) \wedge (m_1, \ldots, m_n) \in \mathtt{chains}(S, M_1, \ldots, M_n))$, so that $\mathtt{flows}(e, m_1, \ldots, m_n)$.

Can-Only Semantics: (**Case 1**) Let $E = \langle eid, \mathtt{E}, \phi \rangle$ be an exception, $M = \langle mid, \mathtt{M}, \phi \rangle$ be a module, $\oplus$ be a relation in {`raise, reraise, signal, handle`}, and S be a set of implementation classes. Rules of type "*mid* `can` $\oplus$ `only` *eid*" are violated if $\exists\ (m \in \mathtt{methods}(M,S) \wedge e \in S \setminus \mathtt{map}(E,S))$, such that $\oplus(m,e)$. (**Case 2**) Let $E = \langle eid, \mathtt{E}, \phi \rangle$ and $F = \langle fid, \mathtt{E}, \phi \rangle$ be exceptions, $M = \langle mid, \mathtt{M}, \phi \rangle$ be a module, and S be a set of implementation classes. Rules of type "*mid* `can remap only` *eid* `to` *fid*" are violated if $\exists\ (m \in \mathtt{methods}(M,S) \wedge ((e \in \mathtt{map}(E,S) \wedge f \in S \setminus \mathtt{map}(F,S)) \vee (e \in S \setminus \mathtt{map}(E,S) \wedge f \in \mathtt{map}(F,S)) \vee (e \in S \setminus \mathtt{map}(E,S) \wedge f \in S \setminus \mathtt{map}(F,S)))$, so that $\mathtt{remap}(m,e,f)$. (**Case 3**) Let $E = \langle eid, \mathtt{E}, \phi \rangle$ be an exception, $M_1 = \langle mid_1, \mathtt{M}, \phi \rangle, \ldots, M_n = \langle mid_n, \mathtt{M}, \phi \rangle$ be a list of n modules, and S be a set of implementation classes. The rules of type "*eid* `can flow oly` $mid_1, \ldots,$"

mid_n" are violated if $\exists\ (e \in \mathtt{map}(E,S)\ \wedge\ (m_1,\ldots,m_k) \notin \mathtt{chains}(S,M_1,\ldots,M_n))$, so that $\mathtt{flows}(e,m_1,\ldots,m_k)$ with $k > 1$.

In ArCatch.Checker, all source code information relevant for the checking process is extracted using the Design Wizard[2] tool and the Java Compiler Tree API[3]. The Design Wizard provides means to extract the program class dependencies, such as class inheritance trees and method call-graphs to feed our design rules checking algorithm. The Compiler Tree API provides support to inspect the AST (Abstract Syntax Tree) of Java programs, helping in the identification whether raising, re-raising, and remapping cases occurs in the source code.

4   Case Study

In this section, we describe the design employed to conduct the case study (Sect. 4.1), the associated results (Sect. 4.2) and threats to validity (Sect. 4.3).

4.1   Case Study Design

The Case and Unit of Analysis. The case and unit of analysis is an open source system called Health Watcher (HW), which was developed to improve the quality of the services provided by health care institutions in Brazil. HW is a Java web-based system that allows citizens to register complaints regarding health issues, so that associated health care institutions can promptly investigate the complaints and take the required actions [21]. The HW system was chosen because it has a clear exception handling design and has been used in several empirical studies regarding software modularity and exception handling [9,11, 16] (conveninece sampling). Furthermore, considering the importance of data triangulation in case studies, it was important to select a system whose software architect would be available for a follow-up interview, which was the case of HW.

HW follows a multilayered architectural style composed by 4 layers: view layer (ViL), "the highest layer", distribution layer (DiL), business layer (BuL), and data layer (DaL), "the lowest layer". We analyzed 10 versions of HW. All evaluated 10 versions are available on the Web[4] and it varies from 7070 up to 100054 lines of code, 80 up to 136 classes, and 19 up to 25 packages.

Data Collection. The data used in our analysis was collected through two methods: repository mining and unstructured interview. We employed repository mining to extract the code of HW. We conducted two unstructured interviews with the software architect of HW. The goal of the first interview was to confirm the exception handling strategy employed in HW. In the second interview, we discussed the results of our analysis with the software architect, to collect additional insights about the results. The interviews were conducted via Skype in October and December 2016 and took about 20 and 50 min respectively.

---

[2] https://github.com/joaoarthurbm/designwizard.
[3] https://docs.oracle.com/javase/7/docs/jdk/api/javac/tree/.
[4] http://ptolemy.cs.iastate.edu/design-study/#healthwatcher.

We made notes during the interviews and discussed the notes with the intervie-wee, to ensure that the notes reflected the content of the interview.

Data Preparation. To be able to evaluate our approach, we have to conduct some prepation of the mined source code. Each layer of HW architecture was represented as a module (Listing 1.1, line 1) and mapped to the corresponding implementation classes at the source code level. Listing 1.1 shows this map-ping[5] performed to the v1 version of HW. The viL module was mapped (List-ing 1.1, line 2) to all classes of package "healthwatcher.view.servlets". The diL module was mapped to all classes of package "lib.distribution.rmi" and the IFacade, HealthWatcherFacade, and HealthWatcherFacadeInit classes (Listing 1.1, line 3). The buL module was mapped to all classes of subpackages of "healthwatcher.business" (Listing 1.1, line 4). Finally, the daL module was mapped to all classes of packages and subpackages of "healthwatcher.data" and "lib.persistence" (Listing 1.1, line 5).

Listing 1.1. Health Watcher Layers Mapping.

```
1 ModuleElement viL, diL, buL, daL;
2 viL = module("ViL").matching("healthwatcher.view.servlets.\\w*").build();
3 diL = module("DiL").matching("(lib.distribution.rmi.\\w*|healthwatcher.
      view.IFacade|healthwatcher.business.(HealthWatcherFacade|
      HealthWatcherFacadeInit))*").build();
4 buL = module("BuL").matching("healthwatcher.business.(complaint|employee|
      healthguide).\\w*").build();
5 daL = module("DaL").matching("(healthwatcher.data|lib.persistence).(\\w*.)
      *\\w*").build();
```

All exceptions defined in version v1 are in the package lib.exceptions. Based on the HW documentation and the source code analysis, six groups of exceptions were defined and mapped, as shown in Listing 1.2. The diLEx excep-tion represents the user-defined exceptions (i.e., defined by the programmer) related to the DiL layer, buLEx exceptions are related to the BuL layer, and daLEx exceptions are related to the DaL layer. The svtEx and sqlEx are platform-defined exceptions and allEx represents all user-defined exceptions.

Listing 1.2. Exceptions Mapping.

```
1 ExceptionElement diLEx, buLEx, daLEx, sqlEx, svtEx, allEx;
2 diLEx = exception("DiLE").matching("(java.rmi.RemoteException|lib.
      exceptions.CommunicationException)*").build();
3 buLEx = exception("BuLE").matching("lib.exceptions.(ObjectAlready)\\w*").
      build();
4 daLEx = exception("DaLE").matching("lib.exceptions.(Persistence|ObjectNot|
      Repository|Transaction)\\w*").build();
5 sqlEx = exception("SQLE").matching("java.sql.SQLException").build();
6 svtEx = exception("SVTE").matching("javax.servlet.ServletException").build
      ();
7 allEx = exception("AllE").matching("lib.exceptions.(\\w*.)*\\w*").build();
```

Note that once the system evolves, the mappings of classes into layers also changes. Thus, for each HW version, it was necessary to perform some fine-tunes in the mapping to capture changes occurred from one version to other.

---

[5] The symbol "\w" represents a word character: [a-zA-Z_0-9].

Another step in the data preparation was to define an exception handling policy to evaluate the HW exception handling design based on the intention of HW's software architect (collected via an unstructured interview) and good practices recommended by the Oracle's BluePrints Design Patterns[6] for multi-layered architectures of Java systems. This policy states that an exception can be raised in or signaled by an arbitrary layer. When a specific layer (callee) signals an exception, such exception can only propagate to the immediately upper layer (caller), which is responsible for catching the exception and performing handling actions (*catch-and-handle* strategy). This puts the system back in its normal control flow. If this exception cannot be handled in this scope, the caller layer must perform an exception type remapping and signal the new exception type to the next upper layer (*catch-and-remap* strategy). This process repeats until the exceptional situation is finally handled at an upper layer. Exceptions signaled by third-party components to a specific layer must be handled in this layer or be remapped and propagated to the next upper layer.

Table 1 shows all design rules defined to enforce the established policy. Each rule enforces a specific aspect of the exception handling policy. For instance, the rule R01 enforces that exceptions signaled by the under layer diL must be handled by the upper layer viL (*catch-and-handle*). The rules R06 and R10 have a similar purpose. The rules R07 and R11 ensure that the *catch-and-remap* strategy is used. The rules R14 and R15 enforce that sqlEx exceptions signaled by third-party components must be handled by daL module. The rule R03 enforces that no user-defined exception can be signaled by viL. Finally, the R16 enforces that daLEx exceptions cannot flow through modules daL, buL, and diL.

4.2   Results and Discussion

Table 1 summarizes the evaluation results. Each HW version is checked against the same set of 16 design rules. All versions fully comply with six design rules (R02, R04, R07, R11, R12 e R14) and do not conform to 7 design rules (R01, R05, R06, R08, R09, R10, and R16). On one hand, R03 and R13 start to be violated in versions 10 and 4, respectively. On the other hand, R15 is violated in version 9 and starts be satisfied in the last version. In short, versions v1–v3 and v4–v10 has a 50% and 44% of conformance degree respectively.

Looking at the ArCatch.Checker conformance report (Listing 1.3), the R03 is violated in version 10 because the method initFacade() of class HWServlet starts to signal the exception CommunicationException after the modularization of exception handling code. The R013 starts to violate in version 4 because the implementation of Observer pattern, after that the method notify() of class Subject starts signaling the exceptions (Listing 1.4) ObjectNotFoundException, RepositoryException, ObjectNotValidException e TransactionException.

---

[6] http://www.oracle.com/technetwork/java/patterns-139816.html.

Table 1. Exception handling design rules and checking results.

ID	Exception handling design rule	Health watcher versions									
		01	02	03	04	05	06	07	08	09	10
R01	module(viL).mustHandle(diLEx).build()	✗	✗	✗	✗	✗	✗	✗	✗	✗	✗
R02	only(viL).canSignal(svtEx).build()	✓	✓	✓	✓	✓	✓	✓	✓	✓	✓
R03	module(viL).cannotSignal(allEx).build()	✓	✓	✓	✓	✓	✓	✓	✓	✓	✗
R04	only(diL).canRaise(diLEx).build()	✓	✓	✓	✓	✓	✓	✓	✓	✓	✓
R05	only(diL).canSignal(diLEx).build()	✗	✗	✗	✗	✗	✗	✗	✗	✗	✗
R06	module(diL).mustHandle(buLEx).build()	✗	✗	✗	✗	✗	✗	✗	✗	✗	✗
R07	only(diL).canRemap(buLEx).to(diLEx).build()	✓	✓	✓	✓	✓	✓	✓	✓	✓	✓
R08	only(buL).canRaise(buLEx).build()	✗	✗	✗	✗	✗	✗	✗	✗	✗	✗
R09	only(buL).canSignal(buLEx).build()	✗	✗	✗	✗	✗	✗	✗	✗	✗	✗
R10	module(buL).mustHandle(daLEx).build()	✗	✗	✗	✗	✗	✗	✗	✗	✗	✗
R11	only(buL).canRemap(daLEx).to(buLEx).build()	✓	✓	✓	✓	✓	✓	✓	✓	✓	✓
R12	only(daL).canRaise(daLEx).build()	✓	✓	✓	✓	✓	✓	✓	✓	✓	✓
R13	only(daL).canSignal(daLEx).build()	✓	✓	✓	✗	✗	✗	✗	✗	✗	✗
R14	only(daL).canHandle(sqlEx).build()	✓	✓	✓	✓	✓	✓	✓	✓	✓	✓
R15	module(daL).cannotSignal(sqlEx).build()	✗	✗	✗	✗	✗	✗	✗	✗	✗	✓
R16	exception(daLEx).cannotFlow(daL, buL, diL).build()	✗	✗	✗	✗	✗	✗	✗	✗	✗	✗

Listing 1.3. Rule R03 Example Report (HW v10).

```
1   -Rule Violations
2    -The method [healthwatcher.view.servlets.HWServlet.initFacade()] is
        signaling the exception [lib.exceptions.CommunicationException]
```

Listing 1.4. Rule R13 Example Report (HW v4).

```
1  -Rule Violations
2    -The method [lib.patterns.observer.Observer.notify(lib.patterns.observer
        .Subject)] is signaling the exception [lib.exceptions.
        ObjectNotFoundException]
3    -The method [lib.patterns.observer.Observer.notify(lib.patterns.observer
        .Subject)] is signaling the exception [lib.exceptions.
        RepositoryException]
4    -The method [lib.patterns.observer.Observer.notify(lib.patterns.observer
        .Subject)] is signaling the exception [lib.exceptions.
        ObjectNotValidException]
5    -The method [lib.patterns.observer.Observer.notify(lib.patterns.observer
        .Subject)] is signaling the exception [lib.exceptions.
        TransactionException]
```

The R15 is violated from versions 1 until version 9, starting to be satisfied in version 10. These violations occurred because some classes of daL signal the exception SQLException. However, after the modularization of exception handling code in version 10, such violations no long occurred. The full set of conformance checking reports for all 10 versions of HW can be found on the paper's website[7].

---

[7] https://github.com/juarezmeneses/ArCatchExperiment.

Listing 1.5. Rule R15 Example Report (HW v1–v9).

```
1  -Rule Violations
2    -The method [healthwatcher.data.rdb.ComplaintRepositoryRDB.
         accessComplaint(java.sql.ResultSet,healthwatcher.model.complaint.
         Complaint)] is signaling the exception [java.sql.SQLException]
```

To further validate the results, we interviewed the HW's software architect. First, we discussed the seven design rules that are violated in all versions. Thus, after looking at the violation report, he recognized that all violations represented clear deviations from his intention as software architect, confirming the existence of exception handling erosion problems in HW.

Second, we discussed the violation of R03 and R13. Regarding R03, the architect recognized that such violation introduced in version 10 is a mistake made by a developer and a possible solution could be create a try-catch bock on method `initFacade()` to catch the exception `CommunicationException` and perform an log operation or a page redirection to proper present the error. Regarding R13, the architect argued that such violation is not a proper violation itself, but a side effect caused by implementation of Observer design pattern. However, he decided that it must be fixed in a future version. Finally, looking at the violation report of R15, the architect had no doubt that such violation represents a deviation from his intention, which was fixed in version 10.

No evaluation regarding performance and usability of ArCatch was conducted in this paper. However, in the evaluation scenario, ArCatch takes about 50 s (average) to perform the source code analysis and check the conformance of each design rule in each HW version. After define the exception handling policy, the specification of all design rules using ArCatch.Rules takes less then 1 h. The mapping process was the most time consuming part, once we were not familiar with its source code; we needed to analyze manually the source code of each version. The first version analysis took more than 5 h, while the sum of all other versions analysis took about of 5 h, i.e. the entire mapping process took 10 h.

4.3   Threats to Validity

The threats to validity associated with our investigation are discussed using the classification by Runeson and Höst [18]. Since no causal relationship was investigated in the case study, we do not discuss internal validity threats.

Reliability validity threats are related to the repeatability of a study, i.e. how dependent are the research results on the researchers who conducted it [18]. We minimized this threat by involving several researchers in the design and execution of our investigation. Furthermore, our observations and findings were verified by HW's software architect to avoid false interpretations.

Construct validity threats reflect whether the measures used really represent the intended purpose of the investigation [18]. To mitigate this threat, we collected data using multiple methods (data triangulation). Moreover, some information about source code is extracted and represented as a static call-graph. However, some relations represented in the static call-graph can never occur in actual program runs. In fact, it is an undecidable problem. The static call-graph provides over-approximative information, which can lead ArCatch to find rule violations that may never happen at runtime (i.e., false alarms).

External validity threats limit the generalization of the findings of the investigation [18]. Since we employed the case study method, our findings are strongly bounded by the context of our study. In addition, the investigated case involved only one product, which is not used intensively by different users. To mitigate this threat, we made an attempt to detail the context of our study as much as possible. However, this is a strong limitation of our study, which we intend to address by evaluating our approach by conducting other case studies.

5   Related Work

We have reviewed the state of the art on architecture conformance checking solutions focusing on their support to the exception handling conformance checking.

The Semmle .QL [15] is a conformance checking solution where design constraints are specified as queries performed in the software source code. The .QL syntax is inspired in the SQL language. The LogEn [8] solution is based on dependency relations between implementation elements of different levels of granularity. LogEn provides a visual DSL as an Eclipse IDE plug-in to specify the mapping between architectural and implementation elements and express dependency constraints. Both solutions adopt Datalog, a logical query language, to perform the conformance checking. Regarding the exception handling conformance checking, LogEn only provides support to deal with raising and handling relations, while .QL only provides support to handling relation.

The DCL Suite [22], TamDera [11], and Dictō [5] provide a textual external DSL to describe dependence constraints between system modules and a checker to verify the compliance between the implemented and intended architectures. TamDera provides means to deal with architectural degradation in terms of erosion and drift problems, while DCL Suite and Dictō only provide support to deal with architectural erosion problems. In contrast to DCL Suite and TamDera, which provides their own conformance checker implementation, Dictō performs the conformance checking using existent conformance tools (e.g., JPF and PMD). Both DCL Suite and TamDera have been developed as a plug-in for Eclipse IDE. Therefore, programmers can carry out the conformance checking process as the source code is being written. The Dictō has been developed as an IDE agnostic solution that can be easily integrated in a static analysis tools such as SonarQube. Regarding the exception handling conformance checking, TamDera and Dictō only provide support to signaling and handling relations, while DCL Suite only provide support for signaling relations.

The EPL [1] is a conformance checking solution devoted to check the conformance of exception handling policies in Java programs. In EPL, an exception handling policy is a set of design decisions governing the exceptions usage in a software project. EPL provides an external DSL to describe exception handling policies involving exceptions and compartments, which is a language constructor used to express which classes and methods are taken into account in the conformance checking process. EPL has been developed as a plug-in for Eclipse IDE and the conformance checking can be performed as the source code is being written. EPL provides its own conformance checker based on the Eclipse JDT. Regarding the exception handling conformance checking, EPL is the most complete of the solutions we analyzed, only without support to express and check dependency constraints related to the exceptional control flow.

6   Conclusion and Future Work

In this paper, we have presented ArCatch, a conformance checking solution that tackles the exception handling erosion problem (RQ1). ArCatch aims at enforcing exception handling design decisions in Java projects, by providing: (i) a declarative language (ArCatch.Rules) for expressing design constraints regarding exception handling; and (ii) a rule checker (ArCatch.Checker) to automatically verify the exception handling conformance. Furthermore, ArCatch provides support for several kinds of dependence relation concerning the exception handling design, such as raising, re-raising, remapping, signaling, handling, and flow.

To evaluate our approach (RQ1.1 and RQ1.2), we conducted a case study and identified that: (i) at least 7 design rule violations in each version were detected; (ii) all versions conform to 6 design rules; and (iii) three violations appear in three different versions. ArCatch proved useful in the identification of existing exception handling erosion problems and its causes. This erosion can be avoided if adopting our approach in the system project since the beginning.

As future work, we plan to perform a user-centric evaluation to analyze ArCatch in terms of performance, scalability, usability, and learning curve. We also want to analyze if it is possible to use the ArCatch.Rules specifications to derive software tests for the exception handling code. Finally, we intend to conduct other case studies involving companies from different domains.

References

1. Barbosa, E.A., Garcia, A., Robillard, M.P., Jakobus, B.: Enforcing exception handling policies with a domain-specific language. IEEE Trans. Softw. Eng. **42**(6), 559–584 (2016)
2. Brunet, J., Guerrero, D., Figueiredo, J.: Design tests: an approach to programmatically check your code against design rules. In: 31st International Conference on Software Engineering, pp. 255–258, May 2009
3. Cacho, N., Barbosa, E.A., Araujo, J., Pranto, F., Garcia, A., Cesar, T., Soares, E., Cassio, A., Filipe, T., Garcia, I.: How does exception handling behavior evolve? an exploratory study in Java and C# applications. In: ICSME 2014, pp. 31–40. IEEE (2014)
4. Cacho, N., César, T., Filipe, T., Soares, E., Cassio, A., Souza, R., Garcia, I., Barbosa, E.A., Garcia, A.: Trading robustness for maintainability: an empirical study of evolving c# programs. In: Proceedings of the 36th International Conference on Software Engineering, ICSE 2014, pp. 584–595 (2014)

5. Caracciolo, A., Lungu, M., Nierstrasz, O.: A unified approach to architecture conformance checking. In: Proceedings of the 12th Working IEEE/IFIP Conference on Software Architecture (WICSA), pp. 41–50. ACM Press, May 2015

6. Chang, B.M., Choi, K.: A review on exception analysis. Inf. Softw. Technol. **77**(C), 1–16 (2016)

7. Ebert, F., Castor, F., Serebrenik, A.: An exploratory study on exception handling bugs in java programs. J. Syst. Softw. **106**(C), 82–101 (2015)

8. Eichberg, M., Kloppenburg, S., Klose, K., Mezini, M.: Defining and continuous checking of structural program dependencies. In: Proceedings of the 30th International Conference on Software Engineering, ICSE 2008, pp. 391–400. ACM (2008)

9. Ferrari, F., Burrows, R., Lemos, O., Garcia, A., Figueiredo, E., Cacho, N., Lopes, F., Temudo, N., Silva, L., Soares, S., Rashid, A., Masiero, P., Batista, T., Maldonado, J.: An exploratory study of fault-proneness in evolving aspect-oriented programs. In: Proceedings of the 32nd ACM/IEEE International Conference on Software Engineering, ICSE 2010, pp. 65–74. ACM, New York (2010)

10. Garcia, A.F., Rubira, C.M., Romanovsky, A., Xu, J.: A comparative study of exception handling mechanisms for building dependable object-oriented software. J. Syst. Softw. **59**(2), 197–222 (2001)

11. Gurgel, A., Macia, I., Garcia, A., Staa, A., Mezini, M., Eichberg, M., Mitschke, R.: Blending and reusing rules for architectural degradation prevention. In: Proceedings of the 13th International Conference on Modularity, pp. 61–72. ACM (2014)

12. van Gurp, J., Bosch, J.: Design erosion: problems and causes. J. Syst. Softw. **61**(2), 105–119 (2002)

13. Kechagia, M., Spinellis, D.: Undocumented and unchecked: exceptions that spell trouble. In: Proceedings of the 11th Working Conference on Mining Software Repositories, MSR 2014, pp. 312–315. ACM, New York (2014)

14. Lee, P.A., Anderson, T.: Fault Tolerance: Principles and Practice. Dependable Computing and Fault-Tolerant Systems, 2 edn., vol. 3. Springer, Wien (1990)

15. Moor, O.d., Verbaere, M., Hajiyev, E., Avgustinov, P., Ekman, T., Ongkingco, N., Sereni, D., Tibble, J.: Keynote address: .ql for source code analysis. In: SCAM 2007, pp. 3–16. IEEE Computer Society, Washington, DC (2007)

16. Oizumi, W.N., Garcia, A.F., Colanzi, T.E., Ferreira, M., Staa, A.V.: On the relationship of code-anomaly agglomerations and architectural problems. J. Softw. Eng. Res. Dev. **3**(1), 1–22 (2015)

17. Passos, L., Terra, R., Valente, M., Diniz, R., Mendonça, N.C.: Static architecture-conformance checking: an illustrative overview. IEEE Softw. **27**(5), 82–89 (2010)

18. Runeson, P., Höst, M., Rainer, A., Regnell, B.: Case Study Research in Software Engineering: Guidelines and Examples. Wiley, Hoboken (2012)

19. Shah, H., Gorg, C., Harrold, M.J.: Understanding exception handling: viewpoints of novices and experts. IEEE Trans. Softw. Eng. **36**(2), 150–161 (2010)

20. de Silva, L., Balasubramaniam, D.: Controlling software architecture erosion: a survey. J. Syst. Softw. **85**(1), 132–151 (2012)

21. Soares, S., Laureano, E., Borba, P.: Implementing distribution and persistence aspects with aspectj. In: OOPSLA 2002, pp. 174–190. ACM, New York (2002)

22. Terra, R., Valente, M.T.: A dependency constraint language to manage object-oriented software architectures. Softw. Pract. Exper. **39**(12), 1073–1094 (2009)

Considerations About Continuous Experimentation for Resource-Constrained Platforms in Self-driving Vehicles

Federico Giaimo[1]([✉]), Christian Berger[2], and Crispin Kirchner[3]

[1] Chalmers University of Technology, Göteborg, Sweden
giaimo@chalmers.se
[2] University of Göteborg, Göteborg, Sweden
christian.berger@gu.se
[3] RWTH Aachen University, Aachen, Germany
crispin.kirchner@rwth-aachen.de

Abstract. Autonomous vehicles are slowly becoming reality thanks to the efforts of many academic and industrial organizations. Due to the complexity of the software powering these systems and the dynamicity of the development processes, an architectural solution capable of supporting long-term evolution and maintenance is required.

Continuous Experimentation (CE) is an already increasingly adopted practice in software-intensive web-based software systems to steadily improve them over time. CE allows organizations to steer the development efforts by basing decisions on data collected about the system in its field of application. Despite the advantages of Continuous Experimentation, this practice is only rarely adopted in cyber-physical systems and in the automotive domain. Reasons for this include the strict safety constraints and the computational capabilities needed from the target systems.

In this work, a concept for using Continuous Experimentation for resource-constrained platforms like a self-driving vehicle is outlined.

Keywords: Software architecture for cyber-physical systems · Continuous Experimentation · Software evolution · Middleware

1 Introduction

Constant efforts in technology and software development by various research and commercial institutions are making autonomous cars gradually a reality. While this final objective is still out of reach in the nearest future, many features that can replace the human driver in ordinary driving tasks are already available.

Due to its safety constraints the software in vehicles needs to be very high in quality. This will prove even more true for autonomous vehicles, which will have the responsibility to assess the real world around them to decide a course of action while always meeting the safety requirements. For this reason it is

© Springer International Publishing AG 2017
A. Lopes and R. de Lemos (Eds.): ECSA 2017, LNCS 10475, pp. 84–91, 2017.
DOI: 10.1007/978-3-319-65831-5_6

imperative to find and enable a process that allows continuous software quality improvements, possibly even after the vehicle is sold to the customers.

Continuous Experimentation (CE) is an Extreme Programming practice that could satisfy these needs by running so-called "experiments" to collect meaningful data. These experiments are usually either variants of the deployed software or additional software features. The goal is to collect and use the resulting real-world data in order to decide in an objective way which of the possible variants or features is the most successful one. A CE setup begins with the target-base divided in sets, one of which is the *control set*, running unmodified software, and one or more *experimental sets*, which will run an experiment each. The software in all sets then collects relevant usage and performance data that will be relayed back to the developers. The best-performing set will decide which software variant or feature will be further developed and deployed to all the other targets.

CE is increasingly adopted in the context of software-intensive web-based applications, and the current state-of-practice is outlined in Sect. 2. With a focus on autonomous vehicles, we outlined in our previous work the design criteria for the software architecture to enable experimentation on Cyber-Physical Systems (CPS) as well [1]. However, challenges related to safety considerations are still unresolved and pose a significant obstacle for the adoption of software experimentation on vehicles. Scarcity of resources plays also an important role in this sense since the hardware in the car is carefully dimensioned in terms of performances to provide "just enough". Further challenges like scalability issues in case of several systems conducting experiments have also been identified in our previous study [2].

The Research Goal of this work is to assess the challenges related to the scarcity of resources that prevent the widespread adoption of CE in the automotive context, and to propose strategies to overcome them.

This goal is further elaborated into the following Research Questions:

RQ1 : What impact does the lack of resources in cyber-physical systems impose on the design and application of continuous experimentation?

RQ2 : What design criteria should the software architecture satisfy in order to enable continuous experimentation for a resource-constrained cyber-physical system?

2   Related Work

Several works are present in literature focusing on Continuous Experimentation. One of these is Fagerholm et al. [3], which describes a CE model that takes into account the roles, tasks, infrastructure and information artifacts involved by this practice. In this paper, the authors developed and extended their model, validating it against the results of two empirical case studies conducted in startup companies.

Another article of interest is Olsson and Bosch [4], which describes the steps that should be taken to move a traditional software development process to a "continuous" one. These steps involve the gradual introduction of Agile practices and the modification of the organization and their strategies in order to align them to the ones that better support continuous product evolution and delivery.

Several articles related to CE report the advancements and characteristics of the experimentation processes and platforms in industrial settings. An example of these works is Tang et al. [5] that described the experimental setting at Google Inc. where, in order to improve the experimentation process and execution, experiments that involve independent factors are overlapped. Further examples are Kohavi et al. [6], that described Microsoft Bing's own solution to run "over 200 experiments concurrently", and Amatriain [7], that outlined Netflix's approach to experimentation.

At the best of the authors' knowledge, and perhaps hinting at the novelty of the field, some of the major academic databases, i.e. IEEE Xplore, ACM Digital Library, Scopus, Web of Science, were searched for articles regarding Continuous Experimentation in the context of CPS, but unrelated or no results at all were found at the time of writing.

3 Assessing the Scarcity of Resources

Running experimental software alongside production software requires additional computational resources. In contrast to web-based applications running in server farms, where additional virtual servers can be spawned if needed, acquiring additional computational power in CPS is not trivial, as their hardware cannot be changed after delivery to the customers.

To assess these limitations, different *execution strategies* for acquiring unused computational power are proposed, taking into consideration different initial conditions that we have explored in the context of one of our research projects [8]. These strategies are explained in the following paragraphs and depicted in Fig. 1. The automotive software in the proposed execution scenarios is assumed to be structured in modules, which are recurrently executed in time slots, either *data-* or *time-triggered* [9]. This means respectively that a module is either executed whenever new information arrives, or at a fixed frequency even if new data has not been gathered or if new data was queued waiting to be processed. The ideal way to test an experimental version of a production software module would be to run it in parallel to the production version in order to provide the same input to both modules. However, due to safety reasons and lack of computational resources the experimental module may be forced to run on a less frequent schedule than the production module and its communications capabilities may be reduced (for example its output could be logged instead of forwarded to the intended recipients). In order to make the experimental software "believe" that it is being run without such handicaps it is required to encapsulate the time and the communication resources that the software modules can access.

Due to the necessary level of control needed over the software modules in the authors' understanding it is not enough to simply delegate the experiment's execution schedule to the operating system's Process Scheduler. Firstly because the choice of whether to run an experimental module and what execution schedule to adopt depends on several factors that are only known at high levels of abstraction. Secondly and more importantly, executing an experiment can imply the execution of a software module at the potential "expenses" of another selected one when computational resources are scarce, and to unfairly favor a software module over another is against the Process Scheduler's goal to serve resources in a fair way among all processes.

In the following the identified execution strategies will be described.

Parallel Execution. In the simplest case, even though either time or computational resources are scarce on a particular core or processor alongside the production module, a third software module can be paused or stopped in order to reuse its resources to run the experiment. In this case it is possible to assume that an unused processor is available, and the experimental module can be executed in *parallel* to the production module. As both modules run on independent computing units, they are not necessarily coupled in terms of execution frequency. This case has been described for completeness but it is unlikely to be applicable.

Serial Execution. In the typical case that there is no additional computing unit available to independently execute an experimental module, the computing time needed by the experiment could come from the unused time of a production module. In this case the experimental module could be executed *serially*, i.e. always after the production module has finished its computation and until the production module is executed again in its next time slot.

When production and experimental modules are functionally related and are supposed to operate as synchronously as possible, two different cases with different implications can be identified: whether the experimental module can or cannot conclude its calculations in the unused time left in the production module's time slot. In the simplest case, the experimental module can finish its tasks inside the time window left over by the production module, in the second case, the time left unused by the production module is not enough for the experimental module to complete its operations, which results in an interruption of the experimental module. It is worth noting that whenever the execution of the experimental module needs to be stretched over two non-contiguous time slots due to the lack of unused time in the current slot, the result is that the experimental module will be executed less frequently than the production module, potentially resulting in time synchronization issues and affecting the comparability of metrics in the case of A/B testing.

Downsampled Execution. The third execution strategy, called *downsampling*, is applicable if there is no additional computing node available and no computation time is left in the time slice of a module. As computational power on cars is limited, it can be expected to also be the most likely applicable strategy. This approach is based on the assumption that conditions exist under which the execution of a production module can periodically be skipped (analog to suspending the production module from time to time), freeing computational resources to be used for experimentation purposes. Skipping execution cycles of a production module may result in compromising safety-critical aspects of the vehicle, hence great care must be taken to ensure that the planned downsampling is safe. A possible way to ensure its safety could be to run preliminary tests before applying this strategy, to verify in advance that it is viable in practice and at which rate the production module can skip computation cycles before dependent modules downstream in the data-processing chain are affected. Furthermore, the conditions under which the downsampling rate has been tested need to be fixed and the execution of the experiment must only be carried out when the vehicle operates under those conditions. As with this strategy the time slots available to the experimental module are non-contiguous, the considerations about time synchronization and logic coherence that were expressed for the serial execution strategy apply to this case as well.

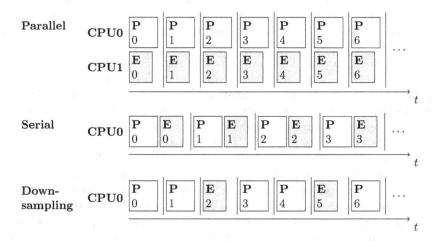

Fig. 1. Execution strategies. "P" and "E" stand for Production and Experimental software module. Picture based on Kirchner [8].

The proposed strategies may also be composed and adjusted at runtime. For example, it could happen that an experiment might initially require the analysis of relatively small amounts of data, thus making the serial execution strategy feasible. If however more intensive calculations would later be required and the conditions would allow it, the strategy could be changed to downsampling in order to allocate more time to each experimental iteration at the cost of a less frequent execution schedule.

4   Software Architecture

Section 3 has identified three potential strategies to execute an experimental software module next to a product module. Furthermore, we have pointed out that the production and experimental modules need to be decoupled from the real system time and from their respective potential communication vector with downstream modules. The reason is that the production and experimental module should believe that they are triggered at the very same point in time by the same input data; while the execution strategy in effect must be entirely transparent for the modules. Also, the communication of data into and from the production and experimental modules must be controlled entirely. While the ingoing communication may not be critical, a strict control of any outgoing communication is needed to avoid unwanted interference with the dependent downstream software modules. Furthermore, any time stamping related to sending data from the production and experimental modules to other modules must be potentially adjusted to make the rest of the system believe that these modules have not been executed with different execution strategies. The possibility of *rewriting* time stamp information for communication is another indicator why the regular Process Scheduler provided by the operating system does not meet the requirements for conducting experiments on a resource-constrained computational environment.

Chalmers University of Technology hosts a vehicle laboratory called Revere, "Resource for Vehicle Research" [10], with the goal of conducting and developing research for self-driving vehicles and active safety. The Revere laboratory uses our middleware OpenDaVINCI[1], which allows the realization of distributed microservices communicating via Protobuf-encoded messages. The activation of software modules realized with OpenDaVINCI complies to the time-triggered or data-triggered principle described in Sect. 3. OpenDaVINCI by default encapsulates the system time via an object called `TimeStamp` that either invokes the POSIX time API returning the "real" time or transparently replaces the real system clock with a virtual one. The communication facilities available to the software modules are also encapsulated. OpenDaVINCI uses by default UDP multicast as communication principle. In OpenDaVINCI a so-called `ContainerConference` is provided as the data to be exchanged is wrapped into `Container` containing the actual data to be exchanged and some meta-information like time stamps for sending, receiving, and sample time point.

To enable CE using these building blocks, both the production and experimental modules will be handled by an *Experimenter* software module that will manage them to realize the aforementioned execution strategies by forwarding input data to both modules, activating and suspending them according to the respective execution strategy, and receiving data containers to be distributed for both delivery or logging purposes.

5   Discussion

For the current state-of-practice of CE in web-based systems, which usually involves validation of user feedback, small scale approaches are not viable since less generalizable. However, in the automotive domain the experiments would

---

[1] http://code.opendavinci.org.

focus on algorithmic problems and their verification in realistic scenarios, making the results easier to generalize even if collected by a small number of vehicles.

This work proposes a new element to consider in order to apply CE on cyber-physical systems, which is the execution strategy. This element is introduced to account for the possible lack of computational resources, and can critically impact the amount of collected results or the overall viability of the experiments. For this reason we propose an addition to the CE model proposed by Fagerholm et al. [3] when it involves experiments on CPS: the *domain expert*, a person or team with deep knowledge of the system and its capabilities. The domain expert's main role is to advise the experimenter and data scientist while devising and planning the experiment to be run. The insights this figure could provide would not be limited only to the choice of the execution strategy but could range for example from deciding if an experiment could be run "live" on customers' vehicles, or if preliminary measurements would be needed to ensure its viability, and so on. As a direct application of the "web-based" continuous experimentation would prove difficult or even impossible in the context of CPS due to the several key differences between the two fields, we claim that the presence of an intermediary figure can smoothen or in some cases enable the experimentation process thanks to its knowledge of both the system and the proposed techniques to obtain the additional computational time needed to run experiments.

We report about threats to the validity of this study according to Runeson and Höst [11]. Our current work in the lab concerns the validation of the proposed strategies using our self-driving vehicles to increase the external validity of the suggested architectural design considerations. It is also impossible to completely eliminate the threat to reliability, i.e. whether different researchers would come out with the same solution if they were to assess the same problem. To mitigate this threat, we carefully described our reasoning to motivate our suggested design decisions.

6   Conclusions and Future Work

The present work aims at contextualizing the Continuous Experimentation process into the Cyber-Physical System field, assessing the lack of surplus resources that would be needed for the system to run the additional experimental code. In order to assess this deficit, three different execution strategies have been proposed that would allow to run an experimental software module alongside a production module. The different characteristics of the strategies enable the adaptation of the solution for different application scenarios.

In order for a software architecture to enable and make use of the proposed strategies it must be possible to strictly control two crucial types of information that are accessible to both the production and experimental software module, which are the time and the communication resource. Controlling the modules' access to these resources acts as enabling criteria ensuring the transparency of the execution strategy to the software modules themselves.

Future efforts will focus on evaluating the contributions in a setting closer to the specific challenges encountered in industry, by continuing the research in the

COPPLAR project, which is Chalmers University of Technology's contribution to the DriveMe context[2]. The DriveMe project is an autonomous driving pilot project by Volvo Cars that aims at releasing 100 cars capable of self-driving capabilities on selected public roads in 2017.

Acknowledgment. This work has been supported by the COPPLAR Project – CampusShuttle cooperative perception and planning platform [12], funded by Vinnova FFI, Diarienr: 2015-04849.

References

1. Giaimo, F., Berger, C.: Design criteria to architect continuous experimentation for self-driving vehicles. In: Proceedings of the International Conference on Software Architecture, ICSA 2017. IEEE, New York (2017)
2. Giaimo, F., Yin, H., Berger, C., Crnkovic, I.: Continuous experimentation on cyber-physical systems: challenges and opportunities. In: Proceedings of the Scientific Workshop Proceedings of XP2016, p. 14. ACM (2016)
3. Fagerholm, F., Guinea, A.S., Mäenpää, H., Münch, J.: The right model for continuous experimentation. J. Syst. Softw. **123**, 292–305 (2017)
4. Olsson, H.H., Bosch, J.: Climbing the stairway to heaven: evolving from agile development to continuous deployment of software. In: Bosch, J. (ed.) Continuous Software Engineering, pp. 15–27. Springer, Heidelberg (2014)
5. Tang, D., Agarwal, A., O'Brien, D., Meyer, M.: Overlapping experiment infrastructure: more, better, faster experimentation. In: Proceedings of the 16th ACM SIGKDD International Conference on Knowledge Discovery and Data Mining, pp. 17–26. ACM (2010)
6. Kohavi, R., Deng, A., Frasca, B., Walker, T., Xu, Y., Pohlmann, N.: Online controlled experiments at large scale. In: Proceedings of the 19th ACM SIGKDD International Conference on Knowledge Discovery and Data Mining, KDD 2013, pp. 1168–1176. ACM, New York (2013)
7. Amatriain, X.: Beyond data: from user information to business value through personalized recommendations and consumer science. In: Proceedings of the 22nd ACM International Conference on Information & Knowledge Management, pp. 2201–2208. ACM (2013)
8. Kirchner, C.: Assessing safety aspects for continuous experimentation on the example of automated driving. Master's thesis, RWTH Aachen, February 2017
9. Navet, N., Simonot-Lion, F.: Automotive Embedded Systems Handbook. CRC Press, Boca Raton (2008)
10. ReVeRe - Research Vehicle Resource at Chalmers. https://www.chalmers.se/safer/EN/projects/pre-crash-safety/projects/revere-research-vehicle. Accessed 14 Jan 2017
11. Runeson, P., Höst, M.: Guidelines for conducting and reporting case study research in software engineering. Empirical Softw. Eng. **14**(2), 131 (2009)
12. COPPLAR Project - CampusShuttle cooperative perception and planning platform. https://www.chalmers.se/safer/EN/projects/pre-crash-safety/projects/copplar-campusshuttle. Accessed 14 Jan 2017

---

[2] http://www.chalmers.se/en/areas-of-advance/Transport/news/Pages/Chalmers-joins-the-Drive-Me-project.aspx.

Automatic Generation

An Architecture Framework for Modelling and Simulation of Situational-Aware Cyber-Physical Systems

Mohammad Sharaf[1]([⊠]), Moamin Abughazala[2], Henry Muccini[1], and Mai Abusair[1]

[1] DISIM Department, University of L'Aquila, L'aquila, Italy
massharaf@yahoo.com, henry.muccini@univaq.it, mai.abusair@gmail.com
[2] Computer Science Department, An-Najah National Univesity, Nablus, Palestine
m.abughazaleh@najah.edu

Abstract. Situational Aware (SiA) Cyber-physical systems (CPS) harmoniously integrate computational and physical components to being aware of what is happening in the surroundings and using this information to decide and act. Architecture description of SiA-CPS can be a valuable tool to reason about the selected solutions, and to enable code generation and simulation. This paper presents an architecture framework that automatically generates from a SiA-CPS architecture description, an executable code used to simulate the architecture model and evaluate it in terms of data traffic load, battery level and energy consumptions. The framework makes use of a model transformation approach where, three SiA-CPS domain-specific modeling views are automatically transformed into the input language of CupCarbon, an open source tool supporting the simulation of sensor network architectures.

1 Introduction

An architecture description is the practice of recording software, system, and enterprise architectures so that architectures can be understood, documented, analyzed and realized [1]. Accordingly, a number of architecture frameworks, architecture description languages, and different views and viewpoints have been proposed in the years [2–5], each one focussing on a specific application domain, set of views and viewpoints, or concerns. As clearly remarked since more than two decades, an architecture description is essential to the analysis of the high-level properties of a complex system [6]. It can expose various kinds of problems that would otherwise go undetected [7].

This paper proposes a means to simulate *situational-aware cyber-physical systems*, based on a multi-view architecture description.

Situational-aware cyber-physical systems (SiA-CPS) are cyber-physical systems that, by transforming sensed data into actionable intelligence, has the ability to observe the (user's) surroundings and make detailed assessments about his environment. SiA-CPS involves being aware of what is happening in the vicinity

© Springer International Publishing AG 2017
A. Lopes and R. de Lemos (Eds.): ECSA 2017, LNCS 10475, pp. 95–111, 2017.
DOI: 10.1007/978-3-319-65831-5_7

to understand how information, events, and one's own actions will impact goals and objectives, both immediately and in the near future [8].

Architecting SiA-CPS requires the description of novel architectural views, were the physical environment, as well as its cyber dimension, plays a key role [9]. Software components, implemented on top of SiA-specific hardware IoT devices (e.g., sensors and actuators, CCTV cameras, beacons), are required to interact in a prescribed open or closed physical space (e.g., a parking lot, a classroom, a hallway) under observation [10]. In previous work [11], some of the co-authors presented an architecture description for SiA-CPS. Designed according to the IEEE/ISO/IEC 42010 standard [1], the CAPS architecture description supports an architecture-driven development of SiA-CPSs, and comprises three (plus two) modeling views, and namely: the software architecture structural and behavioral view (SAML), the hardware view (HWML), and the physical space view (SPML). The latter implements an architecture description for what typically referred as cyber physical space [12–14]. In order to create a combined software, hardware, and space view of SiA-CPS, the three proposed modelling views are linked together via two auxiliary views, denoted as Mapping Modelling Language (MAPML) and Deployment Modelling Language (DEPML).

This work builds on top of [11] by proposing a code generation framework that, by transforming CAPS models into the CupCarbon [15] simulator input, will support the CAPS architecture simulation in terms of data traffic and load and battery consumptions. The framework, through a group of code generators, transforms SAML model (and then, HWML and SPML) into a completely functional code. This paper will focus on the CupCarbon simulator language named Senscript. The CAPS modeling and simulation framework is realized by exploiting advanced Model-Driven Engineering (MDE) techniques, such as metamodelling, model weaving and model transformation.

The main contributions of this paper can be summarized as follows:

- A technical process, comprising four main processes (parsing, analyzing, generating script, and generating project) to manipulate CAPS models;
- A set of model to text transformations, that transforms SAML, HWML, and SPML models into CupCarbon files;
- The initial application to the UnivAq Street Science situational awareness application.

The rest of the paper is organized as follow: Sect. 2 provides background information on the CAPS modeling framework, the CupCarbon Simulator, and the UnivaAq Street Science application scenario. Section 3 details the code generation framework: its process and the transformational approach. Section 4 applies the CAPS simulation approach to the NdR system, while simulation results are presented in Sect. 5. Section 6 concludes the paper.

2   Background

2.1   The CAPS Modeling Framework

The CAPS modeling framework supports the engineer of SiA-CPS. It is based on a multi-view architectural approach designed according to the IEEE/ISO/IEC 42010 standard [1]. The aim of this framework is to support the architecture description, reasoning, and design decision process.

The CAPS is designed and implemented taking into account three architectural views: the software architecture structural and behavioral view (SAML), the hardware view (HWML), and the physical space view (SPML). We decided to have all things related to Software in one view (as well for HW and SPML) in order to provide a cohesive modeling environment. In addition, the CAPS has two auxiliary views, denoted as Mapping Modeling Language (MAPML) and Deployment Modeling Language (DEPML), are used to link together the three views. While details are provided in [11], we here summarize the main modeling elements.

The *software architecture view* supports architects in the definition of the software architecture of the SiA-CPS application through the *SAML* modeling language. This view looks exclusively to software elements, with a specific focus on the architecture structure and its behavior [16]. Briefly, the *SAML* view describes how `components` and `connections` exchange messages through `message ports`. Each component in *SAML* model can declare a set of `modes`, and each mode can contain a list of `events`, `conditions`, and `actions`, that all together represent the behavior of the component (an example is provided in Sect. 4). Moreover, `application data` manipulated by actions are defined inside the component.

The *hardware view* describes the hardware characteristics of each `hardware element` to be used within a SiA-CPS. A model in the hardware modeling language (HWML) encompasses specific low-level, node-specific information, like its `memory`, `energy source`, `processor`, installed `sensing units` and `actuating units`. A description of the HWML metamodel is reported in [11].

The *physical space view* describes the physical site, in the real world, where the SiA-CPS equipment will be deployed. The space modeling language (SPML) provides support for developing 3D model editors. The CAPS modeling framework enables engineers to specify 3D syntaxes for SPML in a declarative way which will reduce the amount of effort and need for low-level expertise. It aims to support the standardization of a language for declarative specification of 3D concrete syntaxes for SiA-CPS. This view is especially useful for developers and system engineers when they have to consider the network topology, the presence of possible physical obstacles (e.g., walls, trees) within the network deployment area, and so on. More details are available in [11].

2.2   CupCarbon Simulator

CupCarbon [15] is an open source simulator dedicated for wireless sensor network. It is used for scientific and educational purposes. It assists scientists in testing their wireless topologies and protocols, while it assists trainers in clarifying how wireless sensors work. Moreover, in CupCarbon, a network can be designed and sensors can be deployed directly onto the map by using OpenStreetMap that is provided through its interface. For more specific sensor nodes configurations, CupCarbon provides a scripting language called *SenScript* that can be used for this purpose. Moreover, its environment allows users to design mobility scenarios through which they generate different events. After deploying sensor nodes, one can use CupCarbon to simulate the energy consumption.

In this paper, the CupCarbon simulator will receive the input files generated by the CAPS code generator. Those files, encoding information coming from CAPS in the SenScript language, will be used to simulate energy consumption, battery level and data traffic of model nodes associated with the CAPS architectural model.

2.3   UnivAq Street Science System

The UnivAq Street Science is the European Researchers' Night (NdR) event organized by the University of L'Aquila. In this event, the research community and public are brought together from the afternoon until late at night to share a combination of entertainment and information. As an exemplification scenario we will take the NdR held in L'Aquila city center, in which performances, lectures, demonstrations, workshops take place in its squares, main streets, and buildings. From our experience in organizing this event in L'Aquila, we captured some source of evidence. First, about 20,000 visitors are coming to the NdR every year. Second, late hours usually have more crowded than early hours. Third, the weather changes the visitor's preferences in what to see and where to stay more. Forth, visitors are unable to easily locate activities and though they miss some of them.

Our research group has been invited to provide new services to improve the quality of the visiting experience. For this purpose, we developed (and we are refining for the 2017 edition) a SiA-CPS with a mobile application as the first step towards a better NdR experience. Through the environmental physical sensors that we are deploying in the NdR area, and the mobile application used by visitors on their smartphones, we are providing the following services: (i) access control to rooms, laboratories, and parking lots, (ii) open and closed spaces monitoring, (iii) balance people crowd among different events and spaces, by using the mobile app to inform visitors about the degree of crowd in a place, (iv) make a planner that creates a tour while minimizing the waiting time and crowd in an area, (v) urban security, specifically in the case of earthquakes, fires and over crowd.

In this paper we focus on two situational-aware services that are planned for the NdR. These services are related to rooms access control and safe airflow. A SAML model will be presented in Sect. 4. We will also describe the related HWML and SPML models. By using the CAPS code generator, the models will be transformed into CupCarbon Scripts. After all, the model generated code will be sent to the CupCarbon simulator in order to evaluate the architecture's energy consumption, battery level, and data traffic.

3   CAPS Code Generation

CAPS code generation framework is a framework in which CAPS models pass through different interpretations in order to build a code project that is able to be inserted in CupCarbon simulator. By running this code project on Cup-Carbon, we will be able to evaluate CAPS architecture in terms of data traffic load, battery level and energy consumptions of its nodes. This framework starts from interpreting SAML model and its components into Senscript files. Then, HW specifications and the deployment locations of nodes will be extracted from HWML and SPML models, respectively, and used to set up configuration files. All files result from CAPS models will be used in building CupCarbon project.

As depicted in Fig. 1, the framework has four activities: parsing, analyzing, script generation and project generation. These activities are detailed in the following sections.

3.1   Parsing

In this activity we use as input the SAML model that is typically stored in XMI file. This file encompasses a lot of information that are not needed for code generation. Thus, this information needs to be filtered out in order to acquire a relevant subset of SAML model values that conforms to SAML meta model. These values are used to instantiate templates. Templates and filtering pattern is one of several patterns that are usually followed in implementing code generators, as described in [17].

The parser is in charge of parsing the SAML XMI file to get all the information needed based on templates definitions. Templates are defined based on SAML meta model, and there are different templates defined for different SAML sub models. For example, there are templates for Software Architecture elements (SAML components and connectors), ports, modes and data. This parser, will create an object of software architecture, that in turn carries the SAML model description in java.

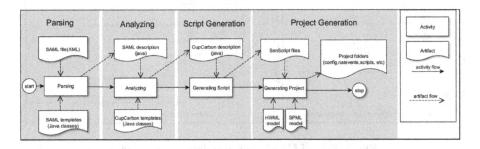

Fig. 1. CAPS automatic code generation framework

Accordingly, the resulting software architecture object contains the structural and behavioral part of the model. For the structural part, it contains the declarations of components, their data, their ports (as defined in the SAML meta model). Moreover, according to the definition, each port can be an IN message port or an OUT message port. The IN port defines APIs for messages to be received from other components. The OUT port defines a set of APIs for messages to be sent for other components [18].

For the behavioral part, each component has a group of modes, or states. The mode is represented as a method that carries the name of the mode. The mode method can contain if statements that perform logical tests. If a test evaluates to true, the mode method performs an action. The action can change variables values defined in the component scope and/or can call another mode method. Exit and entry modes are represented by calling methods of different types. Furthermore, this behavioral part of the code generator provides helpers to navigate through the diverse SAML metaclasses that are responsible for modeling the behavior.

The assumption we have in this work, that, each component in CAPS must be built to have at most one sensing unit (humidity sensor, or temperature sensor, or etc.). The reason of this assumption is, in the current state, CupCarbon is able to manage one sensing unit inside its sensor node. Hence, CupCarbon sensor node can contain many radio modules, a battery and a sensing unit. As it will be shown later, the component in CAPS will be represented as a sensor node in CupCarbon. More complex representation for several sensors in CAPS component will be handled in the future.

3.2 Analyzing

This activity takes as an input the software architecture object and the SAML model description in java, that result from the previous parsing activity. The input must be transformed into CupCarbon compatible information, in order to build CupCarbon Senscript files.

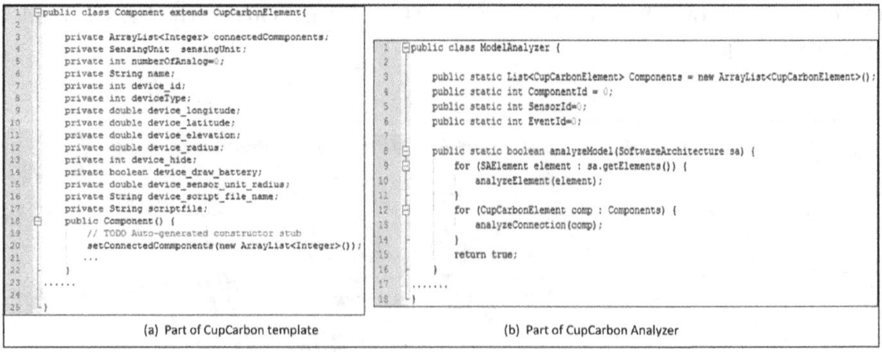

(a) Part of CupCarbon template   (b) Part of CupCarbon Analyzer

Fig. 2. Part of CupCarbon template and analyzer

The Analyzer (ModelAnalyzer) depicted in Fig. 2(b), represents the core section in code generation. The method *analyzeModel* takes the Software Architecture object as a parameter and analyzes each element to create the corresponding objects that will be used later for generating CupCarbon sensors and scripts. The CupCarbon template depicted in Fig. 2(a) represents the structure of CupCarbon element that will be used in this conversion.

The Analyzer is composed of two main parts:

(1) **Element Analyzer:** this part of the code (line 10 in Fig. 2(b)), takes an *SAElement* object as a parameter (that retrieves the parsed SAML software architecture elements) and then checks each element type and creates new objects that will represent the element in CupCarbon. For example if the element is a component, it will create an object from the Component class. If the element is a connection, it will create an object from the Connection class. Another important task of this part, is the mode analyzer. It is responsible for analyzing each mode in a component.

Modes (that were represented as methods) and mode transitions (represented as calling methods), will be interpreted as a group of *while* and *if* statements (a Senscript code, that result from a component of two modes, is described in Sect. 4, Fig. 5). The behavioral elements (event-condition-action) contained in the mode will be interpreted into other objects (composite objects) for a component. Thus, the result from this step, is a list of CupCarbon components, each CupCarbon component (CupCarbon element) has a sensing unit, radio module parameters and instructions that will be used in the creation of SenScript file for this CupCarbon component.

(2) **Connection Analyzer:** this part of the code (line 13 in Fig. 2(b)), is used to check the connection between components that already have been generated, in the previous part, and deciding their target and source components (connected components). Moreover, it denotes connections that occur between two components on the same platform or separated by a network, and it can decide how messages are controlled when they are moving between two components on different communication channels. The communication over these connections can be synchronous and asynchronous [19]. Asynchronous communication is acquired through using buffers (declaring communication array), while synchronous communication is acquired through using the buffer and setting its size to 0. For the sake of simplicity, the communication on the connection is made unidirectional and one communication is used for each different exchanged message. The buffer size is set into 1 in asynchronous communication, but during the code generation, the user can change this size of the buffer depending on the requirements of the application to be analyzed.

Finally, the result of analyzing activity is a list of CupCarbon components defined with their connections. The object that carries this information is shown in Line 3 on Fig. 2(b). These objects represent CupCarbon elements description in java, and will be an entry to the script generation activity.

3.3 Generating Script

This activity takes as an input the list of CupCarbon components objects produced from the analyzing phase. This activity is in charge of preparing the Senscripts code. A Senscript file for each component will be produced.

Part of the code responsible of Senscript generation is shown in Fig. 3. Figure 3(a), Lines 5, 6, 7, and 8, show how each component in the list of Cub-CarbonElement is sent to SenscriptGenerator. Figure 3(b), Line 10, shows the generateSenscript method that receives the component. This method uses several helpers and command instructions to translate the content of component object into Senscript code. In Fig. 3(c) an example of helper methods that translate read and write variables statements are shown.

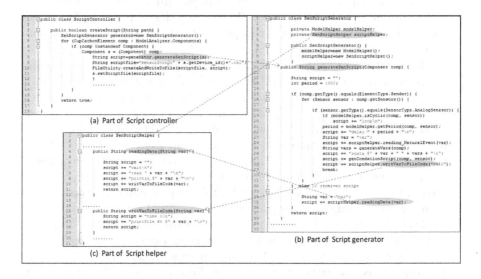

(a) Part of Script controller

(c) Part of Script helper

(b) Part of Script generator

Fig. 3. Part of generating senscripts code

The script controller in Fig. 3(a), is responsible for putting all the translated statements for each component in a distinct Senscript file.

For each component, the script controller depicted in Fig. 3(a), is in charge of storing all the code translated for a component into a senscript file (.csc). The name of the file is distinguished by the device id (component id).

Thus, the result of this activity is a group of SenScripts files that represent all the components in the CupCarbon simulator (the CupCarbon component is represented as a CubCarbon node in the CupCarbon simulator).

3.4 Generating Project

This activity is responsible for creating files readable by the CupCarbon simulator. These files include configuration parameters and radio modules needed to run a CupCarbon project. Examples of device parameters are: device type, device id, device longitude, device latitude, and device elevation. Examples of device radio modules are: radio standard, radio radius, and radio data rate [15].

The location parameters for each device (device longitude, device latitude, device elevation) will be automatically extracted from the SPML model (XMI file). Other parameters and radio modules will be extracted from the HWML model (XMI file). Then, an automatic generation of parameters and radio modules files are created. Each device has parameters file and a radio module file. An example of parameters and radio modules extracted from these models into CupCarbon files are shown in Figs. 6 and 7 in Sect. 4.

Parameters and radio modules files, along with the generated Senscript files, will form the final project to be loaded in the CupCarbon simulator workspace.

Finally, after loading the project and before running the simulation process on CupCarbon, few more configurations are needed to be done through its interface. First, set some device (node) parameters through its interface (like, setting up the *energy max* value that represents the initial energy of the battery). Second, create natural events for each sensing unit. This in turn will create a natural event file for each sensing unit and store it in the natevent folder in the project workspace.

4   Application of CAPS Models, Code Generation and Simulation to the NdR Case Study

In this section, we will simply represent a partial example of NdR case study introduced in Sect. 2. A simple scenario describes the monitoring of people count and oxygen level in a NdR room will be introduced. We will show its SAML model that plays a major role in SenScript code generation. We will show the needed part of its related HWML and SPML models that will be transfered to CupCarbon configuration files.

Figure 4 shows the SAML model of the CAPS. It is important to note that this figure is actually a screen-shot of our CAPS tool [20]. From a structural point of view, the shown SiA-CPS model is composed of five main components; OxygenSensor, RoomPeopleCounter, RoomController, EntranceLockActuator, WindowsLockActuator, and Server.

The OxygenSensor component is responsible for monitoring the Oxygen breathing percentage in a room. It includes two modes: (1) Normal mode: in this mode the oxygen sensor reads Oxygen breathing percentage (O2) in a room every 100 s. A timer is set in this mode to schedule the reading from the oxygen sensor. A message carrying the O2 value is sent from the output message port of the OxygenSensor component to the in port of the RoomController component. Moreover, if the reading of O2 is less than 0.19 that means the state of the room will enter the critical mode. (2) Critical mode: in this mode the oxygen sensor reads Oxygen breathing percentage (O2) in a room every 1 s, since this mode indicates the unsafe level of oxygen. Also in this mode, a timer is set to schedule the reading from the oxygen sensor. A message carrying the O2 value is sent

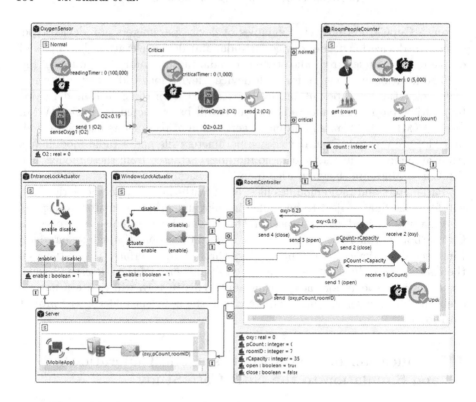

Fig. 4. The Software architecture of simple scenario in NdR case study

from the output message port of the OxygenSensor component to the in port of the RoomController component. Moreover, if the reading of O2 is more than 0.23 that means the state of the room will go back to the normal mode.

The RoomPeopleCounter component is responsible for counting the people in a room. This counter work all the time to count people in a room. But, it updates this information to the RoomController only every 5 s. When a timer is fired, it sends a message containing the people count in a room (count) from the out port of the RoomPeopleCounter component to the in port of the RoomController component.

The RoomController component is responsible for receiving sensors data in a room and take decisions based on its values. The decisions in this example are related to send a control messages to the actuators to open and/or close, windows and doors. The description shown in RoomController component is a simplified version of its supposed work. In this example, RoomController component receives two types of messages from its out ports:

(1) Message contains Oxygen breathing percentage: if the received value is less than 0.19, this component sends through its out port a message to the in port of the WindowsLockActuator component. This message contains a Boolean variable (open), the value of this variable is set to true. Otherwise, if the

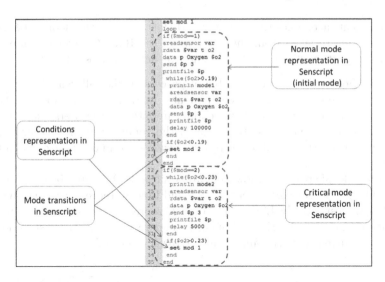

Fig. 5. SenScript generated by CAPS code generator for OxygenSensor component

received value is more than 0.23, this component sends through its out port a message to the in port of the WindowsLockActuator component. This message contains a Boolean variable (close), the value of this variable is set to false.

(2) Message contains people count: if the received value is less than room capacity (rCapacity = 35), this component sends through its out port a message to the in port of the EntranceLockActuator component. This message contains a Boolean variable (open), the value of this variable is true. Otherwise, if the received value is more than rCapacity, this component sends through its out port a message to the in port of the EntranceLockActuator component. This message contains a Boolean variable (close), the value of this variable is false.

The RoomController component is in charge of sending a message contains the values of the Oxygen (oxy), people counter (pCounter), and ID of a room (roomID) to the Server, in port, from the out port of the RoomController.

WindowsLockActuator component is the one responsible for performing the correct action of opening or closing the windows. If it receives from its in port a message containing a true value coming from the out port of the RoomController component, it enables the actuator and thus it opens the windows. Otherwise, if the value received from the out port of the RoomController component, to its in port, containing a false value, the actuator closes the windows.

EntranceLockActuator component is liable for performing the correct action of opening or closing the doors. If it receives from its in port a message containing o true value coming from the out port of the RoomController component, it enables the actuator and thus it opens the doors. Otherwise, if the value received from the out port of the RoomController component, to its in port, containing a false value, the actuator closes the doors.

Finally, Server component is liable of processing the different data received through its in ports from other components. In this example, we restrict the Server component responsibility in sending updates to the users running NdR mobile application. This update indicates the rooms state if they are full or not, depending on the roomID and pCount received from out port of RoomControllers.

For the sake of space, we show in figure 5 the code generated by CAPS generator for OxygenSensor component. Line 3 and Line 20 represent the normal and critical mode respectively. Line 14 and Line 27 represent the timers in the normal and critical modes, respectively. Line 4, 10 and 23 represent the instructions of reading the current oxygen value from the oxygen sensor.

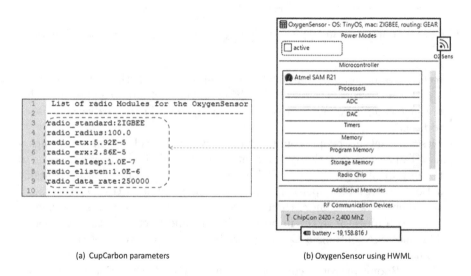

(a) CupCarbon parameters   (b) OxygenSensor using HWML

Fig. 6. An Example of HWML model and its representation in CupCarbon

According to the HWML model, we take the OxygenSensor component as an example to show the configuration information needed for it in CupCarbon simulator. Figure 6(b), shows part of HWML model that represents hardware specifications for OxygenSensor component in CAPS. This OxygenSensor is equipped with O2 sensor for sensing the percentage of oxygen in a room. It uses Texas Instruments ChipCon 2420 RF transceiver and it uses batteries of two AA with up to 19159 Joules. The sensor radio standard is 802.15.4 and radio radius is 20. Figure 6(a), shows a screenshot for an Oxygen Sensor radio modules configuration file.

Referring to SPML model. The example, depicted in Fig. 7, represents part of the physical environment of our NdR scenario. Figure 7(b), shows part of the

SPML model that describes the deployment physical position of OxygenSensor device. Figure 7(a), shows CupCarbon parameters needed from the OxygenSensor SPML model, these parameters are: device longitude (x), device latitude (y) and device elevation (Elevation).

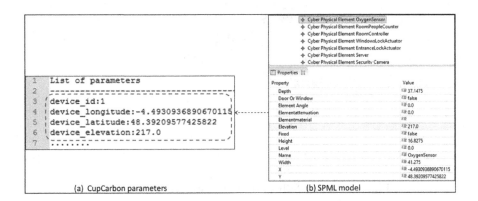

(a) CupCarbon parameters   (b) SPML model

Fig. 7. An Example of SPML model and its representation in CupCarbon

In addition to the described models, there are two auxiliary models: (i) MAPML is Mapping Modeling Language used to link SAML and HWML, (ii) DEPML is Deployment Modeling Language (DEPML) used to link SAML and SPML. For the sake of simplicity, they are not described here. For better details about these auxiliary models, please see [11].

5 Results

In this section we will describe the results of running our project in CupCarbon simulator. We applied three different behaviors for the NdR case study example. These behaviors are, first, the OxygenSensor runs with normal mode only. Second, the OxygenSensor runs with critical mode only. Third, the OxygenSensor runs in normal and critical modes, that is originally described in Sect. 4. These three different behaviors are applied in our CAPS modeling framework tool. Then, we used our CAPS automatic code generation framework tool to produce three CupCarbon projects. After all, we ran the simulator under the three behaviors and compare data traffic, energy consumption and battery level of it nodes.

For all simulation experimentations, we fixed simulation time to 6000 s, and energy max for all nodes to 19159 J. For OxygenSensor natural events, we selected random generation between 0.10–0.35. For people counter natural events, we selected random generation between 15–45. The Fig. 8, shows a screen shot of running the NdR project (applying third behavior) on CupCarbon simulator.

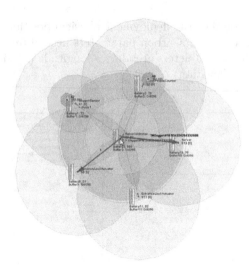

Fig. 8. Running NdR project on CupCarbon simulator

Table 1. Messages exchanged in components during simulation

Component ID	Component Name	# of sent messages			# of received messages			Data traffic in KB		
		Normal mode	Critical mode	Normal+ Critical	Normal mode	Critical mode	Normal+ Critical	Normal mode	Critical mode	Normal+ Critical
S1	OxygenSensor	81	1459	123	0	0	0	3	40	4
S2	RoomPeopleCounter	151	151	151	0	0	0	5	5	5
S3	RoomController	403	2628	460	232	1610	274	17	97	19
S9	WindowsLockActuator	0	0	0	55	902	70	1	4	1
S11	EntranceLockActuator	0	0	0	117	117	117	1	1	1
S13	Server	0	0	0	231	1609	273	7	47	8

In all the behaviors applied, the OxygenSensor and RoomPeopleCounter components are always sending messages and they don't receive any. While, WindowsLockActuator, EntranceLockActuator and server components are always receiving messages and they don't send any. But, In RoomController, the traffic is in both direction, it sends and receives messages. This explains some zero values appear in the table depicted in Table 1, this table shows the exchanged messages through the IN and OUT ports of the components during running the three behaviors in CupCarbon, it also shows the data traffic in Kilo Bytes that occur at each component.

Further, from Table 1, we conclude that the data traffic of OxygenSensor, RoomController, and server node receive the highest traffic when we run the critical mode behavior. This is due to the high messages they exchange during this mode. The normal mode receives a low amount of traffic but it could be not safe enough for detecting Oxygen level in a room. Thus, we can notice that using the critical and normal modes give also a low range of data traffic compared to using only critical mode. Moreover, using critical and normal modes together is still a safe behavior. Thus, this proves how small changes in the architecture can affect on the efficiency concern.

According to the battery levels and power consumption. The Figs. 9(a), (b) and (c), show the battery level when running the simulator under the three behaviors. The Figs. 9(e), (d) and (f), show the energy consumption when running the simulator under the three behaviors. From these figures, if we want to consider for example the two nodes, OxygenSensor (S1 in blue) and RoomController (S3 in red), we notice that S3 received the highest battery level drain when running the three modes. That is expected since the controller receives the highest data traffic among them. A minor improvement is noticed on RoomController when running the two modes together. While, for OxygenSensor we can notice how it experience the lowest battery level drain when it runs only the normal mode, the highest drain is when it runs critical mode, but we can also notice that running the two modes together gain better battery level improvements than critical mode. If we notice also the same nodes in the energy consumption charts, we can see how running critical and normal modes together shows a good improvements comparing to running only critical mode. Moreover, we notice how the energy consumption in normal mode is close to energy consumption in normal and critical modes together.

Therefore, to recognize the tradeoff between safety, energy and data traffic concerns. We notice that using only normal mode achieves energy efficiency by

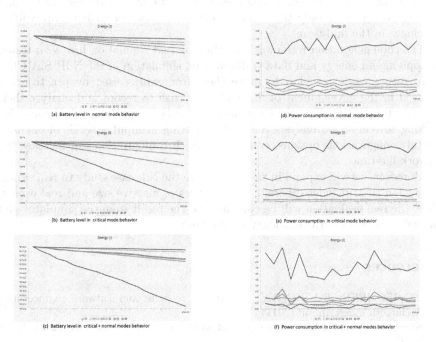

Fig. 9. CupCarbon results for battery level and power consumption in different modes (Color figure online)

having the least data traffic. The energy efficiency is inversely proportional to the data traffic size (number of messages exchanged). However, in normal mode, the safety concern will be less than it in critical mode. Therefore, using normal mode with critical mode provide a better compromise between those concerns.

Our simulation results show that by using CAPS modeling framework, CAPS code generation framework, and CupCarbon simulation for SiA-CPS, we can get the early evaluation for energy and data traffic savings while developing SiA-CPS. This vision of testing the architecture in the early stage will improve the process of architecting such systems.

According to the real experimentation, it is a work that we are planning to do. It requires a long process of deploying sensors and actuators. We will use the arduino code, that result from cubcarbon, to be installed in real sensors. The Ndr event runs in L'Aquila every year in September, so our first experimentation is supposed to be in September 2017.

6   Conclusions and Future Work

In this paper we proposed a modelling platform supported by a code generation framework, and integrated with CupCarbon simulation for engineering situational-aware cyber-physical systems.

This frameworks allows engineers to run a trade-off analysis between energy consumption and performance indices like sensor nodes throughput, reliability and network latency. The modeling framework, automatic code generation, and simulations represent only the starting point of a series of goals we are willing to achieve in the mid-term.

The code generation framework functioning and simulation has been tested by applying an energy and data traffic-related simulation of the NdR SiA-CPS.

In future work, we plan to make these frameworks used by practitioners involved in the development of SiA-CPS. We wish to record and analyze their usage patterns and collect their feedback for further improvements. We are also working to realize an analysis that, while getting in input a series of environmental configurations options, can tell us which configuration can increase the network life-time.

Moreover, we will expand in the near future the Ndr case study to real experimentation that includes different architectures of massive size and real events. Thus, the real evaluation will be compared to the result from the simulator and this will clearly state the efficiency of our work.

References

1. ISO/IEC/IEEE: ISO/IEC/IEEE 42010:2011 Systems and software engineering - Architecture description (2011)
2. Kruchten, P.B.: The 4+1 view model of architecture. IEEE Software **12**(6), 42–50 (1995)

3. Rozanski, N., Woods, E.: Software Systems Architecture: Working With Stakeholders Using Viewpoints and Perspectives. Addison-Wesley Professional, Boston (2005)
4. Kruchten, P., Capilla, R., Dueñas, J.C.: The decision view's role in software architecture practice. IEEE Softw. **26**(2), 36–42 (2009)
5. Emery, D., Hilliard, R.: Every architecture description needs a framework: expressing architecture frameworks using ISO/IEC 42010. In: WICSA/ECSA 2009 (2009)
6. Shaw, M., Garlan, D.: Software Architecture: Perspectives on an Emerging Discipline. Prentice-Hall, Upper Saddle River (1996)
7. Perry, D.E., Wolf, A.L.: Foundations for the study of software architecture. SIGSOFT Softw. Eng. Notes **17**(4), 40–52 (1992)
8. Jajodia, S., Liu, P., Swarup, V., Wang, C.: Cyber Situational Awareness, vol. 14. Springer, Heidelberg (2010)
9. Malavolta, I., Muccini, H., Sharaf, M.: A preliminary study on architecting cyber-physical systems. In: Proceedings of the 2015 European Conference on Software Architecture Workshops, vol. 20. ACM (2015)
10. Muccini, H., Sharaf, M., Weyns, D.: Self-adaptation for cyber-physical systems: a systematic literature review. In: Proceedings of the 11th International Symposium on Software Engineering for Adaptive and Self-Managing Systems, pp. 75–81. ACM (2016)
11. Muccini, H., Sharaf, M.: Caps: architecture description of situational aware cyber physical systems. In: 2017 IEEE International Conference on Software Architecture (ICSA), pp. 211–220. IEEE (2017)
12. Menon, V., Jayaraman, B., Govindaraju, V.: The three rs of cyberphysical spaces. Computer **44**(9), 73–79 (2011)
13. Malavolta, I., Muccini, H.: A survey on the specification of the physical environment of wireless sensor networks. In: 2014 40th EUROMICRO Conference on Software Engineering and Advanced Applications, pp. 245–253 (2014)
14. Tsigkanos, C., Kehrer, T., Ghezzi, C.: Architecting dynamic cyber-physical spaces. Computing **98**(10), 1011–1040 (2016)
15. Bounceur, A.: Cupcarbon: a new platform for designing and simulating smart-city and IOT wireless sensor networks (SCI-WSN). In: Proceedings of the International Conference on Internet of things and Cloud Computing, p. 1. ACM (2016)
16. Crnkovic, I., Malavolta, I., Muccini, H., Sharaf, M.: On the use of component-based principles and practices for architecting cyber-physical systems. In: 2016 19th International ACM SIGSOFT Symposium on Component-Based Software Engineering (CBSE), pp. 23–32 (2016)
17. Voelter, M.: A catalog of patterns for program generation. In: EuroPLoP, pp. 285–320 (2003)
18. Bucchiarone, A., Di Ruscio, D., Muccini, H., Pelliccione, P.: From requirements to code: an architecture-centric approach for producing quality systems. arXiv preprint arXiv:0910.0493 (2009)
19. Pelliccione, P., Inverardi, P., Muccini, H.: Charmy: a framework for designing and verifying architectural specifications. IEEE Trans. Softw. Eng. **35**(3), 325–346 (2009)
20. Muccini, H., Sharaf, M.: Caps: a tool for architecting situational-aware cyber-physical systems. In: 2017 IEEE International Conference on Software Architecture (ICSA). IEEE (2017)

Control of Self-adaptation Under Partial Observation: A Modular Approach

Narges Khakpour[✉]

Linnaeus University, Växjö, Sweden
narges.khakpour@lnu.se

To realize correct adaptive and reconfigurable systems, we need techniques to assure that the behavior of an adaptive system during dynamic adaptation is correct. In this paper, we propose a modular approach to synthesize a symbolic reconfiguration controller that guides the behavior of a system during adaptation under partial observations. The reconfiguration controller observes the system behavior partially during an adaptation and controls it by allowing/disallowing actions in a way to ensure that a given property is satisfied and a deadlock is avoided.

1 Introduction

Partial observability arises often in self-adaptive systems, because not all parts of a system are under the control of the adaptation logic, or the observation cost of some certain parts can be high (e.g. for security or performance reasons) [6], or there is uncertainty in the observed behavior (e.g. imprecision in the data sensed by sensors). Hence, an adaptive system with partial observations should be designed in a way that can make a reasonable decision based on its observations to control the adaptation behavior.

In order to have a safe structural adaptation in component-based systems, we must address some challenges [12]. A structural adaptation may involve simultaneous changes in several independent components that do not occur instantaneously. The system is likely to move through several invalid configurations before reaching a final valid configuration and some safety properties can become violated in transient states. Therefore, correct design of a system such that the system satisfies some specific properties during adaptation is crucial. Furthermore, it is often assumed that a newly added component starts its execution in a predefined initial state, while it is required for the new state to be consistent with the system state before the reconfiguration, e.g. the state of a replaced component should be transferred to the new component properly. In addition, there must not be a deadlock in the adaptation phase.

To address the above mentioned shortcomings, in this paper, we propose a modular symbolic approach to control the behavior of a system under partial observations during a reconfiguration phase, i.e., while the system is in a transient state, undergoing a structural reconfiguration, which may involve sequences of actions that affect different components of the system, as the unaffected parts of the system continue to run concurrently [12]. The full version of this paper is published in [10].

© Springer International Publishing AG 2017
A. Lopes and R. de Lemos (Eds.): ECSA 2017, LNCS 10475, pp. 112–119, 2017.
DOI: 10.1007/978-3-319-65831-5_8

The behavior of the system during a reconfiguration is defined as a set of configurations where one of the configurations is active at a time and the system switches among them. We specify the system behavior in each configuration using a symbolic state transition system. Afterwards, the undesirable states or bad states that must be avoided during a reconfiguration are described using a predicate on the system state variables, e.g. no message should be lost. We also define the observation of the system in each configuration, and propose an algorithm that computes the bad states of each configuration and synthesizes a local controller for each configuration using the supervisory controller synthesis method proposed in [9]. The result is then a reconfiguration controller used to control the behavior of the system during an adaptation, i.e. the controller runs in parallel with the system, monitors the system, and allows/disallows the controllable events to avoid the bad states. An event is uncontrollable if it cannot be prevented from occurring in a system, e.g. the event of a component crash is uncontrollable, as we cannot prevent it from happening.

Our contributions in this paper are two-folded:

- We propose the first method to synthesize a controller to support adaptations in self-adaptive systems under partial observations where some information is invisible, uncertain or imprecise.
- Compositional analysis and symbolic methods are the two common ways to handle the scalability issues. To enhance the scalability, we propose a modular symbolic method to synthesize a (non-blocking) controller to enforce safety properties that can be used to control infinite systems.

Structure of the Paper. This paper is organized as follows. We present a brief review of the symbolic supervisory controller synthesis method in Sect. 2. Section 3 discusses specification of a system during the adaptation phase. We introduce our synthesis approach in Sect. 4. Section 5 discusses related work, and finally in Sect. 6, we conclude and discuss our plans for future work.

2   Symbolic Controller Synthesis

In this section, we briefly review the symbolic supervisory controller synthesis with partial observation approach [9]. In this method, the system behavior is represented by a symbolic transition system.

Definition 1 (Symbolic Transition System). *A symbolic transition system (STS) is a tuple $\mathcal{T} = \langle V, \Theta, \Sigma, \rightarrow \rangle$ where $V = \langle v_1, \ldots, v_n \rangle$ is a tuple of variables, $\Theta \subseteq \mathcal{D}_V$ is a predicate on V defining the initial condition on the variables, Σ is a finite alphabet of actions, and $\rightarrow$ is a finite set of symbolic transitions $\delta = \langle \sigma_\delta, G_\delta, A_\delta \rangle$ where $\sigma_\delta \in \Sigma$ is the action of δ, $G_\delta \subseteq \mathcal{D}_V$ is a predicate on V, which guards δ, $A_\delta : \mathcal{D}_V \mapsto \mathcal{D}_V$ is the update function of δ, defines as a set of assignments, and $\mathcal{D}_V$ represents all possible (infinite) valuation of the variables in V.*

A partial observation of the system means that the current state is unclear, and it's defined in term of a mask function $M : \mathcal{D}_V \rightarrow Y$, that maps the system states to the states of the observation space Y. The actions $\Sigma = \Sigma_c \cup \Sigma_{uc}$ are partitioned into the set of controllable actions Σ_c, and the set of uncontrollable ones Σ_{uc}. In [9], a symbolic method is used to compute a controller $\mathcal{C} = \langle \mathcal{S}, \Theta_0 \rangle$ where the function $\mathcal{S} : Y \rightarrow 2^{\Sigma_c}$ defines a set $\mathcal{S}(y)$ of controllable actions to forbid in any state ν such that $y = M(\nu)$, for an observation $y \in Y$, and $\Theta_0 \subseteq \mathcal{D}_V$ is the set of forbidden initial states. This controller avoids the system $\mathcal{T}$ to reach the bad states $\mathcal{B}$ and guarantees that for all reachable states of the controlled system, there is a transition δ from that state (i.e. the system is non-blocking). To this end, a set $I(\mathcal{B})$ is computed using fix-point computations that contains the states that lead to $\mathcal{B}$ enabling only uncontrollable actions, or it would lead to the blocking states in the controlled system (see Fig. 1). Then a controller is designed to disable all the controllable actions that may lead to a state in $I(\mathcal{B})$, for each observation $y \in Y$, by restricting the transitions' guards in the controlled system.

3   Moldeing a Reconfiguring System

A system is composed of a set of components in addition to a global reconfigurator. The reconfigurator is a component that describes different strategies (sequences of guarded actions) to reconfigure a system structure toward a target structure. A reconfigurator contains two types of actions: structural actions to modify the system structure and behavioral actions used to interact with the system components.

A reconfigurator can partially observe the components' variables, and influence their values by synchronizing on the common actions. A structural reconfiguration is performed by synchronization of the reconfigurator and the involving component on the structural actions. We build an abstract model of the global reconfigurator, called *abstract reconfigurator* $\mathcal{K}$, that describes the system from a pure structural perspective [10]. Figure 2(ii) represents the abstract reconfigurator of Fig. 2(i). A state g_i of $\mathcal{K}$ is a graph that shows the system structure in the configuration g_i, and a transition $\langle g_i, l, g_i \rangle$ models a structural change, if $g_i \neq g_j$.

We define the system behavior during a reconfiguration as a set of configurations where one of them is active at a time. The system is formally defined as a tuple $\langle \mathcal{K}, \mathbb{T}, \Psi \rangle$, where $\mathcal{K}$ is the abstract reconfigurator that shows how the system should be reconfigured, $\mathbb{T}$ is a set of STSs specifying the configurations behavior, and $\Psi(g_i)$ maps a configuration g_i to its corresponding STS in $\mathbb{T}$. A configuration with the system structure g_i is modeled as a symbolic state transition system. The behavior of a system in a specific configuration is obtained by composing the behavior of the involving components in addition to its the behavior of the global reconfigurator in that configuration [10].

Example 1. We use a consumer-producer example as our running example that consists of one producer, one buffer and one consumer. The producer produces

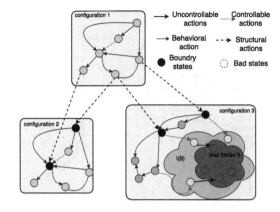

Fig. 1. The method overview

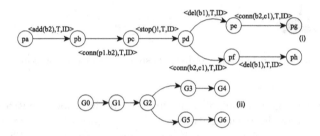

Fig. 2. The reconfigurator

data and puts them in the buffer where the consumer fetches data. Figure 2 (i) shows a global reconfigurator that replaces the buffer b1 with a larger buffer b2. In this figure, the action $add(c)$ adds a new component c, $del(c)$ removes the component c and $con(c, c')$ connects c to c'. Figure 3 partially shows the behavior of our example in the configuration pa (see Fig. 2(ii)) where a state identifier shows the concatenation of the first two characters of the components' states followed by the configuration ID. A transition label is of the form $\langle \sigma, \phi, a \rangle$ where σ is the action, ϕ is the transition guard and a is the set of updates.

4   Modular Synthesis of a Controller

We call a reconfiguring system $\langle \mathcal{K}, \mathbb{T}, \Psi \rangle$ *structurally progressive* if and only if, its abstract reconfigurator $\mathcal{K}$ contains no cycle, i.e. there is no path from a state to itself. This type of systems progress their structure toward the final configurations. Given a structurally progressive reconfiguring system $\langle \mathcal{K}, \mathbb{T}, \Psi \rangle$, and a function $\mathcal{B}(g)$ that defines the bad states in the configuration g, we present an algorithm to synthesize a (non-blocking) controller that avoids the bad states of the system.

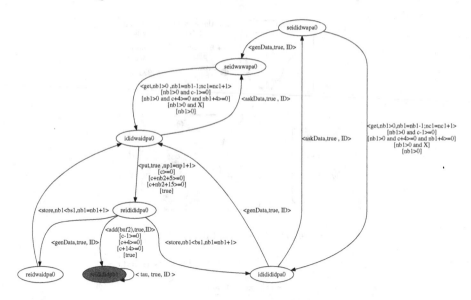

Fig. 3. The system behavior and synthesis results in the configuration pa0

To synthesize a global controller, we first synthesize a local controller for each configuration using the basic controller synthesis method introduced in Sect. 2, and then construct a global controller to guide an adaptation. The forbidden states $(I(\mathcal{B}))$ is constructed by propagating the bad states backwardly along the incoming uncontrollable transitions. The forbidden states of a configuration will not be propagated to the states of its children configuration, because the abstract reconfigurator of a structurally-progressive system has no cycle and there is no transition from a configuration children to its states, e.g. there is no transition from the configuration 3 to 1 in Fig. 1. This enables us to start computing the forbidden states of the system from its final configurations that have no outgoing transitions in the abstract reconfigurator, then compute the forbidden states of its parent configurations in a recursive way until we reach the initial configurations. Algorithm 1 shows our algorithm to synthesize the local controllers modularly that allows us to construct some of the local controllers concurrently. The bad states of a configuration (g) are determined by the bad states of that configuration defined in $\mathcal{B}(g)$ in addition to the forbidden boundary states of its next configurations. A boundary state is a common state between two configurations connected in $\mathcal{K}$ (See Fig. 1) (See [10] for more details).

Let $\langle \mathbb{C}, \Psi' \rangle$ be a tuple where $\mathbb{C}$ is the set of controllers synthesized for the configurations and Ψ' be a function that determines the corresponding controller of each configuration. We design the global controller as a multi-controller system where one of the local controllers is active at a time. As soon as the system switches to a new configuration, the current controller is deactivated and that of the new configuration becomes activated.

Algorithm 1. Modular Controller Synthesis

Input: A structurally progressive reconfiguring system $\langle \mathcal{K}, \mathbb{T}, \Psi \rangle$.
Output: A pair $\langle \mathbb{C}, \Psi' \rangle$ where $\mathbb{C}$ is a set of controllers and the function Φ'
        returns the controller of a configuration

$\mathcal{K}' = \mathcal{K}$;
repeat
    // Synthesize controllers for the leaves concurrently
    for *each* $g \in leaves(\mathcal{K}')$ **do**
        $B = compute(\mathcal{K}, g, \Psi', \mathcal{B}(g))$ // Obtain the bad states of g
        $C = synthesize(\Psi(g), B)$;
        $\Psi'(g) = C$;
        $\mathbb{C} = \mathbb{C} \cup C$;
    end
    $\mathcal{K}' = remove\_leaves(\mathcal{K}')$;
until $\mathcal{K}' \neq \emptyset$;

Example 2. Let no-data-loss be a property that should be enforced. We define a bad state predicate as $\Sigma_{i \in P} np_i - \Sigma_{i \in C} nc_i > \Sigma_{i \in B} nb_i$ which states that the number of produced data by the producers minus the number of the consumed data is greater than the number of data stored in the buffers, i.e. there is a data loss. The synthesized controller to ensure this property depends on its observations and the controllablity of events. If the controller does not have proper observations or control over actions, it can become very preventive and may forbid any event. For example, if the controller in the illustrating example has full observations and can only control the structural actions, the controller forbids all events. Similarly, if the controller cannot observe np_1 (or any other variable of the bad state predicate), the synthesized controller becomes empty.

If we consider interaction actions and structural actions as controllable, then the controller becomes more permissive. In the configuration $pa0$ of our example, the structural action is $add(buf2)$ and the interaction actions are get and put. A guard is generated for each of the controllable actions that are shown in Fig. 3 where $c = np_1 - nc_1 - nb_1 - nb_2$ and $X = -19nb1 - 34nc1 + 34np1 - 49$. For each controllable transition, five labels are shown in this figure where the first is the original transition label, the second shows the synthesized guard to forbid the transition in case of full observations, the third is for the case that the imprecision of nb_1 is about 5 unites, the fourth denotes the synthesized guard when the value of nb_1 is unknown in the range $[20, 35]$, and the last represents the results for the case that np_1 and the buffer sizes are hidden.

5   Related Work

In [11,12], we adapted the Ramadge-Wonham (RW) framework [14], a classical automaton-based framework, to synthesize a non-blocking adaptor to control the behavior of a system during a reconfiguration phase. This method does not support partial observations and is not scalable enough to be applied to complex systems where the state space is very large. The aim of reconfiguration control synthesis in [1,2,15] is to coordinate the interaction behavior of the components in order to avoid undesirable behavior such as deadlocks. The interaction behavior of the system and the desirable behavior are modeled using labeled transitions systems. Then, some algorithms are proposed to synthesize (distributed) adaptors to coordinate the components' interactions. Furthermore, supervisory control theory is used to synthesize behavioral adaptors to adjust the communication between services such that a certain behavioral property holds in the composed system [8]. The main difference between our approach and the above approaches is that they are mainly concerned with synthesizing the behavioral adaptors to coordinate the interactions of components/services, while we are interested in correct-by-construction design of controllers to guarantee the safe structural adaptations. Compared to [1,2] we can synthesize a centralized adaptor and we do not deal with real-time properties such as latency, performance, etc., as done in [15].

The authors of [3,13] proposed an approach based on the concept of proof lattice to verify if a system is in a correct state during and after adaptation in terms of satisfying the transitional-invariants. In this approach, the behavior of a system during adaptation is specified using an adaptation lattice in which a node is an automaton denoting the behavior of a possible intermediate program. Although verification identifies undesirable behavior, one has to fix errors manually while using synthesis techniques, we can generate a controller to control the adaptation phase. In this work, the properties to be verified are only about the behavior of the system while we consider both structural and behavioral properties.

Discrete Control Theory has recently been applied to computing systems. We presented the works done in the area of dynamic adaptation and component-based system in [12]. In an approach related to reactive systems and synchronous programming, discrete controller synthesis, as defined and implemented in the tool Sigali, is integrated in a programming language compiler BZR [7], used in component-based software [4]. Furthermore, interface synthesis [5] is also related to Discrete Controller Synthesis, and consists of generating interfacing wrappers for components, in order to adapt them for the composition into given component assemblies, with respect to the communication protocols between them.

6   Conclusions

We proposed a modular approach for synthesizing a symbolic controller to control dynamic reconfigurations in adaptive systems under partial observations. As a future work, we will extend the method to synthesize a controller that guides the system to successfully finish the adaptation by converging to its final states.

References

1. Autili, M., Flammini, M., Inverardi, P., Navarra, A., Tivoli, M.: Synthesis of concurrent and distributed adaptors for component-based systems. In: Gruhn, V., Oquendo, F. (eds.) EWSA 2006. LNCS, vol. 4344, pp. 17–32. Springer, Heidelberg (2006). doi:10.1007/11966104_3
2. Autili, M., Mostarda, L., Navarra, A., Tivoli, M.: Synthesis of decentralized and concurrent adaptors for correctly assembling distributed component-based systems. J. Syst. Softw. **81**(12), 2210–2236 (2008)
3. Biyani, K.N., Kulkarni, S.S.: Assurance of dynamic adaptation in distributed systems. J. Parallel Distrib. Comput. **68**(8), 1097–1112 (2008)
4. Bouhadiba, T., Sabah, Q., Delaval, G., Rutten, E.: Synchronous control of reconfiguration in fractal component-based systems - a case study. In: Proceeding of ACM Conference on Embedded Software, EMSOFT, Taiwan (2011)
5. Chakrabarti, A., Alfaro, L., Henzinger, T.A., Mang, F.Y.C.: Synchronous and bidirectional component interfaces. In: Brinksma, E., Larsen, K.G. (eds.) CAV 2002. LNCS, vol. 2404, pp. 414–427. Springer, Heidelberg (2002). doi:10.1007/3-540-45657-0_34
6. Cmara, J., Lopes, A., Garlan, D., Schmerl, B.: Adaptation impact and environment models for architecture-based self-adaptive systems. Sci. Comput. Programm. **127**, 50–75 (2016). Special issue of the 11th International Symposium on Formal Aspects of Component Software
7. Delaval, G., Rutten, E., Marchand, H.: Integrating discrete controller synthesis into a reactive programming language compiler. Discret. Event Dyn. Syst. **23**(4), 385–418 (2013)
8. Gierds, C., Mooij, A.J., Wolf, K.: Reducing adapter synthesis to controller synthesis. IEEE Trans. Serv. Comput. **5**(1), 72–85 (2012)
9. Kalyon, G., Le Gall, T., Marchand, H., Massart, T.: Control of infinite symbolic transition systems under partial observation. In: 2009 European Control Conference (ECC), pp. 1456–1462 (2009)
10. Khakpour, N.: Control of self-adaptation under partial observation: A modular approach. Technical report, Linnaeus University (2017)
11. Khakpour, N., Arbab, F., Rutten, E.: Supervisory controller synthesis for safe software adaptation. In: Proceedings of the 12th IFAC Workshop on Disceret Event Systems (2014)
12. Khakpour, N., Arbab, F., Rutten, É.: Synthesizing structural and behavioral control for reconfigurations in component-based systems. Formal Asp. Comput. **28**(1), 21–43 (2016)
13. Kulkarni, S.S., Biyani, K.N.: Correctness of component-based adaptation. In: Crnkovic, I., Stafford, J.A., Schmidt, H.W., Wallnau, K. (eds.) CBSE 2004. LNCS, vol. 3054, pp. 48–58. Springer, Heidelberg (2004). doi:10.1007/978-3-540-24774-6_6
14. Ramadge, P.J., Wonham, W.M.: Supervisory control of a class of discrete event processes. SIAM J. Control Optim. **25**(1), 206–230 (1987)
15. Tivoli, M., Fradet, P., Girault, A., Goessler, G.: Adaptor synthesis for real-time components. In: Grumberg, O., Huth, M. (eds.) TACAS 2007. LNCS, vol. 4424, pp. 185–200. Springer, Heidelberg (2007). doi:10.1007/978-3-540-71209-1_16

Architectural Decisions

On Cognitive Biases in Architecture Decision Making

Andrzej Zalewski[(⊠)], Klara Borowa, and Andrzej Ratkowski

Institute of Control and Computation Engineering,
Warsaw University of Technology, Warsaw, Poland
a.zalewski@ia.pw.edu.pl

Abstract. The research carried out to date shows that architectural decision-making is far from being a rational process. Architects tend to adopt a satisfying approach, rather than looking for the optimal architecture, which is a result of many human and social factors. The results of a workshop, carried out with 14 software engineering practitioners show that cognitive biases are commonly present in architecture decision-making. A systematic approach to analysing the influence of biases on decision making has been introduced. Twelve cognitive biases identified during the workshop were analysed with regard to the elements of the decision-making context that affected the aspects of architectural decision making. Finally, we analyse the interactions between cognitive biases and the conditions of real-world software development.

Keywords: Cognitive biases · Architectural decisions · Architectural decision-making

1 Introduction

The concept of architectural decisions enables the design rationale and architectural knowledge to be captured, but equally important is the focus it places on the act of deciding on software design [20]. This has shaped anew our perception of software development as a decision-making process, and triggered research into its nature.

The research on how architectural decisions are made revealed that, despite the intrinsic complexity of architecting, architects as decision makers remain normal human beings: their judgement is more often bounded rational than fully rational, which is a result of the inherent properties of the human mind.

As normal human beings, architects are subject to cognitive biases [4, 7–18]. This exploratory paper, which has been motivated by the outcomes of a workshop carried out with 14 software engineering practitioners, investigates how cognitive biases influence architectural decision-making. Our research focuses on answering the following research questions:

- RQ.1. Are biases in architecture decision making commonly observed by software engineering practitioners?
- RQ.2. What are the most significant cognitive biases that influence architecture decision making?

© Springer International Publishing AG 2017
B.A. Lopes and R. de Lemos (Eds.): ECSA 2017, LNCS 10475, pp. 123–137, 2017.
DOI: 10.1007/978-3-319-65831-5_9

- RQ.3. Which of these biases result from cognitive biases inherent to the conditions of the human mind?
- RQ.4. Which elements of the decision-making context can bias architects' decisions?
- RQ.5. Which aspects of architectural decision making are influenced by the biases that have been identified?
- RQ.6. How do practical conditions influence the extent of the influence of the biases on architectural decision making?

The research presented in this paper shows that biases are commonly observed by software practitioners (Sect. 3.1). In order to capture how cognitive biases influence architectural decision making, we propose a model comprising contextual factors that are transformed by the biases into influence on the identified aspects of the architectural decision-making process (Sect. 3.2). The identified cognitive biases are presented and discussed according to this model (Sect. 3.2). The ways in which the practical conditions of architecture decision making affect the 'mechanics' of biases' influence is presented in Sect. 4. The discussion of the findings (Sect. 5) is presented in Sect. 6, the summary of the paper and the research outlook in Sect. 7.

2 Related Work

The social and human factors in software engineering have been studied since the advent of software engineering as a scientific discipline – compare reports from NATO conferences from 1968 and 1969 [1, 2]. Probably the earliest observation of the influence of social factors on software architecture is the now famous Conway's law [2].

The research on cognitive biases was pioneered by Tversky and Kahneman (e.g. [4, 7, 11]), and the latter was awarded a Noble Prize. Their research has been later extended by many researchers, e.g. [7–18]. Kahneman and Renshon [19] define cognitive biases as "predictable errors in the ways that individuals interpret information and make decisions".

The dual process theory, as stated by Kahneman [4], is one widely known and accepted in psychology and helps to explain the mechanisms of the human mind. According to the theory, our thoughts are controlled by two parallel systems: System 1 and System 2.

System 1 controls the part of our mind that is fast, runs effortlessly, and completely out of our control. It is very useful, letting us, for example, instantly react to danger and save our lives in a dire situation. Sadly, its associative nature may make our line of thought illogical, often creating associations where there are none. System 1 is unable to process rule-based logic, and thus does not always perform well.

System 2 is the complete opposite of System 1. It is slow, requires a great amount of conscious effort to use, and is very logical. Since the use of System 1 is something unavoidable, System 2 serves the purpose of correcting the premature conclusions of System 1, but only if we put effort into it. It is when this correction does not happen, or is not strong enough, that cognitive biases occur.

The process of architectural decision making has been thoroughly investigated by Zannier et al. [3] in 2007. Their research shows that architects use naturalistic (looking for a satisfactory solution) or rational decision making (looking for an optimal solution). The naturalistic approach is common for poorly-structured problems, while the rational one for well-structured problems.

In 2015, Tang and van Vliet observed [5] that most architects need only a few reasons before concluding a decision, which is a result of satisficing behaviour of naturalistic decision making.

The research record on the role of biases in software engineering in general, and in software architecture, is rather small. Tang and van Vliet, in 2016 [6], indicate only a couple of papers that can be related to the role of biases in design processes. They show some examples of anchoring, framing and confirmation biases in software engineering, and conclude that "biases do play a role; and we probably cannot fully prevent them from occurring; they are simply too human."

The research presented in this paper aims to expand upon these observations, and to systematise the way we analyse how cognitive biases influence architectural decision making.

3   Investigating Biases in Architectural Decision Making

3.1   Workshop on Biases in Architecture Decision-Making

Fourteen software engineering practitioners with a wide variety of professional experience (8 novices – 1–2 years of experience and 6 experts with at least 10 years of experience) were gathered on a workshop. The purpose was to gather data about biases that may have an influence over the process of software development and sort out those that affect architecture-decision making. A few days before the workshop, participants were provided with a list of 105 cognitive biases with their definitions and examples that purposefully weren't connected to software architecture. They were supposed to get acquainted with them as a form of preparation. The workshop agenda was as follows:

1. Short presentation on cognitive biases – the notion of 'cognitive bias' was explained and most important biases, such as Anchoring [11], the Bandwagon Effect [18], the Dunning-Kruger Effect [21] and the Law of the Instrument [14], were discussed;
2. Poll of the participants – they were asked to write down any examples of biases that they could have observed from their previous projects;
3. Survey and an open discussion on biases indicated by the participants, aimed at improving the understanding of people's statements;
4. Rating of the biases - each participant was asked to rate the frequency of cases when they experienced the effect of every cognitive bias listed (on a scale from 0 to 3, where 0 means something that was never observed, and 3 means an often experienced phenomenon);
5. Identifying related cognitive biases;
6. Wrap-up and conclusion.

The results of the workshop are summarised in Table 1.

Table 1. Biases relevant to architecture decision making indicated by the workshop participants

Reported bias	Related cognitive bias	Average frequency assessment
Judging the quality of a system by the form of its presentation by marketing specialists	Framing effect	2.58
Estimating the time needed to complete a task wrongly, because of the expectations placed on the development team by the client, rather than the true complexity of the problem	Confirmation bias	2.33
Excessive overvaluation of a solution that we created ourselves	IKEA effect	2.33
Spending long hours on meetings discussing trivial problems (like whether we should use spaces or tabs in our code) instead of truly important ones	Parkinson's Law of triviality	2.25
Insisting on continuing using certain COTS despite the long record of errors	Anchoring	2.25
Errors created by miscommunication between the technical staff and a client, because of them having a completely different background	Curse of knowledge	2.16
Focusing mainly on a set of standards, believing that if they are met, then the quality of the product will be good	Anchoring	2.16
Belief that "new is better". Quick abandonment of old tools and technologies while they are still properly working	Pro-innovation bias	2.08
Dismissing serious issues as trivial, without any further thought	Parkinson's Law of triviality	2.08
Evasion of solutions that were not used previously in our industry	IKEA effect	2.00
Underestimating a problem by assuming that it could be solved by "writing some code", even with no detailed plan of the implementation	Planning fallacy	1.91
Wrongly assuming that a solution found on the web is correct and appropriate for our problem, especially if it is popular	Bandwagon effect	1.83
Avoidance of redoing work on a system that was already done – even if it was done poorly	Irrational escalation	1.75
Being unable to admit that there is an error. Logic similar to "it's not a bug, it's a feature"	Anchoring	1.75
Applying the design patterns that we know everywhere - even if it's not the best solution	Law of the instrument	1.66
Underestimating the possible load put on a system. Guessing without any evidence to support our claims	Optimism bias	1.66
Focusing only on hardware when solving optimisation problems	Anchoring	1.36

3.2   Influence of Cognitive Biases on Architecture Decision-Making

Expanding on the workshop results, we discussed and analysed the identified biases in order to identify how they influence the decision-making process. As a result we developed the model presented in Fig. 1.

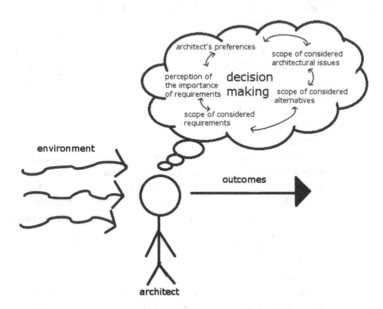

Fig. 1. How biases influence architecture decision making

Figure 1 shows that cognitive biases subconsciously influence the decision-making process by associating some contextual factors with a given architectural problem. These factors usually have no connection, or just a limited connection, with the analysed issue itself. The biases include these factors into the decision-making process and alter the critical aspects of the decision-making process. Analysing the biases on the basis of our experience we identified sets of:

- *contextual factors affecting architecture decision making*, for example: form of presentation, architect's beliefs, "topics of the year", time spent on a given design, order, etc. – for a complete list see Table 2, Column (3).
- *aspects of architecture decision-making process affected by the biases*, for example such architect's preferences (expressed by a decision's rationale), scope of considered architectural issues, etc. – for a complete list see Table 2, Column (4).

Below we describe and study in a greater detail the cognitive biases indicated in Table 1.

Framing Effect
The example that achieved the highest average rating in the experiment was representative of the framing effect. The bias itself happens when information is judged

Table 2. Influence of cognitive biases on architecture decision making

Bias (1)	Description (2)	Main contextual factors that influence architect's judgment (3)	Influenced aspects of architecture decision making (4)
Framing effect	Drawing different conclusions from the same information depending on the form of presentation [7]	Form of presentation	Architect's preferences, scope of considered architectural issues and alternatives
Confirmation bias	Focus on searching for facts that confirms one's beliefs, while ignoring opposing information [8]	The architect's beliefs	All the aspects
IKEA effect	Overvaluing items that were created or assembled by us personally [9]	Who was the author of a given design; time spent on a given design	Scope of considered alternatives, preferences
Parkinson's Law of triviality	Focusing time and effort on trivial matters while often omitting the truly important ones [10]	None	All the aspects
Anchoring	Relying on one piece of information more heavily than any other, usually on the first one that we were exposed to [11]	Order of obtaining information	Scope and perception of importance of considered requirements; preferences
Curse of knowledge	When individuals, due to having a different level of knowledge, interpret facts differently [12]	The knowledge, experience and background of the stakeholders	All the aspects
Pro-innovation bias	An overly optimistic approach in adopting innovative solutions [15]	The architect's state of mind with respect to innovative solutions	Preferences, scope of considered alternatives
Planning fallacy	Underestimation of the time it will take to complete a task [16]	Problem complexity	Preferences
Bandwagon effect	The phenomenon of people more likely adapting ideas/buying products that have already been widely accepted [18]	Existing widely accepted solutions	Preferences

(*continued*)

Table 2. (*continued*)

Bias (1)	Description (2)	Main contextual factors that influence architect's judgment (3)	Influenced aspects of architecture decision making (4)
Irrational escalation	Continuing an action/investment, because of a similar prior one, even if the previous one turned out to be a wrong decision [17]	Existence of an initial solution, course of action contradicting the use of an initial solution	Preferences
Law of the instrument	Using a tool/skill that you possess everywhere, even in contexts where it is not appropriate [14]	Architectural solutions focal for an architect	Scope of considered alternatives, preferences
Optimism bias	Overestimating the probability of favourable outcomes of our decisions [13]	The architect's state of mind	All the aspects

differently on the basis of how it was presented. This effect was examined thoroughly by Tversky and Kahneman [7]. In the course of their research, they discovered that slight differences in the formulation of the choice problem may significantly impact decision making.

The exact scenario that the workshop participants pointed at was that software products are often purchased not on the basis of their quality, but of the way they are advertised, for example: properly advertised products (like COTS) are more likely to be chosen, even if they are less suited to the needs of the project. The framing bias affects mainly architect's preferences, scope of considered architectural issues and alternatives.

Confirmation Bias
Another widely appearing case is an example of conformation bias. Confirmation bias itself, as stated by Nickerson [8], is a natural tendency to look for evidence supporting our claims, because we believe that this is an effective way of showing what is right, if it really is right.

The subjects linked the wrong estimation of the time needed to complete a project with their superiors' (or clients') expectations. Concerning architectural decision making, it is easy to observe a tendency to look for arguments confirming our beliefs that certain solutions are better than others. Believers of microservices would always find evidence to confirm it is a best choice. In order to confirm their beliefs, architects may narrow the scope of considered architectural issues, requirements and alternatives. Such an architect would prefer to choose the options, which comply with his beliefs.

IKEA Effect

Easily associated with the phenomenon of the globally-known producer of ready-to-assemble furniture – the IKEA effect is one that makes us biased when it comes to items we have created or assembled ourselves [9]. What makes the furniture bought in IKEA so special, is that when you assemble it yourself, the false belief that it's worth more than you paid for it is created. All because you had to put your own time and effort into it. A similar effect can be observed in almost every domain, not only the furniture business. When comparing to the products of our competitors, even if they are renowned professionals in their field, we are easy to prey for the unstoppable gut feeling that our creation is the best.

The participants also pointed to the reverse form of this effect – that we tend to avoid solutions that have not been yet used in our industry, thus boxing ourselves in a small pool of alternative choices. It is a popular phenomenon that authors of a given system (application etc.) are rather reluctant to replace it even if a definitely better one is currently available. This will certainly narrow the set of considered alternatives and obviously affect architect's preferences.

Parkinson's Law of Triviality

According to Parkinson's Law: 'work expands to fill the time available'. This unavoidable effect rules over most workplaces, although most managers would prefer to overlook it. Parkinson's Law of triviality is a narrower version of Parkinson's Law stating that we spend an enormous amount of time debating over trivial unimportant issues [10].

Most of our subjects had the unfortunate displeasure of taking part in meetings that seemed to be endless and led to nothing. Although wasting time does not have to lead to wrong decisions by itself, it does shorten the time available to resolve more complex issues. This may result in 'system 1' being used to resolve the crucial problems instead of 'system 2'. This may indirectly affect all the aspects of architectural decision making.

Anchoring

The effect of anchoring is created by the way in which the human brain estimates probabilities. Naturally, we tend to cling to the first fact that comes to our mind when contemplating an issue. This means that the first piece of information we obtained, or one that we have a particularly fond memory of, heavily influences decision making [11]. When 'anchored' to an idea, it becomes hard to notice different solutions, and even if we do, it is very unlikely that we will choose them.

Although examples of the anchoring effect were rated very differently by the participants, it is worth noting that this was the bias for which they found the greatest amount of examples. Anchoring seems to have an influence over almost every kind of decision: hardware, technologies, design and even implementation. It influences mainly architect's preferences but also possibly the scope and perception of importance of requirements.

Curse of Knowledge

We may be put in a situation when we have to communicate with someone of a completely different background, or with a different level of experience, or even simply someone younger than us. We fall prey of the curse of knowledge, if at some point we falsely assume that the other side possesses the same knowledge that we have about any kind of issue. This may be more apparent in contacts between children and adults, when the young ones find it hard to grasp concepts that are new to them, but adult relations are not free from this effect [12].

The curse may cause misunderstandings at any level of human interaction, which is especially crucial when understanding the requirements of our client and choosing appropriate solutions for their problems. Team members with different experience levels can also be influenced when an issue is not explained properly, they can misunderstand the way in which their tasks should be handled. Therefore, the curse of knowledge bias influences the scope of requirements and the architect's perception of their priorities, as well as scope of considered architectural issues and alternatives, and as a result this may also alter architect's preferences.

Pro-innovation Bias

The false belief that innovation should always be adopted is what we call the pro-innovation bias [15]. Humans naturally have a positive attitude associated with innovation. However, it does not mean that innovation should always be pursued.

The pursuit of a novel solution is not always necessary; sometimes it may even be harmful. What needs to be taken into account is the high risk of every innovative project. If a stable and reliable system is to be created in a reasonable timeframe, usually innovation should be avoided. As one of the subjects pointed out, it is not always the case that potentially high rewards await those that successfully bring new ideas to life. Relating these observations into architectural decision making, we observe that pro-innovation bias means that innovative design alternatives are considered and preferred.

Planning Fallacy

The planning fallacy is the tendency to underestimate the time required to complete a task. Interestingly, it seems to affect the individuals who are supposed to complete the tasks more than observers – of course, if they have information about the individuals' past performance [16].

This cognitive bias has a great influence over the planning phase of any project. The amount of information needed to avoid it is so big that it is almost impossible to process it, especially if a problem is complex. Although various methodologies have their ways of soothing this problem (e.g. Planning Poker in Scrum), there are almost none that can prevent it on the early decision-making level. Let us also observe that the planning fallacy may affect the preferences of an architect who may choose solutions which are more difficult to implement than he thought when making a decision.

Bandwagon Effect

The bandwagon effect is a universal phenomenon that appears in almost any domain where human beings are given a choice. People naturally want to wear, buy, do, consume and behave like their fellows, thus becoming part of a group [18]. This results in popular choices and popular decisions becoming even more popular.

The danger this bias poses should not be downplayed – it puts our mind in a small box, limiting our possibilities and potentially forces bad decisions on us. Especially in cases of pressure from higher-ups to solve a problem in the way they wish us to. In some cases even, due to the organisation culture in a company, it may even be impossible to have any influence on this kind of decisions, which could result in choosing solutions being very far from perfect. Therefore the bandwagon makes an architect to prefer the same solutions that have already been widely accepted by a similar organisations, by an industry branch or our community.

Irrational Escalation

Irrational escalation takes place when one continues to commit to an initial course of action, even if it is obviously no longer the most beneficial choice [17].

As the participants noticed, this may affect performance when old technologies, code or components that are unfit for the task, are forced on us. Often these old products should have been abandoned long ago due to their doubtful quality, but since at some point they were invested in, there is a stubborn reluctance to let go of them. Irrational escalation means that architect gets fixed on an existing solution.

Optimism Bias

We do not usually assume failure before trying something. Most healthy people's brains are hardwired that way [13]. When writing his example, one of our participants told us a story where a client he worked for judged how many messages his system would have to handle daily. Unfortunately, in reality, the estimated value turned out to be a hundred times too low, which triggered later multiple serious issues. As this example shows, being overly optimistic can hurt badly not only planning, but the architected system's quality as well. Architect's optimism can potentially influence all the aspects of architectural decision-making.

Law of the Instrument

Known in software architecture as the Golden Hammer anti-pattern [14] - when a single technology or design pattern is used in every possible place. This obviously results in the creation of numerous inefficient and mismatched solutions. The bias experienced here may simply be a symptom of the lack of necessary skill or knowledge that forces us to use well-known solutions. Such cases were pointed out by the participants of the workshop. Furthermore, there is one more scenario that requires further consideration – does spending money on a technology in the past force us to use it? This seems to be the case in many big companies, where decisions to invest in expensive technologies are often made independently of the technical context of specific projects.

The above findings have been summarised in Table 2. Note that in Column (3), only the most important factors influencing the decision making have been listed. Naturally, there are numerous other factors that may modulate (magnify or diminish) the influence posed by a give cognitive bias, for example the architect's knowledge/experience, organisation's culture.

4 Cognitive Biases in the Practical Conditions of Architectural Decision Making

Having established that cognitive biases are a common phenomenon in architecture decision making, we explore real-world factors that can influence their manifestation or affect the magnitude of their influence on architecture decision making.

Biases and Time
Cognitive biases are an integral element of human nature. They have been shaped by the evolution of the human mind, and as such are a result of the adaptation to the conditions of the environment. Although they possibly distract architects from crafting a fully rational, thoroughly deliberated design, they potentially enable the qualities desirable by today's hectic software industry: rapid architecting and quick response to changes or emergencies.

As the "need for speed" concerns more and more software engineers, the role of System 1 will certainly be increasing at the cost of diminishing the role of System 2. It means that even more decisions will be made intuitively without a thorough deliberation. This may substantially hinder the quality of a software architecture. At the same time, architecting efficiently under the pressure of time is something very desirable in the frenetic software industry, as well as in emergency cases.

It seems that there are two basic ways of addressing this challenge:

1. Applying debiasing techniques – this seems to be generally difficult, as the main factor limiting rational judgement is the lack of time and other external pressures. In order to ensure rational decision making, we have to give architects more time to conclude a decision and to restrain the external pressures. This is in many cases impossible, as we have limited or no control over the conditions that are external to architectural decision making;
2. Accepting "the rules of the game" (biases) and trying to exploit them to our advantage – this requires the development of techniques that lead to reasonable architectures under pressure of time. Hypothesising further, they could take the form of a specific training for architects, probably similar to those used by students preparing for programming competitions: this training supposedly makes system 1 closer to system 2 with regard to algorithms and computer programming, as trained students decide at a glance which algorithms should be used in order to solve their exercise.

Biases and Teams
Applying group architecture decision making techniques has the potential to limit the influence of biases, as decisions are made by people with different mindsets. This justifies assessing an architecture by a group of stakeholders, such as in ATAM. At the same time, group decision making brings with it the risk posed by the 'law of triviality' bias.

Biases and Cultural Factors
Cultural factors may magnify or diminish the influence of cognitive biases. For example, in many cultures it is difficult for people to admit they cannot understand

something or accomplish a certain design. This will certainly strengthen the curse of knowledge bias.

Biases and Tools and Methodologies
It is also important to recognise that cognitive biases introduce a feedback between what we create and how it is created, i.e. what we create, what we know influences how it is created by us. This is exactly what most of the biases do – consider, for example, anchoring bias, irrational escalation and the law of instrument biases. Therefore, it is worth investigating how different software development methodologies, architecture decision-making techniques, software development tools etc. interact with cognitive biases and vice versa.

5 Results

RQ.1 Are biases in architecture decision making commonly observed by software engineering practitioners?
It turned out that the participants commonly observe biases in deciding on software design. Both novices (less than 2 years of experience) and experts (more than 10 years of experience) in software engineering noticed biases. Novices indicated on average 1 bias each, experts about 4 biases each. Experts have a much broader experience than novices, which explains the observed difference.

RQ.2. What are the most significant biases in architecture decision-making?
As a result of our research, we identified 12 cognitive biases that influence architecture decision making. The list of these can be found in Tables 1 and 2.

RQ.3. Which of these biases result from cognitive biases inherent to the conditions of the human mind?
All these biases, concerning architectural decision making, indicated by the workshop participants and listed in Table 1, can be related to well-known cognitive biases.

RQ.4. Which elements of the decision-making context can bias architects' decisions?
These identified elements of the decision-making context that bias architects' decisions are: form of presentation, the architect's beliefs, who was the author of a given design, the time spent on a given design, the order of obtaining information, the knowledge, experience and background of the stakeholders, the architect's state of mind, the problem complexity, the existing widely-accepted solutions, the course of action contradicting the use of an initial solution, and architectural solutions focal for an architect.

RQ.5. Which aspects of architectural decision making are influenced by the biases that have been identified?
The above aspects of architectural decision making are: the architect's preferences (finally expressed by the rationale for a decision), the scope of the considered architectural issues, alternatives and requirements, and the perception of the importance of requirements (compare Sect. 3.2 and Table 2).

RQ.6. How do practical conditions influence the extent of the biases' influence on architectural decision making?

Time, teams, cultural factors as well as tools and methodologies used for software development can affect the extent of the biases' influence on architecture decision making.

6   Discussion, Limitations

The volume of research on cognitive biases in software engineering is rather small (compare Sect. 2). Let us observe that our research confirms the findings of Tang and van Vliet [6], namely, that anchoring, framing and confirmation biases are among the most often observed by software engineering practitioners as influencing architectural decision making.

The contribution of this paper comprises:

- the proposition of a model of how biases influence architectural decision making, which enables a systematic, uniform analysis of various biases;
- the identification of 12 cognitive biases that influence architectural decision making;
- an analysis of how each bias affects decision making, by identifying the elements of the model mentioned above (elements of the context affecting decision making and aspects of the decision-making process influenced by each bias);
- an analysis and identification of real-world factors that can potentially influence the extent of the influence of biases on architecture decision making.

The obvious limitation of the presented results are:

- the number of workshop participants may influence the representativeness of the results;
- although the claims of Sect. 4 seem to be logically sound, the analysis of real-world factors is only exploratory, hence it requires empirical substantiation to strengthen the claims of Sect. 4.

To provide an environment that would, as much as possible, neutralize the effects of additional biases and mistakes from the participants, all of them were informed thoroughly about the topic of cognitive biases both before and during the workshop which is described in more detail in Sect. 3.1.

7   Summary and Research Outlook

Cognitive biases are commonly present in architecture decision making. By asking practitioners, we identified 12 cognitive biases that can be observed most frequently. In order to analyse their influence on architectural decision making in a uniform way, we have developed a model of how biases 'work'.

The common presents of cognitive biases is both virtue and vice. On one side, they enable rapid architecting by an intuitive resolution of the architectural issues, on the other, they may lead to suboptimal solutions and in extreme cases to a design disaster.

We can either try to accept and exploit them, or fight them. Probably, we need a kind of a decision-making approach that balances 'system 1' and 'system 2' decision making.

The further research outlook includes:

- obtaining a more statistically significant confirmation of the above results by interviews with a larger group of practitioners or by a broader industrial survey;
- investigating the interactions that may exist between the biases;
- developing techniques of using the knowledge about biases and their influence on decision-making process, in order to align the architecting process with the stakeholders' expectations;
- carrying out an in-depth analysis of each of the identified biases.

References

1. Naur, P., Randell, B.: Software engineering techniques. In: Report on a Conference Sponsored by the Nato Science Committee, Garmisch, Germany, 7th to 11th October 1968
2. Buxton, J.N., Randell, B.: Software engineering techniques. In: Report on a conference sponsored by the Nato Science Committee, Rome, Italy, 27–31 October 1969
3. Zannier, C., Chiasson, M., Maurer, F.: A model of design decision making based on empirical results of interviews with software designers. Inf. Softw. Technol. **49**(6), 637–653 (2007)
4. Kahneman, D.: Thinking, Fast and Slow. Penguin, London (2011)
5. Tang, A., Vliet, H.: Software designers satisfice. In: Weyns, D., Mirandola, R., Crnkovic, I. (eds.) ECSA 2015. LNCS, vol. 9278, pp. 105–120. Springer, Cham (2015). doi:10.1007/978-3-319-23727-5_9
6. Van Vliet, H., Tang, A.: Decision making in software architecture. J. Softw. Syst. **117**, 638–644 (2016)
7. Tversky, A., Kahneman, D.: Rational choice and the framing of decisions. J. Bus. **59**, S251–S278 (1986)
8. Nickerson, R.S.: Confirmation bias: a ubiquitous phenomenon in many guises. Rev. Gen. Psychol. **2**, 175 (1998)
9. Norton, M.I., Mochon, D., Ariely, D.: The IKEA effect: when labor leads to love. J. Consum. Psychol. **22**(3), 453–460 (2012)
10. Parkinson, C.N.: Parkinson's Law, or the Pursuit of Progress. Penguin, London (1958)
11. Tversky, A., Kahneman, D.: Judgment under uncertainty: heuristics and biases. In: Wendt, D., Vlek, C. (eds.) Utility, Probability, and Human Decision Making, vol. 11, pp. 141–162. Springer, Netherlands (1975)
12. Birch, S.A.J., Bloom, P.: The curse of knowledge in reasoning about false beliefs. Psychol. Sci. **18**(5), 382–386 (2007)
13. Sharot, T.: Neural mechanisms mediating optimism bias. Nature **450**(7166), 102–105 (2007)
14. Brown, W.H., et al.: AntiPatterns: Refactoring Software, Architectures, and Projects in Crisis. Wiley Inc., Hoboken (1998)
15. Rogers, E.M.: Diffusion of Innovations. Simon and Schuster, New York City (2010)
16. Buehler, R., Griffin, D., Ross, M.: Exploring the planning fallacy: Why people underestimate their task completion times. J. Pers. Soc. Psychol. **67**(3), 366 (1994)
17. Bazerman, M.H., Neale, M.A.: Negotiating Rationally. Simon and Schuster, New York City (1993)

18. Leibenstein, H.: Bandwagon, snob, and Veblen effects in the theory of consumers' demand. Q. J. Econ. **64**(2), 183–207 (1950)
19. Kahneman, D., Renshon, J.: Hawkish biases. In: American Foreign Policy and the Politics of Fear: Threat Inflation Since 9/11, pp. 79–96. Routledge, London (2009)
20. Bosch, J., Jansen, A.: Software architecture as a set of architectural design decisions. In: 5th Working IEEE/IFIP Conference on Software Architecture (WICSA 2005), pp. 109–120 (2005)
21. Kruger, J., Dunning, D.: Unskilled and unaware of it: how difficulties in recognizing one's own incompetence lead to inflated self-assessments. J. Pers. Soc. Psychol. **77**(6), 1121 (1999)

Automatic Extraction of Design Decisions from Issue Management Systems: A Machine Learning Based Approach

Manoj Bhat[1(✉)], Klym Shumaiev[1], Andreas Biesdorf[2], Uwe Hohenstein[2], and Florian Matthes[1]

[1] Technische Universität München, Boltzmannstr. 3, 85748 Garching, Germany
{manoj.mahabaleshwar,klym.shumaiev,matthes}@tum.de
[2] Siemens AG - Corporate Technology, Otto-Hahn-Ring 6, 81739 München, Germany
{andreas.biesdorf,uwe.hohenstein}@siemens.com

Abstract. The need to explicitly document design decisions has been emphasized both in research and in industry. To address design concerns, software architects and developers implicitly capture design decisions in tools such as issue management systems. These design decisions are not explicitly labeled and are not integrated with the architecture knowledge management tools. Automatically extracting design decisions will aid architectural knowledge management tools to learn from the past decisions and to guide architects while making decisions in similar context. In this paper, we propose a two-phase supervised machine learning based approach to first, automatically detect design decisions from issues and second, to automatically classify the identified design decisions into different decision categories. We have manually analyzed and labeled more than 1,500 issues from two large open source repositories and have used this dataset for generating the machine learning models. We have made the dataset publicly available that will serve as a starting point for researchers to further reference and investigate the design decision detection and classification problem. Our evaluation shows that by using linear support vector machines, we can detect design decisions with 91.29% accuracy and classify them with an accuracy of 82.79%. This provides a quantitative basis for learning from past design decisions to support stakeholders in making better and informed design decisions.

Keywords: Software architecture · Design decisions · Machine learning

1 Introduction

Over the last decade, there has been a paradigm shift in how we view software architectures. Since the representation of Architectural Design Decisions (ADDs) as first-class entities [5,17,32], software architecture is considered as a set of architectural design and ADDs [15,18]. The architectural knowledge management (AKM) tools [3,4,21,23] support the documentation of ADDs and its

A. Lopes and R. de Lemos (Eds.): ECSA 2017, LNCS 10475, pp. 138–154, 2017.
DOI: 10.1007/978-3-319-65831-5_10

associated concepts including architectural concerns, alternative architectural solutions, and rationales for ADDs. Moreover, industry standard software architecture templates (for example, arch42[1]) provide placeholders to capture ADDs. Documenting ADDs supports stakeholders to understand and reason about the software architecture during both the development and maintenance phases [6]. However, the manual effort [8,19], time, and cost [31] involved in the documentation process are a concern for practitioners and its immediate benefit is not visible [20]. Hence, industry has often not recognized the value of ADDs, for example, by taking benefit from reoccurring design concerns in similar context.

Furthermore, with the rapid adoption of agile methodologies for software development, ADDs both in large open-source software (OSS) and in industrial projects are scarcely documented [1]. However, stakeholders involved in projects, that follow this agile movement, tend to use agile project management tools such as issue trackers and version control systems [29,30]. In such projects, even though design decisions are not explicitly documented, they are implicitly captured in different systems including project management, issue management, source code version management, and meeting recording systems [25].

The use of issue management systems (for example, JIRA and GitHub issue tracker) for managing issues is becoming popular both in industrial settings as well as in OSS projects [2,12]. An issue is either a task, new feature, user story, or bug. These systems provide a common interface for stakeholders to track, communicate, and visualize the progress of tasks within a project. For instance, a software architect can create a new task (which might implicitly represent a design decision) such as "Remove dependency on Twitter4J repository[2]" and assign it to a developer to complete the task. Furthermore, as a good practice, the developer community maintains a link between the task in the issue management system and the source code commits or pull-requests in version control systems using the task identifier or vice versa. In sum, issue management systems are an excellent source that implicitly captures decisions made by architects and developers [25] and acts as a bridge between stakeholders' requirements and the source code of the corresponding software system. Furthermore, the attributes such as reporter, assignee, and creation date of the issue are also maintained in such systems and can be used to enrich the meta-information of design decisions in AKM tools, for example, to refer to originators and experts.

In this paper, we address the extraction and classification of design decisions that are not systematically documented in AKM tools but implicitly captured in issue management systems. The contribution of this paper is twofold. First, we propose a two-phase machine learning (ML) based approach (cf. Fig. 1). In the first phase, design decisions are automatically detected from issues that are extracted from an issue management system. In the second phase, the identified design decisions are further classified into different decision categories. Second, we make the manually labeled dataset, which was created for training the ML

---

[1] http://arc42.org/.

[2] https://issues.apache.org/jira/browse/SPARK-710.

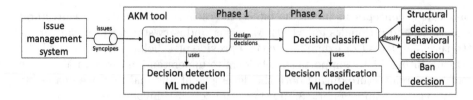

Fig. 1. A two-phase ML-based approach for decision detection and classification

models publicly available[3]. Since, no such labeled dataset exists, this contribution will serve as a starting point and reference for researchers to apply and compare supervised ML algorithms for extracting and classifying design decisions.

As discussed by Kazman et al. [16], architecture needs to be made explicit to avoid knowledge vaporization and to favor the knowledge acquisition process for newcomers and adopters of the project. The extraction of design decisions from issues will support the process of capturing AK in the AKM tools, which will in turn enable various use cases including reasoning, recommendations, traceability, and report generation for stakeholders. In addition, automatically classifying the extracted decisions into different categories such as Structural, Behavioral, and Ban decisions (cf. Sect. 3) will label those decisions to aid the search and the recommendation use cases. In particular, it will allow the creation of a knowledge base that can be used, for instance, to learn from the decisions made in similar past projects. Software architects will be able to rely on decisions made in the past to address design concerns in their current projects. As van der Ven and Bosch [34] put it, "Wouldn't it be great if software architects could get access to the decisions made by other architects, that would allow them to determine what selections were made from a set of alternatives and with what frequency?"

This paper is organized as follows. Section 2 describes the related work. In Sect. 3, we revisit the ADD categories proposed by Kruchten. Section 4 presents the dataset preparation process. Section 5 describes the setup of the ML pipeline used for decision detection and classification. The results of applying different multi-class classification algorithms are discussed in Sect. 6. Finally, we conclude with a short summary and an outlook on the future research.

2 Related Work

The need to systematically capture design decisions to enable reasoning and decision support in AKM tools has been extensively discussed in the past. For instance, Babar and Gorton [3] propose an AKM tool named PAKME for managing architectural knowledge and rationale. The repository within PAKME consists of generic design options and architectural patterns that can be assessed by architects before making architectural decisions. Similarly, tools such as Decision Architect [23] and ADvISE [21] allow architects to capture and analyze

---

[3] https://server.sociocortex.com/typeDefinitions/1vk4hqzziw3jp/Task.

architectural decisions. Capilla et al. [7] in their literature study analyze these tools and their functionalities and indicate that there is a need for substantial improvement in the ability to (semi-) automate use cases for AKM.

The aforementioned tools follow a top-down approach to AKM, that is, they require stakeholders to manually capture data in respective tools which then enables traceability and reasoning based on their meta-models. However, architectural documentation is sparse and stakeholders tend to rather use agile tools such as issue trackers, e-mail clients, PowerPoint, and meeting recording systems to capture their day-to-day decisions [25]. As compared to the top-down approach, we envision a bottom-up approach that focuses on analyzing existing data to automatically extract design decisions and structure them thereafter.

The research in the area of automatic design decision detection and classification is still in its infancy. The approach taken by van der Ven and Bosch [34] is closely related to our work. They propose an approach for analyzing design decisions maintained in the source code commits of OSS repositories. In their work, six subject matter experts manually analyzed 100 different commit messages and indicated that 67% of those commit messages reflected design decisions. Similarly, based on surveys, Dagenais and Robillard [10] identified decisions from developer documentation. In our work, however, we study the issues maintained in issue management systems and apply a ML-based approach to automatically extract and classify design decisions.

Furthermore, in [11,13], authors have successfully applied speech analysis techniques to automatically detect decision-related conversations. We believe that such efforts to automatically detect and extract decisions from systems that are extensively used by architects and developers will aid the adoption of AKM tools to provide significant decision support. Hence, in this paper, we focus on extracting and classifying design decisions from one of the frequently used systems in software development, that is, issue management systems.

3   ADD Categories

In his seminal work [17], Kruchten introduced an ontology of ADDs in software-intensive systems. He classified ADDs into three main categories – existence decisions, property decisions, and executive decisions. Figure 2 shows the taxonomy of the ADD categories with the emphasis on existence decisions, which is the focus of our proposed approach.

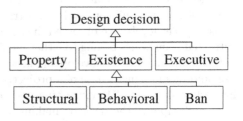

Fig. 2. ADD categories (source: [17])

Existence decisions: Decisions that reflect the existence of an artifact in a system's design or implementation. These decisions are further classified into *structural*, *behavioral*, and *ban* or *non-existence* decisions. Those decisions that indicate the creation or update of artifacts in a system are referred to as structural decisions. Whereas, those decisions that capture, for instance how components interact with each other or discuss the functionality of the system are referred to as behavioral decisions. For example, "Add jets3t dependency to Spark Build[4]" corresponds to a structural decision and the task "Add job cancellation to PySpark[5]" is a behavioral decision. Finally, those decisions that result in the removal of an artifact or interaction between artifacts are referred to as ban or non-existence decisions. For example, the task "remove numpy from RDDSampler of PySpark[6]" is a ban decision. As discussed in [17,25], identifying and then documenting ban decisions is important since these decisions are not traceable to any existing system artifacts.

Property decisions influence the general quality of a system. Design rules, guidelines, and design constraints are considered as property decisions.

Executive decisions are driven by the business environment, management processes, and organizational structures.

Miesbauer and Weinreich [25] demonstrated in their expert survey that the majority of design decisions are existence decisions. In total, they collected 120 examples of design decisions during the interviews. After mapping the examples to the decision categories, they noted that 65% of decisions were existence decisions, 27% were executive decisions (most of them technology decisions), and the remaining 8% belonged to the property decision category. With this as a basis, as well as due to the high manual effort involved in the labeling process for generating the dataset, we start our analysis by considering existence decisions along with its three sub-categories. However, by creating labeled data for the remaining categories and then by training the supervised classifiers, the proposed approach can be extended.

Apart from the aforementioned categories, it should also be noted that design decisions could also be classified according to different abstraction levels. Jansen [14] proposes a funnel of decision-making model to classify decisions at different abstraction levels such as software architecture, detailed design, and implementation. Van der Ven and Bosch [34] relate to these abstraction levels as *high-level*, *medium-level*, and *realization-level* decisions. The decisions at different abstraction levels are related to each other and form a tree structure. Moreover, the decisions at a higher level of abstraction constraint or influence the decisions at lower levels. We observed during the manual analysis that the decisions extracted from issues belong to either medium-level or realization-level decisions. Software architects and developers make these decisions during the implementation and maintenance phase of a project. Moreover, since these decisions are the hardest to make [33,34], extracting and recommending them to software architects will support the decision-making process in similar projects. In order to achieve this, we first need to identify, extract, and classify design decisions from the existing projects. Hence, we formulate the following two hypothesis:

---

[4] https://issues.apache.org/jira/browse/SPARK-898.

[5] https://issues.apache.org/jira/browse/SPARK-986.

[6] https://issues.apache.org/jira/browse/SPARK-4477.

1. Design decisions can be automatically identified and extracted from issues.
2. Design decisions can be automatically classified into ADD categories, namely structural, behavioral, and ban decisions.

To validate the aforementioned hypothesis, we used issues maintained in two large OSS projects. We first extracted the issues from an issue management system into an AKM tool. Then, we applied a ML-based approach to (a) automatically extract design decisions from the already extracted issues and (b) automatically classify the extracted design decisions into three specific categories. The dataset preparation process and the ML pipeline setup for generating the ML models are elaborated in the subsequent sections.

4   Dataset

In this Section, we present the data extraction, curation, and manual labeling processes for generating the dataset for decision detection and classification.

4.1   Data Extraction

We considered two large OSS projects, namely *Apache Spark* and *Apache Hadoop Common* for this study. Apache Spark is a large-scale data processing engine. Since early 2014, contributors of this project have captured more than 19,000 publicly accessible issues in JIRA from version 0.9.0 to 2.1.0[7]. Apache Hadoop, on the other hand, is a distributed computing software and the Hadoop Common component is the core that provides utilities to the other Hadoop components such as YARN and MapReduce. Hadoop Common maintains more than 10,000 issues from version 0.2.0 to 3.0.0-apha1, since early 2013[8]. Both these projects are related to each other, as Apache Spark runs in Hadoop clusters. We selected these two projects for the following reasons:

- Interest to analyze design decisions for building a data analytics platform
- Experts responsible for generating the training dataset for ML had used either one of the systems and were involved in data analytics projects
- Both are long-running projects and have maintained more than 10,000 issues
- Both these projects are extensively used in data management solutions[9]

During the extraction process, we extracted the issues related to these two projects from JIRA while filtering for the following relevant settings. The list of prerequisites for issues to qualify for our study helped us to narrow down the large number of issues to those issues that potentially reflect design decisions. For instance, a *critical task* that has been *resolved* by *implementation* indicates that there is a potential change in the detailed design of a software system.

---

[7] https://issues.apache.org/jira/browse/SPARK – last accessed on 25.01.2017.

[8] https://issues.apache.org/jira/browse/HADOOP – last accessed on 25.01.2017.

[9] https://www.gartner.com/doc/3371732/critical-capabilities-data-warehouse-data.

- Issue Type = Task, New Feature, Improvement, or Epic
- Priority = Blocker, Critical, or Major
- Status = Resolved
- Resolution = Fixed, Implemented, Done, or Resolved

To extract issues from JIRA, we used an OSS component within our AKM tool [4] named SyncPipes[10]. SyncPipes allows end users to map the properties of the source system (JIRA) to the target system (AKM tool). Subsequently, based on the properties mapping, a pipeline is established to enable data integration and synchronization. In total, we extracted 2,259 issues from Apache Spark and 420 issues from Hadoop Common projects.

4.2 Data Curation

We consider the **summary** and **description** attributes of an issue since they elaborately describe an issue's purpose. It should be noted that comments within issues could also be analyzed in this context. However, we restrict our data analysis to the text captured in summary and description attributes and consider the inclusion of comments as part of our future work.

As a first step, the summary and description of all the extracted issues were cleaned by removing the following:

- Code snippets within the text, as well as code inside {{ }} and {code} blocks
- Comments inside {noformat} blocks
- URLs inside the text

We introduced the above restriction so as to ensure that the intent of the issue can be justified only on the basis of textual description without the need for code snippets for explanation.

4.3 Manual Labeling

Two software architects with more than five years of experience individually analyzed the extracted issues in two steps. In the first step, these architects manually classified a set of issues into two classes, namely *Design Decision* and *Not A Design Decision*. In the second step, the decisions identified in the first phase were manually classified into three decision classes, namely *Structural decision*, *Behavioral decision*, and *Ban decision* (cf. Sect. 3). These steps were not necessarily carried out sequentially, but as per the convenience of the experts.

Before starting the labeling process, to ensure a common understanding between the two architects, we set up the rules presented in Table 1 for the manual classification. The classification of design decisions is purely based on the definition of decision categories as discussed in Sect. 3. To the best of authors' knowledge, there does not exist any design decisions dataset that can be used for reference. Hence, we put forth the rules shown in Table 1, for the two architects to support the manual labeling process.

---

[10] https://www.matthes.in.tum.de/pages/2gh0u9d1afap/SyncPipes.

Table 1. Rules for manual classification

Structural decision:

+ Adding or updating plugins, libraries, or third-party systems
+ Adding or updating classes, modules, or files (a class, in this context, refers to a Java class)
+ Changing access specifier of a class
+ Merging or splitting classes or modules
+ Moving parts of the code or the entire files from one location to another (code refactoring to address maintainability issues)
+ Updating names of classes, methods, or modules

Behavioral decision:

+ Adding or updating functionality (methods/functions) and process flows
+ Providing configuration options for managing the behavior of the system
+ Adding or updating application programming interfaces (APIs)
+ Adding or updating dependencies between methods
+ Deprecating or disabling specific functionality
+ Changing the access specifiers of methods

Ban decision:

+ Removing existing plugins, libraries, or third-party systems
+ Discarding classes, modules, code snippets, or files
+ Deleting methods, APIs, process flows, or dependencies between methods
+ Removing deprecated methods

Design decision:

+ An issue that belongs to any one of the above categories

Not a design decision:

+ An issue that does not belong to any of the above categories

Based on the aforementioned rules, both the architects manually analyzed the text in the summary and description attributes of all the extracted issues. Those issues with a missing description and whose intent was not explanatory using the textual description were marked as deleted. The issues that belonged to a specific decision category were labeled respectively, as well as, marked as a *Design Decision*. However, the issues that did not belong to any of the decision categories were marked as *Not A Design Decision*. During this process, we observed that some of the issues were abstract, in the sense that, they were broad issues that could be classified into more than one category. For example, the issue titled "Implement columnar in-memory representation[11]" aims to improve the

---

[11] https://issues.apache.org/jira/browse/SPARK-12785.

memory efficiency of the system and represents a design decision. This issue affects the behavior of the system by introducing a new functionality and affects the structural aspects by introducing new Java classes for its implementation. In this study, we do not apply multi-label classification and focus only on multi-class classification[12] and hence, we restrict the labeling of issues to only one label. Moreover, the majority of issues could be classified into one category since issues are typically concise so that developers can easily understand and implement the tasks. To sum up, architects were requested to mark issues belonging to more than one category as deleted since we argued that applying multi-class classification for detection and classification of design decisions is sufficient to validate the hypothesis set for this study.

Once the architects labeled all the issues individually, the training dataset was consolidated with two focus points in a shared meeting.

- All those issues that were marked as deleted by both the architects were removed from the knowledge base.
- All those issues that had inconsistent decision categories were also removed. Since inconsistent dataset results in unreliable classification results, this step ensured that the issues in the dataset were labeled correctly.

The labeling process resulted in a dataset with 2,139 issues with **781** issues labeled as Design Decisions and 1,358 issues labeled as Not A Design Decision. To avoid skewed results towards Not A Design Decision label (due to a higher number of issues labeled as Not a Design Decision), we randomly selected **790** issues labeled as Not A Design Decision for generating the design decision detection ML model. Furthermore, out of 781 design decisions, 226 were labeled as Structural, 389 were labeled as Behavioral, and the remaining 166 as Ban design decision. To ensure a balanced input for generating the ML model for design decision classification, we randomly selected **160** issues from each category.

5   Machine Learning Pipeline

We used the pipeline shown in Fig. 3 to generate the ML model for decision detection and decision classification. The pipeline itself was divided into two parts. In the first part – "process documents", the labeled dataset was the input and the pipeline generated the term frequency representation of issues. The output of the first part was then consumed by the second part – "Generate model" to produce the classification model and the result of applying the model on the testing dataset. Each issue in the labeled dataset was first tokenized to retrieve words. All the words were then transformed to lower cases. Stop words such as articles, conjunctions, and prepositions were removed. The remaining words were then stemmed to their root words using the Porter stemming algorithm [26]. Subsequently, a list of generated n-grams was appended to the word list. Generating

---

[12] Given that there are multiple labels, in multi-class classification, a document can be assigned to one and only one label. Whereas, in multi-label classification, a document can be assigned to any number of labels.

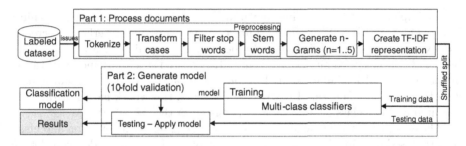

Fig. 3. The machine learning pipeline for design decision detection and classification; Classifiers: SVM, Naive Bayes, Decision tree, Logistic regression, One-vs-rest; n-grams: one to five; Split strategies: 90%, 80%, 70%, 60%, 50%;

n-grams helps to maintain the context of the usage of specific terms by considering its surrounding terms. For the evaluation, we tried different values of n (from 1 to 5) and documented the results as presented in the next section. Finally, the list of words was converted into a term frequency representation. For decision detection with a labeled dataset of 1,571 issues (781 and 790 issues labeled as design decision and not a design decision respectively), we used the term frequency-inverse document frequency (tf-idf) for vector representation. The tf-idf representation evaluates the number of times a word appears in an issue but is offset by the frequency of the word in the corpus. However, for decision classification, we only used term frequency since the dataset was comparatively smaller with 480 design decisions (160 issues in each decision category).

The term frequency representation of issues is provided as input to the second part of the pipeline for generating the classification model. We used different shuffled split strategies (90%, 80%, 70%, 60%, and 50%) and observed the results. That is, the documents were split into training dataset and testing dataset with different split percentages during multiple runs. Furthermore, we used k-fold cross-validation in the model generation process for estimating the accuracy. In our test runs, we used 10-fold cross-validation ($k = 10$) which is common in data mining and machine-learning as it produces less biased accuracy estimations for datasets with small sample sizes [27]. We used different multi-class classifiers on the dataset with the parameters shown in Table 2. The classification model was then applied on the testing dataset to generate the classification results.

Table 2. Classifier parameters

Support vector machines – Kernel: linear; SVM type: C-SVC; Library: LibSVM [9]
Decision tree – Criterion: gain ratio; Depth: 20; Confidence: .25; Minimal gain: .1
Logistic regression – Kernel: dot; ElasticNet: .8; Regularization: .001; Iterations:10
One-vs-rest – Base classifier: Logistic regression
Naive Bayes – Additive smoothing: 1

We implemented the pipeline shown in Fig. 3 using Spark's scalable machine learning library (MLlib) [24]. The MLlib component provides interfaces to create and execute the pipe and filter based pipelines. The pipeline with its configurations and the generated model was eventually persisted as a Spark model instance in the AKM tool for subsequent decision classification. That is, for automatic detection and classification of newly created issues, this Spark model instance is executed and the classification label is persisted in the AKM tool.

The end-to-end workflow of the automatic design decision detection and classification is shown in Fig. 1. Since the output of the first phase (decision detection) is the input to the second phase (decision classification), high accuracy of the results from the first phase is critical. The decision detection component loads the issues, uses the ML model generated for decision detection, and classifies each issue as either a decision or not a decision class. Next, the classification component takes the identified design decisions and classifies them into different categories using the decision classification ML model.

6   Evaluation

In this section, we present the results of applying different classifiers under different configurations for both decision detection and classification using the labeled dataset. In our scenario, the precision (fraction of automatically retrieved documents that are relevant) is as important as the recall (the fraction of relevant documents that were successfully retrieved). For instance, in case of decision detection, it is necessary that all issues that reflect design decisions are retrieved (high recall) and those issues which are not design decisions should not be automatically labeled as design decisions (high precision). Hence, we measure the accuracy as the F-score [28], which is the harmonic mean of precision and recall.

We evaluated multi-class classifiers namely SVM, Naive Bayes, Decision tree, Logistic regression, and One-vs-rest. Since the logistic regression functionality provided by the Spark APIs cannot handle polynomial labels, it was not used for decision classification but only for decision detection (binary). Split strategies from 90% to 50% and n-grams from one to five were analyzed. First, by varying the n-grams from one to five, we expect that the accuracy will proportionally increase. That is, the use of patterns of words, which preserves the context of those words, should positively influence the accuracy of classification. Second, by decreasing the split percentage from 90% to 50%, the accuracy should decrease substantially since lesser number of documents would be used for training the classifiers. In total, 25 individual runs (5 split strategies and 5 n-grams) were executed for each classifier and the corresponding precision, recall, and F-score were calculated. Finally, the average accuracy (average F-score) based on the arithmetic mean of the 25 individual runs for each of the classifiers was analyzed.

Even though the variation of the configuration parameters, namely n-grams and split strategy need not be considered for validating our hypothesis (cf. Sect. 3), we believe that the impact of these parameters on the F-score is interesting for researchers and will help practitioners to reproduce the results.

6.1 Results - Automatic Design Decision Detection

The SVM classifier (average accuracy: 91.29%) outperformed Logistic regression (83.43%), One-vs-rest (79.45%), Decision tree (79.18%), and Naive Bayes (76.04%) classifiers. Since, the tf-idf representation of issues has a high dimensional feature space, sparse vectors, and few irrelevant features due to the data curation process, the SVM outperformed the rest of the classifiers. The maximum accuracy of 94.91% for the SVM classifier was achieved for a larger training set (90% split) with 3, 4, and 5 grams representation and the minimum accuracy of 87.4% with a smaller training set (50% split) and 1-gram settings. The confusion matrix for one specific execution run with 70% split and 3-gram configuration is shown in Table 3. This matrix depicts true and false positives as well as true and false negatives. The true positives (correct classifications) are highlighted on the diagonal of the confusion matrix. The precision for classifying an issue as a design decision is 92.17% and the recall is 90.60%. In addition, the precision for labeling an issue as Not A Design Decision is 90.87% and its recall is 92.41%.

Table 3. Decision detection: the confusion matrix for SVM

	True decision	True not a decision	Class precision
Decision	**212**	18	92.17%
Not a decision	22	**219**	90.87%
Class recall	90.60%	92.41%	

Also, as shown in Fig. 4(a), by reducing the size of the training dataset (from 90% to 50%) the F-score decreases as expected but does not diverge more than 4% points from the average F-score of 91.29%. This indicates that the labeled dataset with 1,571 issues is sufficiently large enough to achieve a consistent

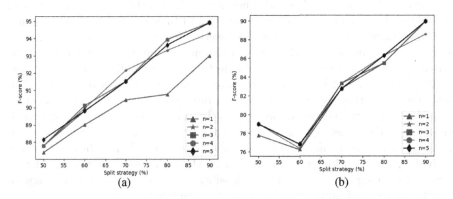

Fig. 4. Influence of n-grams and split strategy on the F-score of SVM: (a) automatic decision detection, (b) automatic decision classification

Table 4. Decision classification: the confusion matrix for SVM

	True ban	True structural	True behavioral	Class precision
Ban	**45**	3	0	93.75%
Structural	4	**41**	13	70.69%
Behavioral	0	6	**39**	86.67%
Class recall	91.84%	82%	75%	

F-score. Furthermore, it can be observed that the variation of n in n-gram generation does not drastically affect the F-score. As expected, the F-score is comparatively lower when we do not consider the combination of words (n = 1) but the F-score slightly improves in the case of 2-grams and 3-grams. However, there does not seem to be any noticeable variations when n is greater than three.

To sum, by using the linear SVM classifier along with n-gram (n >= 2) representation of words, we can automatically extract design decisions from issues (cf. hypothesis 1 in Sect. 3). To the best of authors' knowledge, since no similar study exists with benchmarking results, we consider 91.29% accuracy for automatic design decision detection to be encouraging.

6.2   Results - Automatic Design Decision Classification

Even for the automatic design decision classification, we observed that linear SVM (average accuracy: 82.79%) performed better as compared to classifiers including Naive Bayes (59.09%), Decision tree (60.33%), and One-vs-rest (30%) classifiers. The confusion matrix for linear SVM with 70% training dataset and 30% testing dataset with trigrams is shown in Table 4.

Identifying ban decisions is critical, as they are typically not present in software artifacts (cf. Sect. 3). As shown in Table 4, the precision (93.75%) and recall (91.80%) for automatically classifying design decisions into ban decisions category are above 90%. On the other hand, the precision for structural and behavioral decisions are 70.69% and 86.67% and their recall values are 82% and 75% respectively. We believe that the lower precision and recall for structural and behavioral decisions is due to the existence of similar features (due to the classification rules presented in Table 1) in their corresponding training dataset.

As shown in Fig. 4(b), reducing the size of the training dataset (from 90% to 50%) decreases the F-score as expected (from 89.9% to 76.2%). This variation is justified since the labeled dataset for decision categories is significantly small (160 design decisions in each category). On the contrary, the variation of n-grams does not have any notable affect on the F-score. This indicates that the individual words within issues (or bag of words in the textual representation of issues) play a significant role in the classification as compared to the usage of specific patterns of words and the context of the words.

To conclude, with the linear SVM classifier we can automatically classify design decisions into structural, behavioral, and ban decision categories with an accuracy of 82.79% (cf. hypothesis 2 in Sect. 3). However, we perceive that since the dataset for classifying decisions is relatively small, increasing the sample size will improve the generalization capabilities of the classifiers.

7   Threats to Validity

The results presented in the previous section are based on 1,571 labeled issues for design decision detection and 480 labeled design decisions for classification. The labeled dataset for classification is not as comprehensive as the dataset used for decision detection. Even though, we speculate that the generalization capabilities of design decision classification can be further improved by increasing the sample size of the dataset, providing relevant quantitative evidence is beyond the scope of this paper. However, it should be noted that typically in ML-based approaches for text classification, increasing the sample size of the dataset substantially improves the classification performance [22].

The 1,571 labeled issues are extracted from two large OSS projects, wherein contributors have systematically maintained issues for more than three years. The hypothesis validated using the dataset might not be generalizable for projects where issues are reported scarcely. Hence, understanding what characteristics of the projects could influence the precision and recall of our approach are considered as part of our future work.

In the previous section, we have presented the results of automatic decision detection and classification independently of each other. However, if we consider the workflow described in Fig. 1, the accuracy of the decision detection affects the subsequent decision classification phase. In this work, we do not compute the accuracy for the end-to-end workflow. We plan to perform this evaluation after integrating of the workflow within our AKM tool as part of our future work.

Finally, as explained in the data curation process, analysts did not consider issues that could belong to more than one ADD category. Considering such issues would require further investigation into appropriate classification algorithms for multi-label classification and the study of the corresponding results.

8   Conclusion

In this paper, we presented a two-phase ML-based approach to automatically detect design decisions from issues and to subsequently classify them into three ADD categories, namely Structural, Behavioral and Ban decisions. Furthermore, we made the manually labeled dataset used for supervised learning publicly available. This will act as a starting point for researchers to create their own ML models and to compare the accuracy of the automatic design decision detection and classification process. The results presented in Sect. 6 indicate that we can automatically extract design decisions from issues with an accuracy of 91.29% and classify the extracted decisions into three categories with an accuracy of 82.79% by using the linear SVM classifier. Even though the accuracy can be further improved, we believe that the result is significant enough to demonstrate the feasibility of our approach.

We are currently in the process of integrating our ML pipeline within our AKM tool named AMELIE [4]. This integration will allow us to conduct an extensive evaluation of the ML models in industrial settings. Furthermore, by automatically extracting and structuring design decisions from past projects, we aim to provide recommendations related to semantically similar design decisions in greenfield projects. The process of automatically extracting and classifying design decisions from issues is envisioned to be realized using the end-to-end workflow presented in Fig. 1.

To conclude, since design decisions are not explicitly documented but are rather implicitly captured in systems such as issue management systems, automatically detecting, extracting, and systematically structuring them in an AKM tool will help software architects and developers to refer back to already made design decisions in large-scale software projects as well as in greenfield projects with similar context. Furthermore, classifying them into categories such as Ban decisions will allow stakeholders to reason about those artifacts which no longer exist within the system. Finally, since issues capture both unstructured, as well as structured information, analyzing them, will support the development of decision support systems to address concerns such as "Who took the decision?", "When was the decision taken?", and "Why was the decision made?".

References

1. Ambler, S.: Agile Modeling: Effective Practices for Extreme Programming and the Unified Process. Wiley, New York (2002)
2. Antoniol, G., Ayari, K., Di Penta, M., Khomh, F., Guéhéneuc, Y.G.: Is it a bug or an enhancement?: a text-based approach to classify change requests. In: Proceedings of the 2008 Conference of the Center for Advanced Studies on Collaborative Research: Meeting of Minds, p. 23. ACM (2008)
3. Babar, M.A., Gorton, I.: A tool for managing software architecture knowledge. In: Second Workshop on Sharing and Reusing Architectural Knowledge-Architecture, Rationale, and Design Intent, SHARK/ADI 2007: ICSE Workshops 2007, p. 11. IEEE (2007)
4. Bhat, M., Shumaiev, K., Biesdorf, A., Hohenstein, U., Hassel, M., Matthes, F.: Meta-model based framework for architectural knowledge management. In: Proccedings of the 10th ECSA Workshops, p. 12. ACM (2016)
5. Bosch, J.: Software architecture: the next step. In: Oquendo, F., Warboys, B.C., Morrison, R. (eds.) EWSA 2004. LNCS, vol. 3047, pp. 194–199. Springer, Heidelberg (2004). doi:10.1007/978-3-540-24769-2_14
6. Buchgeher, G., Weinreich, R.: Automatic tracing of decisions to architecture and implementation. In: 2011 9th Working IEEE/IFIP Conference on Software Architecture (WICSA), pp. 46–55. IEEE (2011)
7. Capilla, R., Jansen, A., Tang, A., Avgeriou, P., Babar, M.A.: 10 years of software architecture knowledge management: practice and future. J. Syst. Softw. **116**, 191–205 (2016)

8. Capilla, R., Nava, F., Carrillo, C.: Effort estimation in capturing architectural knowledge. In: Proceedings of 23rd IEEE/ACM International Conference on Automated Software Engineering, pp. 208–217. IEEE Computer Society (2008)

9. Chang, C.C., Lin, C.J.: LIBSVM: a library for support vector machines. ACM Trans. Intell. Syst. Technol. (TIST) **2**(3), 27 (2011)

10. Dagenais, B., Robillard, M.P.: Creating and evolving developer documentation: understanding the decisions of open source contributors. In: Proceedings of 18th ACM SIGSOFT International Symposium on Foundations of Software Engineering, pp. 127–136. ACM (2010)

11. Fernández, R., Frampton, M., Ehlen, P., Purver, M., Peters, S.: Modelling and detecting decisions in multi-party dialogue. In: Proceedings of 9th SIGdial Workshop on Discourse and Dialogue, pp. 156–163. Association for Computational Linguistics (2008)

12. Goth, G.: Agile tool market growing with the philosophy. IEEE Softw. **26**(2), 88–91 (2009)

13. Hsueh, P.-Y., Moore, J.D.: Automatic decision detection in meeting speech. In: Popescu-Belis, A., Renals, S., Bourlard, H. (eds.) MLMI 2007. LNCS, vol. 4892, pp. 168–179. Springer, Heidelberg (2008). doi:10.1007/978-3-540-78155-4_15

14. Jansen, A.: Architectural design decisions. Ph.D. thesis, August 2008

15. Jansen, A., Bosch, J.: Software architecture as a set of architectural design decisions. In: 5th Working IEEE/IFIP Conference on Software Architecture, WICSA 2005, pp. 109–120. IEEE (2005)

16. Kazman, R., Goldenson, D., Monarch, I., Nichols, W., Valetto, G.: Evaluating the effects of architectural documentation: a case study of a large scale open source project. IEEE Trans. Softw. Eng. **42**(3), 220–260 (2016)

17. Kruchten, P.: An ontology of architectural design decisions in software intensive systems. In: 2nd Groningen Workshop on Software Variability, pp. 54–61. Citeseer (2004)

18. Kruchten, P., Capilla, R., Dueñas, J.C.: The decision view's role in software architecture practice. IEEE Softw. **26**(2), 36–42 (2009)

19. Lee, J.: Design rationale systems: understanding the issues. IEEE Expert **12**(3), 78–85 (1997)

20. Lee, L., Kruchten, P.: Capturing software architectural design decisions. In: Canadian Conference on Electrical and Computer Engineering, CCECE 2007, pp. 686–689. IEEE (2007)

21. Lytra, I., Tran, H., Zdun, U.: Supporting consistency between architectural design decisions and component models through reusable architectural knowledge transformations. In: Drira, K. (ed.) ECSA 2013. LNCS, vol. 7957, pp. 224–239. Springer, Heidelberg (2013). doi:10.1007/978-3-642-39031-9_20

22. Manning, C.D., Schütze, H., et al.: Foundations of Statistical Natural Language Processing, vol. 999. MIT Press, Cambridge (1999)

23. Manteuffel, C., Tofan, D., Koziolek, H., Goldschmidt, T., Avgeriou, P.: Industrial implementation of a documentation framework for architectural decisions. In: 2014 IEEE/IFIP Conference on Software Architecture (WICSA), pp. 225–234. IEEE (2014)

24. Meng, X., Bradley, J., Yavuz, B., Sparks, E., Venkataraman, S., Liu, D., Freeman, J., Tsai, D., Amde, M., Owen, S., et al.: MLlib: machine learning in apache spark. J. Mach. Learn. Res. **17**(34), 1–7 (2016)

25. Miesbauer, C., Weinreich, R.: Classification of design decisions – an expert survey in practice. In: Drira, K. (ed.) ECSA 2013. LNCS, vol. 7957, pp. 130–145. Springer, Heidelberg (2013). doi:10.1007/978-3-642-39031-9_12

26. Porter, M.F.: An algorithm for suffix stripping. Program **14**(3), 130–137 (1980)
27. Refaeilzadeh, P., Tang, L., Liu, H.: Cross-validation. In: Liu, L., Özsu, T. (eds.) Encyclopedia of Database Systems, pp. 532–538. Springer, Heidelberg (2009). doi:10.1007/978-0-387-39940-9_565
28. Rijsbergen, C.J.V.: Information Retrieval, 2nd edn. Butterworth-Heinemann, Newton (1979)
29. Stettina, C.J., Heijstek, W.: Necessary and neglected?: an empirical study of internal documentation in agile software development teams. In: Proceedings of 29th ACM International Conference on Design of Communication, pp. 159–166. ACM (2011)
30. Sutherland, J., Viktorov, A., Blount, J., Puntikov, N.: Distributed scrum: agile project management with outsourced development teams. In: 40th Annual Hawaii International Conference on System Sciences, HICSS 2007, p. 274a. IEEE (2007)
31. Tang, A., Babar, M.A., Gorton, I., Han, J.: A survey of architecture design rationale. J. Syst. Softw. **79**(12), 1792–1804 (2006)
32. Tyree, J., Akerman, A.: Architecture decisions: demystifying architecture. IEEE Softw. **22**(2), 19–27 (2005)
33. van der Ven, J.S., Bosch, J.: Architecture decisions: who, how and when. In: Babar, M.A., Brown, A., Mistrik, I. (eds.) Agile Software Architecture, pp. 113–136. Morgan Kaufmann, Boston (2013)
34. van der Ven, J.S., Bosch, J.: Making the right decision: supporting architects with design decision data. In: Drira, K. (ed.) ECSA 2013. LNCS, vol. 7957, pp. 176–183. Springer, Heidelberg (2013). doi:10.1007/978-3-642-39031-9_15

Decision Models for Microservices: Design Areas, Stakeholders, Use Cases, and Requirements

Stefan Haselböck[1]([⊠]), Rainer Weinreich[1], and Georg Buchgeher[2]

[1] Johannes Kepler University Linz, Linz, Austria
{stefan.haselboeck,rainer.weinreich}@jku.at
[2] Software Competence Center Hagenberg GmbH, Hagenberg im Mühlkreis, Austria
georg.buchgeher@scch.at

Abstract. Introducing a microservice architecture is a complex task, requiring many design decisions regarding system architecture, organizational structure, and system infrastructure. Decision models have been successfully used in other domains for design space exploration, decision making and decision documentation. In this paper, we investigate the use of decision models for microservice architecture. As a first step, we identified areas of microservice design and created decision models for some of the identified areas. We then used the created models as part of a technical action research (TAR) process with partner companies to identify important stakeholders and use cases for decision models in this context, as well as to identify requirements on decision model elements and presentation. Results indicate that practitioners perceive decision models for microservices to be useful. Challenges include the large number of interlinked knowledge areas, the need for context-specific adaptations, and the need for processes to manage the decision space over time.

Keywords: Decision models · Microservices · Technical action research (TAR)

1 Introduction

Microservice architecture (aka Microservices) is an architectural style that focuses on modularizing service-oriented software systems in such a way that services and service development teams are as independent from each other as possible [27]. While modularization has always been a means to enable independent development, microservices are also built for independent deployment, scalability, and evolution.

Shifting to a microservice architecture promises faster time-to-market of individual services, less coordination and thus less complexity through development teams that act independently, and more efficient utilization of resources by enabling the possibility to scale individual services independently from each other.

© Springer International Publishing AG 2017
A. Lopes and R. de Lemos (Eds.): ECSA 2017, LNCS 10475, pp. 155–170, 2017.
DOI: 10.1007/978-3-319-65831-5_11

However, introducing a microservice architecture is no easy task. A company undertaking such an endeavor needs to make a variety of decisions touching a wide array of development practices, technologies, and infrastructure to handle the additional challenges and complexity that accompany this architectural style. Examples of such changes are the introduction of an automatic deployment pipeline to deal with the continuous deployment of individual services, the use of a runtime infrastructure that provides isolation and scalability, the introduction of a monitoring infrastructure, and changes to the release process and testing practices, along with organizational and procedural changes (e.g., DevOps [3]). All in all, changing to a microservice architecture may touch nearly every aspect of service development, including design, infrastructure, development practice, and team organization.

To handle this complexity, we investigate the use of decision models to support the establishment of a microservice architecture. Decision models are a well-known approach for exploring the design space, making decisions, documentation, and reuse in software architecture [5,24]. Early work on design space exploration and semi-formal models for representing the design space in human computer interaction (HCI) was performed by MacLean et al. [15,16]. Later, models for representing and utilizing architectural decisions were developed as part of research on rational management [6] and knowledge management [1] in software architecture. In [24], we identified more than 50 approaches to software architecture knowledge management, many of them based on semi-formal decision models. Recent work in this area has also investigated decision models for guiding decision making in different domains, like service-oriented systems [30], cloud computing [29], and cyber-foraging systems [12].

In this paper, we first identify potential areas for microservice decision making. After creating initial decision models for some of the identified areas, we used those models in a technical action research (TAR) process with partner companies to identify important stakeholders and use cases for decision models in the context of microservice architecture. Finally, we identify requirements for the decision models themselves, such as required elements to address the identified use cases, along with specifying requirements concerning the presentation of the decision models to the identified stakeholders.

The remainder of the paper is structured as follows. Section 2 contains background information and outlines related work on decision models. We describe the research design and research questions in Sect. 3. The identified areas of microservice design, stakeholders, use cases, and requirements on microservice decision model elements and presentation are presented in Sect. 4. Section 5 summarizes the main results. Threats to validity are discussed in Sect. 6, and Sect. 7 concludes.

2   Background and Related Work

Bosch and Jansen [4,11] defined software architecture as the result of a set of architectural decisions in one of the first decision-oriented views of software architecture. Since then, design decisions have become important elements of software architecture research, and several models, methods, and tools have been developed to represent, capture, and manage decisions and their rationales in software architecture [5, 23, 24]. Decisions are also a central concept in the ISO/IEC/IEEE 42010 standard on software architecture documentation [10].

Early work on decision models in human computer interaction (HCI) was conducted by MacLean et al. [15, 16], who introduced QOC (Questions, Options, and Criteria) as a semiformal notation to represent the design space around an artifact. QOC focused on representing the basic concepts of design space analysis: questions, options, and criteria. The QOC notation was later adopted in research on architectural knowledge management [1] and used as a basis for decision models in software architecture [14, 28].

Zdun [28] proposed decision models based on QOC for analyzing the software design space. The models are meant to be reusable for multiple design decisions. The work on QOC-based decision models for software architecture was further refined and supported by tools in the ADvISE approach [14].

Zimmermann and Miksovic [30] presented decision models for service-oriented architecture, including the possibility to reuse one or more guidance models in their SOAD meta-model; they described guidance models as reusable assets. In [29], they extended their previous work on decision models, introducing the concepts of problem-space and solution-space modelling.

Lewis et al. [12] presented decision models for cyber-foraging systems with the goal of providing guidance for the architecture and evolution of such systems. In contrast to Zimmermann et al. [29], they did not include a mechanism for capturing decisions made. Their models are comparable to the guidance models proposed by Zimmermann and Miksovic in [30].

Here, we develop decision models for a microservice architecture, specifically using as a basis a metamodel similar to that of Lewis and Zimmermann. Our metamodel includes concerns which relate to questions in the QOC notation and to requirements in other decision models, design options, and implications, which can also be used as criteria to evaluate design options. Implications relate to tradeoffs in the decision model by Lewis et al. [12], but they may not only be related to system qualities but also to organizational structures, economic implications, and infrastructure. We use this metamodel as a basis for developing and refining decision models for various important microservice topics, such as service discovery, service registration, versioning, load balancing, caching, fault tolerance, and so on (see, e.g., [9] on decision models for monitoring microservices). As part of this process, we also identified important areas of microservice design, important stakeholders for these models, potential use cases, and specific requirements for decision models in this domain.

3   Research Design

The goal of this study is to identify areas of microservice design where decision models might be used, stakeholders and use cases for decision models in this context, and requirements for elements of decision models and their presentation. We defined the following research questions to address this goal:

- **RQ1:** What are the main areas of design for a microservice-based system, and how can they be categorized?
- **RQ2:** Which are the important stakeholders of decision models for microservice architectures?
- **RQ3:** What are the intended use cases for decision models for microservice architectures?
- **RQ4:** What elements of a microservice decision model and their presentation are required to support stakeholders in their intended used cases?

3.1 Literature Review

To identify areas of design for microservice architectures and to categorize the identified areas, we reviewed the literature in the digital libraries of IEEE, ACM, and Springer. We first performed an automatic search using the following search terms: microservice*, micro-service*, and "micro service*". We searched for these terms in the titles, abstracts, and keywords of articles published in journals, conferences, and workshops.

After the automatic search, we manually analyzed the results, removing articles not relevant for this study. We then analyzed the remaining articles with main topics regarding different areas of microservice decision-making. Finally, we included several existing mapping studies on microservices [2,7,19] in our analysis.

In addition to the above literature review, we also manually reviewed two well-known books [18,27] and two blogs [13,21] on microservices to validate and refine the list of identified areas of microservice design.

3.2 TAR Study

To identify stakeholders, use cases, and requirements of decision models for microservices, we performed a technical action research (TAR) study as described by Wieringa [26]. The concept of TAR is to design artifacts and validate them under real-world conditions.

The basic structure of the TAR process is shown in Fig. 1, comprising three different cycles. In each cycle, the researcher plays a different role. In the design cycle, the researcher designs an artifact to solve problems in a research context. In the empirical cycle, the researcher validates the designed artifact and tries to answer the defined research questions. The client engineering cycle has two different aims. The client wants to solve a problem with the designed artifact, and the researcher wants to validate his or her artifact. Thus, the researcher helps the client solve their problem by applying the designed artifact. At the same time, he or she collects information to answer the research questions.

We performed the TAR study with two different companies that are currently establishing microservice architectures. The companies operate in two different domains, banking and process automation. The artifacts under study were use cases and stakeholders of decision models for microservices, as well as required elements for decision models and presentation of microservices. To collect data

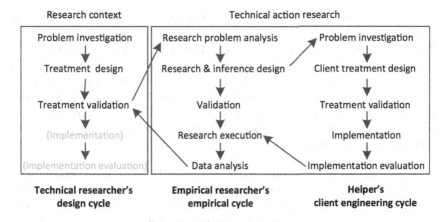

Research context   Technical action research

Fig. 1. The three-level structure of TAR (from [26])

for these points, we performed four client engineering cycles with the two companies. In each cycle, we participated in a design workshop with the clients, each addressing a particular area of microservice design. The workshops were part of regular design sessions at the companies that took place every two weeks as part of Scrum cycles. While we initiated participation in the workshops, we did not initiate the workshops themselves. In preparation for the workshops, we created decision models for the defined areas based on the microservice literature (the helper's role). During the workshop, the participants used the created models to discuss potential design decisions regarding the issues in a particular design area in their company's context, while we (as researchers) acted as pure observers and data collectors. At the end of each workshop, we additionally interviewed workshop participants about potential stakeholders, intended use cases, and the provided models to obtain feedback about the elements and presentation. Interviews were performed either by client staff or by the researchers. The following briefly describes the four different client engineering cycles.

- In the *first client engineering cycle*, we participated in a design workshop on service discovery at a company in the banking domain. During this cycle, the client aimed to get an overview of the topic of service discovery, define requirements for service discovery, and discuss potential design options. We provided initial models for service discovery, service registration, and load balancing, which the workshop participants could use in their discussion, but we did not interfere otherwise.
- The *second engineering cycle* was performed with the same client as was the first cycle. The aim of this cycle was to reflect design decisions already made for service discovery. We used the revised metamodel created during the first client engineering cycle.
- In the *third client engineering cycle*, we participated in a workshop on resilience with the same company. In this cycle, the client had the same aim as in the first engineering cycle. We used a decision model for resilience, which

was based on the refined metamodel from the previous client engineering cycles.

- The *fourth client engineering cycle* was done with a company in the process automation domain. We participated in a meeting with the client on microservice monitoring. The client aimed to get an overview of the topic of monitoring and of available design options, to define requirements for microservice monitoring in the company's context, and to get some information about existing monitoring technologies. We used a set of decision models for microservice monitoring [9] in this workshop.

The main means of data collection were observation and unstructured interviews [22]. We took field notes during the workshops, which we extended with information collected in interviews. For analysis of the collected data, we used the constant comparison method [22] to collect and refine the data in each client engineering cycle. We performed data analysis in two steps. First, we coded the field notes using a provisional "start list" [17] with predefined categories and several subcategories. We then analyzed the coded field notes, finally creating a field memo [22] including the identified stakeholders, use cases, and necessary changes to the elements or presentation. Furthermore, based on the field memo, we redesigned the decision metamodel and the presentation of the model (i.e., the notation of the model) for the next client engineering cycle.

4   Results

In the following section, we present the results that address the research questions presented in Sect. 3, starting with the identified design areas, stakeholders, and use cases (RQ1–RQ3). Section 4.4 presents the requirements for decision models and their elements (RQ4) that emerged during the client engineering cycles in the TAR process.

4.1   RQ1: Design Areas

Figure 2 overviews the design areas that were identified in the literature review. We briefly describe each main design area.

Integration: Microservice architectures comprise potentially thousands of independently developed and operated services, which need to be integrated with each other. Integration of services can occur at different levels, such as the user interface level, the service level, or the data level.

Modularization: Microservice architecture is often primarily seen as a specific, modular approach that aims to design microservices as independently from each other as possible. This may lead to services that provide their own user interfaces and data management facilities. Concepts like domain-driven design can decouple services based on their functionalities. Furthermore, service granularity and size must be considered.

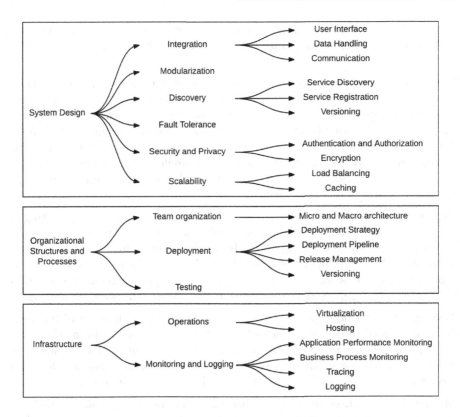

Fig. 2. Areas of microservice design

Discovery: Since microservices are typically spread across different hosts, mechanisms for service registration and discovery are needed to ensure that services can find each other. This also includes mechanisms to find specific versions of services.

Fault Tolerance: To ensure that a local failure of a microservice does not propagate through the whole system and eventually lead to system breakdown, services must be designed to be tolerant against failures at runtime. Furthermore, the infrastructure must provide mechanisms to deal with failing service instances. If required, new service instances should be started automatically.

Security and Privacy: Since microservices provide public interfaces and use remote communication spanning network boundaries, security and privacy must be considered, including subareas like authentication, authorization, and encryption.

Scalability: Scalability is often a central reason for companies to migrate towards a microservice architecture, because it enables independent and selective scaling of single services. Scalability can be achieved on different levels, for instance by replicating services, splitting the functionality for which a service is responsible, or splitting the data for which a service is responsible. To cope with independently scaling services, load balancing and caching mechanisms must also be considered.

Team organization: Design also goes hand-in-hand with team organization. In a microservice architecture, teams operate as independently from each other as possible. Instead of functional teams organized around technical boundaries, teams are mostly cross-functional and organized around business capabilities. A team may develop several microservices, but the development of any single microservice is always the responsibility of a single team. Teams responsible for a microservice may also independently decide the programming language, technology stack, and development process to use.

Deployment: Independent deployment is a central motivation for using a microservice architecture. Independent deployment of a potentially large number of services requires a strategy to bring the services into production with reasonable effort, e.g., by automating the deployment pipeline with continuous deployment. In cases where complete releases require deployment at once, perhaps because of legal restrictions, release management strategies are needed.

Testing: As with deployment, testing a potentially large number of independently developed microservices with frequent releases requires automation. Services should be tested as part of a continuous delivery pipeline. Integration tests should be performed at the end of a continuous deployment pipeline for each service individually, which requires the establishment of test zones.

Monitoring and Logging: Monitoring microservice-based systems is challenging, because of the high number of independent services, which may be located on different hosts. This requires support for the automatic collection, distribution, and combination of the monitoring data from the different services. Monitoring should include application performance, business processes, tracing, and logging.

Operations: A dedicated runtime infrastructure is needed to operate microservice instances, handle the independent scaling of services, support fault tolerance, and support continuous deployment. This may include the use of virtualization and cloud infrastructures.

Some of the above areas are related to each other, such as service discovery and service registration, so making decisions in one design area might require decisions in another design area. In addition, any design area might be related to multiple, other design areas. For example, service versioning may be related to service discovery, because service discovery must handle different versions of a microservice. Also, versioning may be related to service deployment, since different versions of a service must be deployed.

The identified design areas can be further mapped to three main areas of microservice system design, organizational structures and processes, and microservice infrastructure (again see Fig. 2). This highlights that, when establishing a microservice architecture, decisions must be made not only at the level of system design, but also concerning team organization and system infrastructure.

4.2 RQ2: Stakeholders

The second research question aims to identify important stakeholders of decision models for microservices. To answer this research question, we analyzed the roles of the workshop participants in the client engineering cycles and also asked about their roles in interviews after the engineering cycles. We identified six main stakeholders for decision models.

Software Architect: At least one software architect participated in each client engineering cycle. Software architects were responsible either for the architecture of the entire microservice-based software system (i.e., the macro-architecture) or for the architecture of single microservices as part of development teams (i.e., the micro-architecture). Software architects' main interests are to use decision models to explore new design areas, provide decision guidance for other stakeholders, efficiently document design decisions, and review design decisions already made.

Developer: Developers only participated in the fourth client engineering cycle. Typically, developers are involved only in selected areas as part of a cross-functional team. Their main interest is in using decision models to make, document, and review decisions as part of the team.

Application Engineer: This stakeholder was identified during the fourth client engineering cycle. Application engineers are typically responsible for realizing customer projects based on a software platform or product line of an industrial solutions provider. As such, their main interest lies in understanding important platform decisions, along with integrating client solutions with the client's hardware and software infrastructure.

Operations Engineer: This stakeholder was present in three different client engineering cycles, which is no surprise since development and operations usually work together in the context of microservices. They were interested mostly in the design spaces provided for deployment, infrastructural issues like the runtime infrastructure used for load distribution and monitoring, and the available technology options.

Quality Assurer: Stakeholders for quality assurance were present in all client engineering cycles. They were usually part of service development and cross-functional teams and mainly interested in changes to test processes and fault handling.

Manager: This stakeholder was identified during the first and second client engineering cycles. Some workshop participants mentioned that they have to provide support for decision-making that is the responsibility of people at higher management levels. Currently, this is done with the time-consuming method of PowerPoint presentations. They expect to use the structured way of presenting design options and implications together with their rationales to streamline this process.

While the different stakeholders were partly interested in different decision models, typically related to their areas of responsibility and interest, it also became obvious that decision models would typically be used in a team setting, where stakeholders with expertise or interest in a particular topic were present. In addition, other people required for discussion (e.g., experts on specific infrastructure) were integrated on-demand through conference calls.

4.3   RQ3: Use Cases

RQ3 concerns the identification of intended use cases of decision models for microservices. To answer this question, we identified how the decision models were used in the client engineering cycles. In the interviews after the workshops, we also asked study participants to identify additional potential use cases of the presented models. As a result, we identified the following main use cases.

Design Space Exploration: In the first use case, decision models are used to explore a potential design space and to discuss potential design options. Workshop participants used the provided decision models to overview available design options, rationales for selecting particular options, and implications of each option for system qualities and organizational structures and processes. Stakeholders participating in these discussions included software architects, developers, application engineers, quality assurance managers, and operations people. For this kind of discussion, global decision models are typically used. In our case, most of the performed client engineering cycles fell into this category.

Decision Guidance and Documentation: In this use case, decision models are used as a framework to make decisions and efficiently document decisions. The team responsible for a decision uses the models to choose one or several design options. The models provide addressed concerns with, implications of, and the components needed for each possible decision. Potential stakeholders for this use case are cross-functional teams comprising developers, architects, quality assurance, and operations. The participants in our client engineering cycles outlined two use cases in this area: (1) the creation and continuous adaptation of decision models to the local design context of the company, what we termed local or company-specific decision models, which might be used to capture cross-project knowledge in the company and guide the design process as outlined above; and (2) stakeholders at the companies also argued that decision models might be suitable for discussing important decisions with upper management, since it enables a presentation of the rationale for each element and the implications of selecting a particular option in a structured and compact way.

Design Review: In this use case, decision models are used to reflect decisions that have already been made. Therefore, existing decision models created by the decision maker, other teams, or external experts are used. In the client engineering cycles in this case, participants mentioned two intended purposes: (1) to reflect a decision made by the same team, whether architectural or cross-functional; and (2) to reflect decisions made by another team. A concrete example mentioned was the architectural team reflecting decisions made by cross-functional teams. The second client engineering cycle, described in Sect. 3.2, was performed on the basis of this use case. The client's architectural team reflected their decisions about service discovery in the context of a particular infrastructure for service discovery. The researchers created the decision model used.

Requirements Elicitation: This use case was identified in the fourth client engineering cycle of the TAR process. The workshop participants used the provided decision models to determine the requirements of their monitoring infrastructure when discussing different monitoring options.

Evaluation of Technology Options: As expressed in the third and fourth client engineering cycles, decision models may be used to select and evaluate existing technology options for a specific area of design. This requires information about the implemented functionality and the product and runtime costs of different technology options.

4.4 RQ4: Decision Model Elements and Presentation

The following requirements concerning model elements and presentation emerged when using and refining the provided decision models in the TAR process outlined in Sect. 3.2.

Scope: In workshops that aimed at exploring a specific design space, participants added several additional elements to the model, such as concerns, implications, or design options. Some of the added elements were company-specific, but others were also valid in other contexts. Thus, different decision models are needed for different application scopes. So, we introduced the concept of context-dependent (local) and context-independent (global) decision models. Since some of the added elements were also valid in other domains, we further added a feedback loop to continuously incorporate changes to local models into more general, global models, analogous to the feedback loop from application engineering to domain engineering in software product lines described in [20].

Components: Workshop participants were often interested in the system components needed to implement a design option. As a result, we identified a need to include system components as first-level elements in decision models, which can then be linked to concerns and design options.

Technology Options: In two client engineering cycles, one important aim of the client was to identify and evaluate different technology options for implementing a specific design option. Therefore, in the decision models, we need additional elements to model technology options and link them with specific design options.

Reading Direction: To increase the models' comprehensibility, some workshop participants mentioned the need for a clear reading direction. They expressed the need to start at two different points when discussing the design space: either starting with a design option to determine which concerns were addressed or starting with concerns to determine the design options best addressing those concerns. The model's presentation must support both scenarios.

Structuring and Connecting Design Areas: Since areas of microservice design are often related, the model must provide a mechanism to define such relations between different areas. Furthermore, there are many different design areas, requiring a mechanism to structure the whole design space, for example by defining namespaces for decision models and by refining decision models into submodels.

Focusing on Important Elements: In the workshops, we noticed that the presentation of the decision models must be as simple as possible while still providing the full level of detail when needed. Otherwise, a model's users easily become overwhelmed by its complexity. Also, some elements of a particular type turned out to have different levels of importance than others. This became especially evident when showing implications, which we included in the model to show the results of selecting a particular design option. One strategy might be to classify elements according to their levels of importance, showing less important elements only when requested.

5   Discussion

Identified stakeholders were not only the software architects that would be expected in a microservice context, although software architects were often the driving force in discussions in the performed client engineering cycles and were involved in all design areas that discussed in the workshops. Other stakeholders, like developers, operation engineers, and quality assurance, were typically involved only in selected areas, according to their specific roles and interests. However, all stakeholders considered the decision models to be useful, in part because they provided a common ground of understanding and terminology and a means for structuring discussion on a topic.

The most relevant use cases in our client engineering cycles were design space exploration and reviews of already made design decisions. Also, the teams were heavily driven in part by existing microservice technology stacks. Therefore, the decision models were also used to evaluate existing technology options and how they implemented specific design options. In the fourth client engineering cycle, in particular, the company used the decision models to determine requirements for their monitoring infrastructure. The decision models not only enabled a higher level of completeness but also served as a means for weighing the importance of requirements in light of how they addressed design options. Additional use cases like decision guidance, documenting decisions and their rationales, and refining models were identified as equally important in the long term. Finally, participants identified the aspect of sharing as important, including adaptations of local decision models in concrete usage scenarios and the continuous refinement of shared global models based on these context-specific changes.

The decision models we created for the client engineering workshops (e.g., the microservice monitoring models presented in [9]) include the main elements of QOC models (see Sect. 2). In addition, our models included further elements, such as components and technology options, to support the evaluation and selection of technology options and to obtain an impression of what would be required to implement a design option.

The presentation of a single model should mainly provide an overview of the design space, with details shown as needed. Additionally, decision models for a large number of identified design areas must be structured with, for example, namespaces and submodels. We plan further investigation of different forms of model presentation to stakeholders in our ongoing TAR study with both current and new business partners.

6   Threats to Validity

The presented results of the literature review and TAR study may be influenced by several factors.

In our literature review, we did not intend to obtain a complete list of areas of design for microservices. Instead, we wanted an overview of important areas of design that must be considered when introducing microservice architectures and that we could potentially support with decision models. We tried to mitigate threats related to the representativeness of the list of identified design areas by performing an automatic search of the main digital libraries for software engineering using a quite general search string (see Sect. 3.1), followed by manual selection of relevant studies from the results of the automated search. Afterwards, we extended and refined the resulting list of studies with results of mapping studies, augmented with important books and blog posts on this topic.

In our TAR study, we used the data collection methods of observation and unstructured interviews. Seaman [22] mentioned a number of threats to consider for both means of data collection.

For observations, the participants should not feel observed, and the observer should not interrupt in any way. To address these issues, we explained our app-roach and aims to participants before each session, making it clear that we would not interfere with the workshop in any way. During the workshops, we acted as pure observers and data collectors. We only answered questions regarding the meaning of the elements in the discussed decision models.

A potential threat regarding interviews is that interviewees may answer ques-tions in a socially desirable way [25]. To mitigate this threat, interviews should not be performed by the researchers, if possible. In our case, the interviews were partly performed by client staff and partly by the researchers. In cases where we performed the interviews, we made clear that there were no right or wrong answers, as suggested in [22].

For analysis of collected data during the observations and interviews, we used the constant comparison method [22]. Gasson [8] mentioned threats that must be addressed when using this method, namely confirmability, dependability, internal consistency, and transferability. To ensure confirmability, each researcher inde-pendently coded the field notes and discussed the findings. To address depend-ability, we followed the TAR study process, with observations and interviews used as data collection methods and the constant comparison method used for data analysis. To ensure internal consistency, we derived the data from the field memos, which were created based on the independent coding of the field notes. Transferability was addressed by using the artifact under study in several client engineering cycles. In each cycle, the context of design space, use case, participants, or client changed.

Still, our study faces some limitations that may affect the external validity of the findings, most importantly the limited number of clients and client engineering cycles. We tried to mitigate this threat by working with different clients from different domains, as well as by working with different teams at one of the clients. Furthermore, in the client engineering cycles we used decision models for different areas of design.

7   Conclusion

In this work, we identified potential areas of microservice design through a literature review, created decision models based on existing work, decision models in other domains, and microservice literature, and then used the created models in a technical action research process with industrial partners to identify stakeholders, use cases, and requirements for decision models for microservices.

Our results showed that there is a wide range of potential stakeholders in this domain, from software architects and operations personnel to management. Stakeholders outlined a set of use cases, including requirements elicitation, design space exploration, decision guidance, technology evaluation, decision documentation, and decision presentation. Quite interestingly, the provided decision models worked well during workshops undertaken as part of the TAR client engineering cycles, with the models seen not as necessary evils but rather being naturally integrated as useful elements for structuring discussions and supporting the outlined use cases.

Using the models in a real-world context also helped identify specific requirements for the models themselves and their presentation to stakeholders, including the necessity of adapting decision models to a local context, the need for a feedback loop to refactor changes made to local models to models with more global scope, the need to structure a large design space, and the need to model relationships among many design models. The basic elements of the decision models remained broadly similar to what was proposed in QOC; we needed only to add elements like technology options and components to address specific use cases. Finally, we need to give more thought to the presentation of models to support specific use cases, with emphasis placed on presenting only the least amount of information necessary for a potential use case in order to disturb the process at hand as little as possible.

In future work, we plan to perform further workshops as part of our ongoing TAR study. Through these workshops, we aim to refine and validate decision models for the identified areas of microservice design with our partner companies, scientific partners, and possibly with other companies. We are currently working on a tool to support this process of continuous communication and refinement.

Acknowledgement. The research reported in this paper has been supported by the Austrian Ministry for Transport, Innovation and Technology, the Federal Ministry of Science, Research and Economy, and the Province of Upper Austria in the frame of the COMET center SCCH.

References

1. Ali Babar, M., Dingsøyr, T., Lago, P., Van Vliet, H. (eds.): Software Architecture Knowledge Management: Theory and Practice. Springer, Heidelberg (2009)
2. Alshuqayran, N., Ali, N., Evans, R.: A systematic mapping study in microservice architecture. In: 2016 IEEE 9th International Conference on Service-Oriented Computing and Applications (SOCA), pp. 44–51, November 2016
3. Bass, L., Weber, I., Zhu, L.: DevOps: A Software Architect's Perspective. Addison-Wesley Professional, Boston (2015)
4. Bosch, J.: Software architecture: the next step. In: Oquendo, F., Warboys, B.C., Morrison, R. (eds.) EWSA 2004. LNCS, vol. 3047, pp. 194–199. Springer, Heidelberg (2004). doi:10.1007/978-3-540-24769-2_14
5. Capilla, R., Jansen, A., Tang, A., Avgeriou, P., Babar, M.A.: 10 years of software architecture knowledge management: practice and future. J. Syst. Softw. **116**, 191–205 (2015)
6. Dutoit, A.H., McCall, R., Mistrík, I., Paech, B. (eds.): Rationale Management in Software Engineering. Springer, Heidelberg (2006). doi:10.1007/978-3-540-30998-7. http://link.springer.com/10.1007/978-3-540-30998-7
7. Francesco, P.D., Malavolta, I., Lago, P.: Research on architecting microservices: trends, focus, and potential for industrial adoption. In: Proceedings of the 14th International Conference on Software Architecture (ICSA), Gothenburg, Sweden, April 2017
8. Gasson, S.: Rigor in grounded theory research: an interpretive perspective on generating theory from qualitative field studies. In: Whitman, M.E., Woszczynski, A.B. (eds.) The Handbook of Information Systems Research, pp. 79–102. Idea Group, Hershey (2004)
9. Haselböck, S., Weinreich, R.: Decision guidance models for microservice monitoring. In: IEEE International Workshop on Architecting with MicroServices (AMS), International Conference on Software Architecture Workshops (ICSAW 2017), Gothenburg, Sweden, April 2017
10. ISO/IEC/IEEE 42010–2011(E): Systems and software engineering - Architecture description. IEEE (2011). doi:10.1109/IEEESTD.2011.6129467
11. Jansen, A., Bosch, J.: Software architecture as a set of architectural design decisions. In: 5th Working IEEE/IFIP Conference on Software Architecture (WICSA 2005), pp. 109–120 (2005)
12. Lewis, G.A., Lago, P., Avgeriou, P.: A decision model for cyber-foraging systems. In: 13th Working IEEE/IFIP Conference on Software Architecture (WICSA), pp. 51–60, April 2016
13. Lewis, J., Fowler, M.: Microservices, Mar 2014. https://martinfowler.com/articles/microservices.html
14. Lytra, I., Tran, H., Zdun, U.: Supporting consistency between architectural design decisions and component models through reusable architectural knowledge transformations. In: Drira, K. (ed.) ECSA 2013. LNCS, vol. 7957, pp. 224–239. Springer, Heidelberg (2013). doi:10.1007/978-3-642-39031-9_20

15. MacLean, A., McKerlie, D.: Design space analysis and use-representations. In: Carroll, J.M. (ed.) Scenario-Based Design: Envisioning Work and Technology in System Development. Wiley, New York (1995)
16. MacLean, A., Young, R.M., Bellotti, V.M.E., Moran, T.P.: Questions, options, and criteria elements of design space analysis. Hum. Comput. Interact. **6**(3), 201–250 (1991). http://dx.doi.org/10.1207/s15327051hci0603&4_2
17. Miles, M.B., Huberman, A.M.: Qualitative Data Analysis: An Expanded Sourcebook. Sage, Thousand Oaks (1994)
18. Newman, S.: Building Microservices. O'Reilly Media Inc., Sebastopol (2015). http://shop.oreilly.com/product/0636920033158.do
19. Pahl, C., Jamshidi, P.: Microservices: a systematic mapping study. In: Proceedings of the 6th International Conference on Cloud Computing and Services Science - Volume 1: CLOSER, pp. 137–146 (2016)
20. Pohl, K., Böckle, G., van Der Linden, F.J.: Software Product Line Engineering: Foundations, Principles and Techniques. Springer Science & Business Media, Heidelberg (2005)
21. Richardson, C.: What are microservices?. http://microservices.io
22. Seaman, C.B.: Qualitative methods. In: Shull, F., Singer, J., Sjøberg, D.I.K. (eds.) Guide to Advanced Empirical Software Engineering, pp. 35–62. Springer, London (2008). doi:10.1007/978-1-84800-044-5_2
23. Tofan, D., Galster, M., Avgeriou, P., Schuitema, W.: Past and future of software architectural decisions a systematic mapping study. Inf. Softw. Technol. **56**(8), 850–872 (2014). http://www.sciencedirect.com/science/article/pii/S0950584914000706
24. Weinreich, R., Groher, I.: Software architecture knowledge management approaches and their support for knowledge management activities: a systematic literature review. Inf. Softw. Technol. **80**, 265–286 (2016). http://www.sciencedirect.com/science/article/pii/S0950584916301707
25. Wieringa, R., Moralı, A.: Technical action research as a validation method in information systems design science. In: Peffers, K., Rothenberger, M., Kuechler, B. (eds.) DESRIST 2012. LNCS, vol. 7286, pp. 220–238. Springer, Heidelberg (2012). doi:10.1007/978-3-642-29863-9_17
26. Wieringa, R.J.: Design Science Methodology for Information Systems and Software Engineering. Springer, Heidelberg (2014). http://www.springer.com/de/book/9783662438381
27. Wolff, E.: Microservices: Flexible Software Architecture. Addison-Wesley Professional, New Jersey (2016)
28. Zdun, U.: Systematic pattern selection using pattern language grammars and design space analysis. Softw. Pract. Exp. **37**(9), 983–1016 (2007). http://onlinelibrary.wiley.com/doi/10.1002/spe.799/abstract
29. Zimmermann, O., Wegmann, L., Koziolek, H., Goldschmidt, T.: Architectural decision guidance across projects - problem space modeling, decision backlog management and cloud computing knowledge. In: 2015 12th Working IEEE/IFIP Conference on Software Architecture (WICSA), pp. 85–94 (2015)
30. Zimmermann, O., Miksovic, C.: Decisions required vs. decisions made connecting enterprise architects and solution architects via guidance models. In: Aligning Enterprise, System, and Software Architectures, p. 176 (2012)

Software Architecture Risk Containers

Andrew Leigh[✉], Michel Wermelinger, and Andrea Zisman

School of Computing and Communications, The Open University, Milton Keynes, UK
andrew.leigh@open.ac.uk

Abstract. Our motivation is to determine whether risks such as implementation error-proneness can be isolated into three types of containers at design time. This paper identifies several container candidates in other research that fit the risk container concept. Two industrial case studies were used to determine which of three container types tested is most effective at isolating and predicting at design time the risk of implementation error-proneness. We found that Design Rule Containers were more effective than Use Case and Resource Containers.

1 Introduction

According to Bass et al. (2012) 161 historical projects were analysed by Boehm and Turner who found that the bigger the project is, the more architecture risk assessment is needed to avoid rework. No results for the comparative performance of architecture evaluation methods for isolating risks were found in existing work. Not knowing the risk scope limits the ability to estimate the risk impact and cost of mitigations. Our proposition is to investigate whether it is more effective to base risk assessment around *risk containers* that isolate related risk-inducing elements.

In this paper, we test three types of risk containers for their ability to *isolate the risk of implementation error-proneness at the design stage*, namely *Design Rule*, *Use Case* and *Resource Containers*. If container level design metrics that indicate a design might be complex to implement (e.g. coupling metrics), can be used to rank containers, then containers can be used to predict the areas of greatest risk. If the degree of element sharing between containers is low, they are said to be element isolating. Furthermore, if containers are risk predicting and element isolating, they must also be risk isolating because the elements in the container are inducing the risk, and they are not shared with other containers. Risk isolating containers would enable practitioners to identify the risk areas and understand their scope in terms of the affected elements. In this paper we address the following research question:

Can the risk of implementation error-proneness be isolated within risk containers based on the design time architectural description?

The remainder of this paper is structured as follows. Section 2 lists the existing work that most closely fits the risk container concept. Section 3 presents the method used to test three types of containers using two industrial case studies. Section 4 presents analysis of the results. Finally, conclusions are drawn in Sect. 5.

© Springer International Publishing AG 2017
A. Lopes and R. de Lemos (Eds.): ECSA 2017, LNCS 10475, pp. 171–179, 2017.
DOI: 10.1007/978-3-319-65831-5_12

2 Background

We next present existing work that most closely fits the proposed concept of architecture risk containers. This section is organised by the container types we synthesised from the commonalities we found between architecture evaluation techniques.

Attack Graph Containers are tuples containing nodes that an attacker can interact with to exploit a vulnerability in a goal component (Said et al. 2011). UML models are used to estimate component failure probability to assess scenario security risks. Probabilities assigned to graph elements are used to calculate the probability of failure for the goal component. Since the tuple isolates the elements associated with the risk, attack graphs fit the risk container concept.

Design Rule Containers (DRSpaces) proposed by Xiao et al. (2014), are graphs based on the key interfaces (design rules) that split an architecture into independent modules. The vertices are related classes and the edges are the relationships between those related classes. Xiao et al. concluded that if a leading file of a DRSpace is error-prone, a large proportion of the other DRSpace files are likely to be error-prone, and that most error-prone files will be found in just a few DRSpaces. Xiao et al. used a clustering algorithm called Design Rule Hierarchy (DRH) proposed by Wong et al. (2009) to extract DRSpaces from source code. Wong et al. were motivated to develop the DRH algorithm to separate modules of related elements in UML designs to maximise developer parallelism. Leigh et al. (2016) manually populated DRSpaces from UML class diagrams taken from an industrial case study. The term 'Design Rule Containers' is used to standardise terminology in this paper.

Component Containers contain the classes a component is composed of. Stevanetic and Zdun (2016) calculated design metrics from UML to indicate the understandability of components. Their results show that if the internal relationships of a component are difficult to comprehend it might be difficult to maintain and therefore the classes it is composed of isolate the risk. Abdelmoez et al. (2006) estimated requirement maturity and traced it to components to determine component change probability and identify maintainability risks. Goseva-Popstojanova et al. (2003) and Yacoub and Ammar (2002) calculated complexity metrics from designs to assess reliability risks of components. These contributions suggest maintainability and reliability risks could be isolated within Component Containers.

Resource Containers contain the elements dependent on a resource such as a component, service or data store. Stevanetic and Zdun (2016) also showed that if the component functionality is difficult to comprehend, developers might misunderstand how to use it, leading to more errors in dependent code. A Resource Container could be used to isolate elements dependent upon the resource component to isolate the risk.

Scenario Containers contain the elements that support a specific scenario. Williams and Smith (1998) and Cortellessa et al. (2005) used resource estimates (e.g. CPU) to determine whether a scenario is likely to exceed a non-functional requirement. Their methods are limited by their dependency on the accuracy of design time resource estimates and assumptions about the target platform. Their results suggest Scenario Containers could isolate performance related risks at design time.

Use Case Containers contain the elements that support a specific use case. Mustafiz et al. (2008) assign a success probability to each use case step. Use cases are then analysed to compare the achievable reliability with the required reliability. The research by Mustafiz et al. and Goseva-Popstojanova et al. suggests reliability risks can be isolated to the set of operations or classes that fulfil the use case.

Despite the methods found being suggestive of risk containers, little evidence about their risk isolation properties is provided. No results regarding the comparative perform-ance of risk containers types for isolating different risks were found. These limitations mean practitioners have no advice for selecting which containers to use for specific risks. For example, the work of Abdelmoez et al. (2006), Xiao et al. (2014), Leigh et al. (2016), and Stevanovic and Zdun (2016) identifies Design Rule and Component Containers as container candidates for maintainability risks. Whilst we know something about specific cases where each have been effective, their relative performance for isolating risks remains unknown.

Sections 3 and 4 present our most recent work to understand how effectively different design time risk containers isolate the risk of implementation error-proneness.

3   Method

This section describes the method used to test how well three risk container types isolate at *design time* the *risk of implementation error-proneness*. These three risk container types have been chosen due to the different ways they split the architecture. Design Rule (DR) Containers group elements subordinate to modularising design rules, Use Case (UC) Containers group elements supporting use cases, and the Resource Containers group elements that depend upon a database table (as opposed to resources such as CPU).

3.1   Risk Container Creation

DR Containers were constructed using the method described in Leigh et al. (2016). Each design rule class was used as a container basis before expansion with subordinate classes by consulting design relationships. For example, in Fig. 1 element c2 is the basis of DR Container A because it is an abstract class. Elements c3 and c5 are then added to that container because they are sub-classes. One UC Container was created per use case and included each class referenced by the use case. Note how Fig. 1 shows that UC Container D contains all the elements on the use case sequence diagram. Resource Containers were populated with all elements dependent upon a specific database table by seeding with the table encapsulation element and recursively adding elements where the encapsula-tion element is the *child* of a relationship. This can be seen in Fig. 1 where element c4 is the basis for container D and c1 and c3 are added because they are recursively dependent upon c4. Additional implementation classes were added to the initially popu-lated containers using strict name conventions. This was necessary because each design element was realised by an interface and an implementation. Therefore, when an inter-face was allocated to a container its one to one implementation class was also added.

Unlike Xiao et al. (2014) who used automation, our containers were populated by manual analysis.

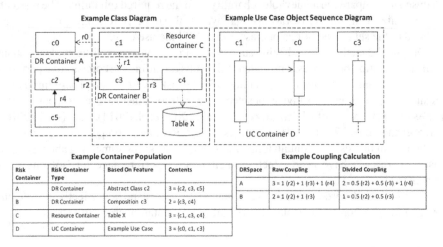

Fig. 1. Example container population and coupling calculation

Control containers were created for each container type by randomly allocating the same elements in the test containers to the same number of control containers. The average number of elements per control container and the average number of containers per element was approximately the same as the test containers. The control containers were used to determine whether basing containers on related elements is a better indicator of error-proneness than random population. The control containers are based on the mean values from ten sets of random assignments per container type.

Coupling is a significant contributory factor in the complexity of software (Bass et al. 2012). Thus, it is expected that containers having elements with greater coupling are more likely to be error-prone during implementation. Such a correlation would imply that error-proneness has been isolated to a degree. That is because the error-proneness is associated with coupling stemming from the architectural feature (e.g. Design Rule, Use Case or Resource) on which the risk container is based. If the architectural feature were to be removed, the risk associated with it would be eliminated (and potentially replaced with risk attached to substitute features). Thus, the presence of a correlation between feature based containers and implementation error-proneness implies isolation to the scope of the features on which the containers have been based.

Tightly coupled elements are more likely to change together when software is developed and maintained due to the ripple effect. As stated by Bass et al. (2012), 'reducing the strength of coupling between two modules A and B will decrease the expected cost of any medication that affects A' (p. 122). Therefore, a more precise answer to our research question can be obtained by determining to what degree containers share elements and how much of the coupling is between elements in the same container. That is because if containers are risk isolating the architectural elements should exist in few containers and elements should have less coupling to other elements outside of their own container.

As per Fig. 1, design coupling is calculated for all elements in the container for relationships like aggregation, composition and dependencies if the element is the relationship parent, and generalisations if the element is the child. This metric indicates how tightly coupled container members are to other elements in the architecture.

Error-proneness is defined as the files having more confirmed bugs per thousand lines of released code (KLOC) than a threshold. We used again the 75th percentile of bugs per KLOC as the threshold (Leigh et al. 2016). Bug identifiers were extracted from the Subversion commit messages for each implementation file.

Using our method, we can compare the container types tested by how well they implicitly isolate error-proneness based on correlation between design time container level coupling and implementation error-proneness, and how well they explicitly isolate individual architectural elements and internal coupling. Thus, a strong and significant correlation between coupling and error-proneness, in combination with high isolation metrics, would answer the research question affirmatively.

3.2   Metric Calculation

The following risk container type metrics were used to test their relative capability for predicting the risk of implementation error-proneness and being element isolating:

- *Number of Containers (N):* number of containers the design has been split into.
- *Percent Container Coverage (PCC):* percentage of all implementation elements that were allocated to risk containers. This metric indicates how much of the implementation was represented in the design.
- *Spearman's rank correlation ρ and confidence level α between design coupling and implementation error-proneness:* Spearman's rank correlation coefficient ρ and confidence level α is computed to indicate the association between container level coupling and percentage of error-prone files. The correlation indicates how well the container type predicts and implicitly isolates error-proneness.
- *Mean Containers Per Class (CPC-M):* mean number of containers each element has been allocated to. This metric indicates the average amount of element sharing between containers and represents the degree of element isolation.
- *Upper Quartile Containers Per Class (CPC-UQ):* 75th percentile of containers each element has been allocated to. This metric is used to confirm the degree of element isolation within containers.
- *Mean Percent Internal Coupling (IC-M):* mean percentage of container level coupling that is between two elements inside the same container. This metric indicates the degree of coupling isolated within containers.
- *Upper Quartile Internal Coupling (IC-UQ):* 75th percentile percentage of container level coupling that is between two elements inside the same container. This metric is used to confirm the degree of coupling isolated within containers.

- *Percent Single Neat Container Change Sets (NCC):* percentage of Subversion change sets that fit neatly inside a single risk container. This metric indicates how well containers isolate source code edits made to change the software and fix bugs.

4   Analysis

Two cases studies from the same software company have been used to evaluate our method. The company prefers to remain anonymous, but their name is registered with the Open University in an intellectual property agreement.

4.1   Case Study 1 – API

The first case study is a bespoke Application Programming Interface (API) that enables clients to integrate with a database in an enterprise solution. The architectural description of the API is a UML model and the implementation contains 87.85 KLOC of object-oriented Java code. Table 1 shows the API results.

Table 1. Case study 1 results

API case study									
API case study	Coverage		Risk predicting		Element isolating				
Container type	N	PCC	ρ	α	CPC-M	CPC-UQ	IC-M	IC-UQ	NCC
Control DR Containers	13	80.90	-0.05	>0.100	1.08	1.00	9.03	12.48	26.40
Control UC Containers	36	12.13	0.38	0.025	5.29	6.60	12.66	17.24	0.49
Control Resource Containers	23	32.81	0.04	>0.100	6.37	9.00	24.09	28.53	0.00
DR Containers	13	**80.89**	**0.85**	**0.001**	**1.08**	**1.00**	**35.33**	**55.56**	**41.33**
UC Containers	36	12.13	0.71	0.001	4.74	5.00	18.52	23.08	2.22
Resource Containers	23	30.81	0.63	0.001	7.77	8.00	**37.37**	**41.54**	0.00

DR Containers have the strongest (ρ) and most significant (α) correlation. The random assignment of elements to containers resulted in a negative correlation for the control DR Containers. DR Containers had the lowest mean containers per class (CPC-M). On average, each element is allocated to just over one DR Container. This contrasts with UC Containers and Resource Containers where each element is allocated on average to approximately 5 and 8 containers respectively. The 75th percentile (CPC-UQ) confirms that elements are distributed across fewer DR Containers than UC and Resource Containers. The mean percentage of coupling where both related elements are inside the same container (IC-M) is greatest for Resource Containers and DR Containers. However, the 75th percentile (IC-UQ) is greater for DR Containers which suggests they typically have less external coupling than Resource Containers.

The percentage of Subversion change sets fitting neatly inside a single container (NCC) is greatest for DR Containers. This result is expected because DR Containers have the highest IC-M/IC-UQ and lowest CPC-M/CPC-UQ, which suggests that DR Containers better isolate the related source code files developers must edit when making changes or fixing bugs in the software. All test containers have stronger correlation and are more risk isolating than their corresponding control containers.

In Leigh et al. (2016) we asked developers to nominate areas of the API that were difficult to implement and maintain. We observed that 2 of 3 nominations fitted neatly inside a DR Container. It is worth noting that none of the nominations could be matched to the API UC Containers. Some elements belonging to the nominated areas could be matched to Resource Containers but a Resource Container that fitted the whole nomination could not be found. This further strengthens the evidence for DR Containers being the most isolating container type in the API case study.

4.2   Case Study 2 – Server

The second case study is concerned with the Server side modules of a COTS data management application. The Server architecture is documented in MS Word documents and the implementation contains 333.55 KLOC of procedural Oracle PL/SQL code. Table 2 shows the Server results.

Table 2. Case study 2 results

Server case study	Server case study								
	Coverage		Risk predicting		Element isolating				
Container type	N	PCC	ρ	α	CPC-M	CPC-UQ	IC-M	IC-UQ	NCC
Control DR Containers	9	12.50	–0.07	>0.100	1.14	1.00	7.45	6.25	23.48
Control UC Containers	68	5.60	0.03	>0.100	6.16	9.70	0.04	0.00	3.26
Control Resource Containers	16	9.48	0.02	>0.100	2.64	5.20	9.19	10.99	0.00
DR Containers	9	**12.50**	**0.92**	**0.001**	**1.14**	**1.00**	**48.61**	**100.00**	**23.19**
UC Containers	68	5.60	0.32	0.005	5.69	8.00	0.00	0.00	3.26
Resource Containers	16	9.48	0.31	0.250	2.77	6.00	15.14	6.00	0.00

DR Containers again had the strongest (ρ) and most significant (α) correlation. The strong correlation observed for UC Containers in the API case study was not reproduced. DR Containers again have the lowest mean CPC-M and CPC-UQ indicating elements are shared between fewer DR Containers than UC and Resource Containers. DR Containers also have the highest IC-M and IC-UQ which again suggests DR Containers have less coupling to external elements. The change set isolating results for the API were not reproduced in the Server because NCC is approximately the same for the test containers as their corresponding controls.

In both case studies DR Containers cover more of the design (PCC) than UC and Resource Containers. This means more of the risk was isolated into DR Containers. The much lower PCC values calculated for the server were due to more time having passed since the design was produced. This meant more implementation elements were present that were not documented in the design.

5   Conclusion

This paper presents the results of testing three types of risk containers to determine their relative efficacy at isolating the risk of implementation error-proneness at design time. The three types tested were Xiao et al.'s (2014) DRSpaces, adapted to split the architectural design by modularising design rules, and two novel containers that group elements supporting use cases, and elements dependent upon databases.

Results from two industrial projects suggest DR Containers are the most effective at isolating the risk of implementation error-proneness at design time. This is due to them having the strongest correlation between container level design coupling and implementation error-proneness and least amount of element sharing and external coupling in both case studies. The results strengthen our previous evidence (Leigh et al. 2016) that DR Containers can be used for design time assessment of software architectures for the risk of implementation error-proneness, based on UML class diagrams or module dependency graphs.

Whilst DR Containers are the most effective of the three container types tested, even more effective risk containers may remain to be found. Further investigation is also needed to understand why the high number of change sets fitting neatly inside a single DR Container in the API was not observed in the Server case study. Furthermore, work is required to determine whether container based risk assessment is generalizable for other risks, and if so, whether the same containers or others work best, and at which levels of architecture abstraction different container types are effective. More work is also required to determine how meaningful different container types are to software practitioners and how durable they are throughout the software development life-cycle. These questions represent opportunities for future work.

References

Abdelmoez, W.M., Goseva-Popstojanova, K., Ammar, H.H.: Methodology for maintainability-based risk assessment. In: Annual Reliability and Maintainability Symposium, RAMS 2006, pp. 337–342. IEEE (2006)

Bass, L., Clement, P., Kazman, R.: Software Architecture in Practice, 3rd edn., pp. 121–124 and p. 280. Addison Wesley, Reading, USA (2012)

Cortellessa, V., Goseva-Popstojanova, K., Appukkutty, K., Guedem, A.R., Hassan, A., Elnaggar, R., Abdelmoez, W., Ammar, H.H.: Model-based performance risk analysis. IEEE Trans. Softw. Eng. **31**(1), 3–20 (2005)

Goseva-Popstojanova, K., Hassan, A., Guedem, A., Abdelmoez, W., Nassar, D.E.M., Ammar, H., Mili, A.: Architectural-level risk analysis using UML. IEEE Trans. Softw. Eng. **29**(10), 946–960 (2003)

Leigh, A., Wermelinger, M., Zisman, A.: An evaluation of design rule spaces as risk containers. In: Proceedings of the 13th Working International Conference on Software Architecture (WICSA), pp. 295–298. IEEE (2016)

Mustafiz, S., Sun, X., Kienzle, J., Vangheluwe, H.: Model-driven assessment of system dependability. J. Softw. Syst. Model. **7**(4), 487–502 (2008)

Said, F.H., Ammar, H.H., Valenti, M.C., Ross, A., Lai, H.J.: Security-based Risk Assessment for Software Architecture, pp. 1–126. West Virginia University Libraries (2011)

Stevanetic, S., Zdun, U.: Exploring the understandability of components in architectural component models using component level metrics and participants' experience. In: 19th International ACM SIGSOFT Symposium on Component-Based Software Engineering (CBSE), pp. 1–6. IEEE (2011)

Williams, L.G., Smith, C.U.: Performance evaluation of software architectures. In: Proceedings of the 1st International Workshop on Software and Performance, pp. 164–177. ACM (1998)

Wong, S., Cai, Y., Valetto, G., Simeonov, G., Sethi, K.: Design rule hierarchies and parallelism in software development tasks. In: Proceedings of the 24th International Conference on Automated Software Engineering (ASE), pp. 197–208. ACM (2009)

Xiao, L., Cai, Y., Kazman, R.: Design rule spaces: a new form of architecture insight. In: Proceedings of the 36th International Conference on Software Engineering, pp. 967–977. ACM (2014)

Yacoub, S.M., Ammar, H.H.: A methodology for architecture-level reliability risk analysis. IEEE Trans. Softw. Eng. **28**(6), 529–547 (2002)

Software Architecture Practice

A Model for Prioritization of Software Architecture Effort

Eoin Woods[1]([⊠]) [iD] and Rabih Bashroush[2] [iD]

[1] Endava Limited, 125 Old Broad Street, London EC2N 1AR, UK
eoin.woods@endava.com
[2] University of East London, University Way, London E16 2RD, UK
r.bashroush@uel.ac.uk

Abstract. As part of our software architecture research and practice we have found that a common difficulty for new architects is knowing where to focus their effort to maximise their effectiveness. This led us to wonder whether successful experienced architects have reusable heuristics or guidelines that they follow to help them prioritise their work. To investigate this we have performed a study using semi-structured interviews to explore how experienced software architects prioritise their activities in order to maximise their effectiveness. From the primary data collected through the interviews we have synthesised a simple model that organises and explains the heuristics that we found to be common across a number of experienced software architects.

Keywords: Software architecture · Software architecture decision making · Software architect effectiveness

1 Introduction

In our research and practice in the field of software architecture, we have noticed and experienced how complex it is for software architects to prioritise their work. The software architect's responsibilities are broad and in principle they can be involved in almost any technical aspect of a project from requirements to operational concerns.

However we observe that successful software architects appear to be very good at focusing their effort effectively, which led us to wonder how they achieve this. They may use generic time management techniques (like [1]) but we were interested in commonly used, role-specific, heuristics which could be taught to new architects.

We decided to investigate this via a questionnaire-based study of a group of experienced architects. We discovered that there are common heuristics which experienced architects use to prioritise their work and we have created a model to capture them.

In this paper, we explain the approach we took and present the model that we created from the results that we obtained. The contribution of our work is not specifically the heuristics in our model, indeed most of them are quite familiar to experienced practitioners, but rather the organisation of the heuristics and the validation that they are used by experienced practitioners to guide their work. We believe that this makes the model potentially useful as a reminder for experienced practitioners and as a teaching aid for new architects who are learning how to fulfil the role.

© Springer International Publishing AG 2017
A. Lopes and R. de Lemos (Eds.): ECSA 2017, LNCS 10475, pp. 183–190, 2017.
DOI: 10.1007/978-3-319-65831-5_13

2   Related Work

When we started investigating this topic, we were primarily interested in how practitioners really worked however we also performed a literature search to find related work from the research community.

We did not find any studies investigating our specific topic, but an architectural method which helps architects to direct their effort is Risk and Cost Driven Architecture (RCDA) [12]. This method transforms the architect's approach from defining finished architectural structures at the start of a project, to use the risk and cost of open decisions to prioritise the architect's work throughout the project. Another practitioner oriented approach that stresses the importance of risk in guiding architecture work is [6]. We were also interested to find some very specific advice from a very experienced architect and researcher [10] that architects should spend 50% of their time on architecting, 25% on inbound communication and 25% on outbound communication.

In the research domain, we found a research community interested in prioritisation of requirements [3, 7], but this only addresses part of an architect's work.

Finally, there is a large amount of mainstream business and self-help literature on time management (such as the well-known [1, 9] and some more focused on software engineering such as [5]) however we were interested in architecture specific approaches and heuristics rather than more general advice.

3   Research Method

When planning this research, we selected a qualitative research approach because we needed to explore the "lived-experiences" of expert practitioners by asking them questions to encourage reflection and insight [13] rather than assessing performance or alignment with specific practices via quantitative means.

We chose to gather our primary data using semi-structured interviews, where we provided the interviewees with a written introduction to the question we wanted to answer and then some specific questions to start their thought processes.

The analysis of the primary data was performed using a simple application of Grounded Theory as it is a suitable method for theory building, to understand the relationships between abstract concepts [4], which described our situation and needs very closely. We performed initial coding on the primary data and then refined this with a focused coding exercise. As suggested in [13] the process of collection and analysis was a parallel, iterative process, rather than a linear one with fixed phases.

This exercise produced a set of themes that classify the heuristics that the architects use, as well as the heuristics themselves. A heuristic had to be mentioned by at least three of the participants (which represented a third of them) for us to consider it significant enough to be included in the model. We combined the themes and heuristics to form a simple model of how experienced architects go about prioritizing their effort.

4   The Study

Our primary data gathering was performed using a semi-structured, face-to-face survey of 8 experienced software architecture practitioners working across 4 countries.

We found the participants by approaching suitable individuals from our professional networks. We were looking for practitioners who had a minimum of 10 years' professional experience and who worked as architects in the information systems domain (rather than architects from – for example – embedded systems).

We focused on the information systems domain because we know from experience that working practices differ between professional domains like information systems and embedded systems. Hence, we thought it more likely that we could create a useful model if we limited ourselves to one broad domain, at least initially.

We deliberately selected candidates that we knew differed from each other in organisation, specialisation and geography to get a reasonably diverse population and avoid obvious sample bias (we discuss the threat of sample bias further in Sect. 6).

Some characteristics of the participants in the study are summarised in the graphs in Fig. 1. As can be seen they represent a range of experience, role type and country.

Fig. 1. Study participants (8 in total)

We used a semi-structured interview format with a written introduction to the question which each interviewee read before being asked a standard set of open ended questions which explored how they went about prioritisation of architecture work and any specific factors that they used to guide them.

The question we asked during the interview was "how can architects concentrate their attention so that they are most effective?" The more specific questions we asked the interviewees to stimulate thought were:

- How do you go about this in your work?
- What factors do you consider when prioritising your attention?
- Do you consider what to focus on? Or what not to focus on?
- For example, how do you prioritise architectural governance compared to other aspects of the project?

The interviewer asked additional questions to understand the answers fully or to encourage the interviewee to add more detail or fill in ambiguous aspects of the answer.

The process of initial coding of the primary data resulted in 25 items, which could be associated with at least one of the interviews. A further focused coding process revealed that there were 9 underlying heuristics which appeared to be significant to the participants in the study and then a further analysis iteration lead to the identification of three categories of prioritisation heuristic which we use to structure our model.

5   A Model for Prioritising Architectural Effort

5.1   The Model

Our heuristic model for focusing architectural effort is shown in Fig. 2.

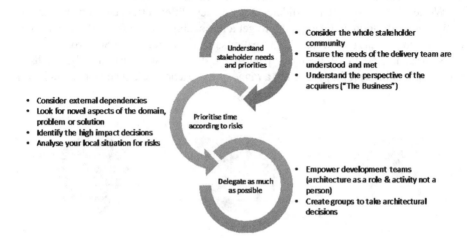

Fig. 2. Model for focusing architectural attention

The three categories of heuristic that the study revealed were firstly, the need to focus on stakeholder needs, secondly, the importance of considering risks when deciding on where to focus effort, and finally the importance of spending time to achieve effective delegation of responsibilities. These categories form the structure of our model, and remind the architect of the general ways in which they should prioritise their efforts. The categories and heuristics are explained in more detail in Sect. 5.2.

It is important to understand the nature of this model and how it should be used. It is not a prescriptive process for architects to follow or a process for developing an architecture. This model is an aide memoire to organise a set of heuristics that experienced practitioners appear to find useful when prioritising their work. While we believe this to be a useful model to teach trainee architects, and a useful reminder for experienced architects, it is necessary to apply the model in a context sensitive manner, within whatever method that the architect is using to develop software architectures.

5.2   Content of the Model

Understand the Stakeholder Needs and Priorities. The first theme which emerged strongly in our study was focusing on the needs and priorities of the stakeholders involved in the situation. The principle that architecture work involves working closely with stakeholders is widely agreed [2, 14] and this theme reinforces that. Architects need to focus significant effort to make sure that stakeholder needs and priorities are understood to maximise focus on the critical success factors for a project and maximise the chances of its success. Three specific heuristics to achieve this which emerged from the study are:

- Consider the whole stakeholder community. Spend time understanding the different groups in the stakeholder community and avoid the mistake of just considering obvious stakeholder groups like end-users, acquirers and the development team. As the architecture methods referenced above note, ignoring important stakeholders (like operational staff or auditors) can prevent the project meeting its goals and cause significant problems on the path to production operation.
- Ensure that the needs of the delivery team are understood and met. Spend sufficient time to ensure that the delivery team can be effective. What is the team good at? What does it know? What does it not know? What skill and knowledge gaps does it have? These areas need attention early in the project so that architecture work avoids risks caused by the capabilities of the team and that time is taken to support and develop the team to address significant weaknesses.
- Understand the perspective and perceptions of the acquirers of the system. Acquirers are a key stakeholder group who judge its success and usually have strategic and budgetary control, so can halt the project before delivery if they are unhappy. Specifically addressing this group's needs, perceptions and concerns emerged as an important factor for some of the experienced architects in our study. Acquirers are often distant from the day-to-day reality of a project and need clear communication to understand their concerns and ensure that they have a realistic view of the project.

Prioritise Effort According to Risks (Driven by Impact x Probability). During a project, an effective approach to prioritising architectural attention is to use a risk driven approach to identify the most important tasks. If the significant risks are understood and mitigated then enough architecture work has probably been completed. If significant risks are open then more architecture work is needed. The specific heuristics to consider for risk assessment are:

- Consider external dependencies. Understand your external dependencies because you have little control over them and they need architectural attention early in the project and whenever things change.
- Look for novel aspects of domain, problem and solution. Another useful heuristic, from the experience of our study participants, is to focus on novelty in your project. What is unfamiliar? What problems have you not solved before? Which technology is unproven? The answers to these questions highlight risks and the participants in our study used them to direct their effort to the most important risks to address.

- Identify the high impact decisions. Prioritise architecture work that will help to mitigate risks where many people would be affected by a problem (e.g. problems with the development environment or problems that will prevent effective operation) or where the risk could endanger the programme (e.g. missing regulatory constraints).
- Analyse your local situation for risks. Consider the local factors unique to your situation, which you will be aware of due to the knowledge you have of the domain, problem and solution. It is impossible to give more specific guidance on this heuristic as every situation is different, but the participants in our study noted the importance of "situational awareness" [15] that allows the architect to find and address the risks specific to the local environment (perhaps due to organisational factors, specific technical challenges, domain complexities or business constraints).

Delegate as Much as Possible. Delegation was an unexpected theme that emerged in the study. The architects who mentioned this theme viewed themselves as a potential bottleneck in a project and delegation and empowerment of others was a way to minimize this. Delegation was also seen as a way of freeing the architect to focus on the aspects of the project that they had to focus on rather than all the other aspects that they could possibly get involved in.

The general message of this theme is to delegate as much architecture work as possible to the person or group best suited to perform it, to prevent individuals becoming project bottlenecks, allow architects to spend more time on risk identification and mitigation, and to spread architectural knowledge through the organisation. The heuristics that were identified to help achieve this are:

- Empower the development teams. To allow delegation and work sharing, architects need to empower (and trust) the teams that they work with. This allows governance to become a shared responsibility and architecture to be viewed as an activity rather than something that is only performed by one person or a small group. This causes architectural knowledge, effort and accountability to be spread across the organisation, creates shared ownership, reduces the load on any one individual and prevents reliance on a single individual from delaying progress.
- Create groups to take architectural responsibilities. A related heuristic is to formalise delegation somewhat and create groups of people to be accountable for specific aspects of architectural work. For example, in a large development programme, an architecture review board can be created to review and approve significant architectural decisions. Such a group can involve a wide range of expertise from across the programme and beyond, so freeing a lead architect from much of the effort involved in gathering and understanding the details of key decisions, while maintaining effective oversight to allow risks to be controlled and technical coherence maintained. Similarly, a specific group of individuals could be responsible for resilience and disaster recovery for a large programme, allowing them to specialise and focus on this complex area, and allowing a lead architect to confidently delegate to them, knowing that they will have the focus and expertise to address this aspect of the architecture.

6   Threats to Validity

There are potential limitations to any qualitative study, including our work, and there are potential threats to its validity. Although we do not believe that any of these seriously threaten the usefulness of our study, it is important to acknowledge them.

There are four main types of threat to the validity of a study like this, namely construct, internal, external and conclusion validity as defined in [11].

Construct and *internal* validity relate to the effectiveness and integrity of the implementation of the research methodology adopted. In our case, sample bias could affect the study due to the small size, specific experience, and regional distribution of our sample of practitioners and author bias could be a problem because the authors of this study are involved in software architecture research and practice. We addressed the former by deliberately inviting a fairly diverse set of practitioners to participate in the study and we plan to address this weakness more robustly by validating the model with a much larger group. Author bias was addressed by careful construction and execution of the interviews, to avoid leading the participants to any specific answers.

External validity ensures the applicability of the results of the study beyond its initial scope and *conclusion* validity ensures the validity of the conclusions drawn. In our case, we believe we avoid these risks through the reasonable diversity we achieved in our participants and because we did not have any preconceived ideas of likely answers and did not suggest any answers to the participants in the written material or verbally and, we drew our conclusions (i.e. the model) using grounded theory and we believe that this process will largely address risks to our conclusion validity.

7   Future Work

We have created a candidate heuristic model for guiding architects through the process of prioritising their effort to maximise their effectiveness. The next step in the work is to construct a simple questionnaire to explore the usefulness and credibility of the model for a much larger number of practitioners. We believe that this will provide us with a strong validation or refutation of it.

If the model proves to be valid and found to be useful by a significant majority of a larger study group then we would aim to publicise it in practitioner circles via conference sessions and short articles in practitioner-oriented web and print publications.

8   Conclusion

Our experience and informal discussion with architects over many years suggested that they find it difficult to decide how to focus their effort to maximise their effectiveness. We were interested in how practitioners solved this problem and if there were commonly used heuristics. To investigate this, we used a semi-structured interview process with eight experienced practitioners and used Grounded Theory to analyse the results.

The conclusion of our initial study is that there are some shared heuristics which practitioners use, but that the community is not aware that the heuristics are widely known. We found that the heuristics clustered into three groups: focus the architects attention on stakeholders, use their time to address specific risks and delegate as much as possible, in order to give them as much time for architecture work as possible.

These findings are not completely unexpected and many of the heuristics are familiar. However, neither the participants or ourselves knew that these were the key heuristics before we undertook the study, so we believe that the model we have created will have value as a teaching aid and as a reminder to experienced practitioners. This is preliminary work based on a small study, so to validate its usefulness, we plan to continue this work with a much wider, questionnaire based study to find out whether a larger group of practitioners finds the model useful and credible.

References

1. Allen, D.: Getting Things Done: The Art of Stress-free Productivity, 2nd edn. Piatkus, London (2015)
2. Bass, L., Clements, P., Kazman, R.: Software Architecture in Practice, 3rd edn. Addison Wesley, Upper Saddle River (2012)
3. Berander, P., Andrews, A.: Requirements prioritization. In: Aurum, A., Wohlin, C. (eds.) Engineering and Managing Software Requirements, pp. 69–94. Springer, Heidelberg (2005)
4. Charmaz, K.: Constructing Grounded Theory: A Practical Guide through Qualitative Analysis. Sage, London (2006)
5. De Marco, T.: Slack: Getting Past Burn-out, Busywork, and the Myth of Total Efficiency. Dorset House, New York (2001)
6. Fairbanks, G.: Just Enough Software Architecture, A Risk Driven Approach. Marshall & Brainerd, Boulder (2010)
7. Herrmann, A., Daneva, M.: Requirements prioritization based on benefit and cost prediction: an agenda for future research. In: Tetsuo, T. (ed.) 16th IEEE International Requirements Engineering, RE 2008. IEEE (2008)
8. Karlsson, J., Ryan, K.: A cost-value approach for prioritizing requirements. IEEE Softw. 14(5), 67–74 (1997)
9. Koch, K.: The 80/20 Principle: The Secret of Achieving More with Less. Nicholas Brearley Publishing, London (2007)
10. Kruchten, P.: What do software architects really do? J. Syst. Softw. 81(12), 2413–2416 (2008)
11. Matt, G.E., Cook, T.D.: Threats to the validity of research synthesis. In: Cooper, H., Hedges, L.V. (eds.) The Handbook of Research Synthesis, pp. 503–520. Russell Sage Foundation, New York (1994)
12. Poort, E.R., van Vliet, H.: RCDA: architecting as a risk-and cost management discipline. J. Syst. Softw. 85(9), 1995–2013 (2012)
13. Reimer, F.J., Quartaroli, M.T., Lapan, S.D.: Qualitative Research: An Introduction to Methods and Designs. Wiley, London (2012)
14. Rozanski, N., Woods, E.: Software systems architecture, working with stakeholders using viewpoints and perspectives, 2nd edn. Addison Wesley, Upper Saddle River (2011)
15. Wikipedia, Situational Awareness. https://en.wikipedia.org/wiki/Situation_awareness. Accessed 10 Apr 2017

Architectural Assumptions
and Their Management
in Industry – An Exploratory Study

Chen Yang[1,2], Peng Liang[1(⊠)], Paris Avgeriou[2], Ulf Eliasson[3,4],
Rogardt Heldal[4], and Patrizio Pelliccione[4]

[1] State Key Lab of Software Engineering, School of Computer Science,
Wuhan University, Wuhan 430072, China
liangp@whu.edu.cn
[2] Department of Mathematics and Computing Science, University of Groningen,
Nijenborgh 9, 9747 AG Groningen, The Netherlands
[3] Volvo Cars, Volvo Jacobs Väg, 405 31 Gothenburg, Sweden
[4] Department of Computer Science and Engineering, Chalmers University
of Technology and University of Gothenburg, 412 96 Gothenburg, Sweden

Abstract. As an important type of architectural knowledge, architectural assumptions should be well managed in projects. However, little empirical research has been conducted regarding architectural assumptions and their management in software development. In this paper, we conducted an exploratory case study with twenty-four architects to analyze architectural assumptions and their management in industry. In this study, we confirmed certain findings from our previous survey on architectural assumptions (e.g., neither the term nor the concept of architectural assumption is commonly used in industry, and stakeholders may have different understandings of the architectural assumption concept). We also got five new findings: (1) architects frequently make architectural assumptions in their work; (2) the architectural assumption concept is subjective; (3) architectural assumptions are context-dependent and have a dynamic nature (e.g., turning out to be invalid or vice versa during their lifecycle); (4) there is a connection between architectural assumptions and certain types of software artifacts (e.g., requirements and design decisions); (5) twelve architectural assumptions management activities and four benefits of managing architectural assumptions were identified.

Keywords: Architectural assumption · Architectural assumptions management · Case study

1 Introduction

The concept of assumption in software engineering is not new. Various types of assumptions have been investigated in the software engineering literature, such as requirement assumptions [1], architectural assumptions [10], and code-level

© Springer International Publishing AG 2017
B.A. Lopes and R. de Lemos (Eds.): ECSA 2017, LNCS 10475, pp. 191–207, 2017.
DOI: 10.1007/978-3-319-65831-5_14

assumptions [2], each focusing on a different aspect of the software development lifecycle. Architectural assumptions (AA[1]) are an important type of architectural knowledge in both architecting and software development in general [5]. Similar to the definition of "assumption" in Oxford English Dictionary[2] and Merriam-Webster[3], we define AA as: architectural knowledge taken for granted, or accepted as true without evidence. The essence of the AA concept is "uncertainty": stakeholders are not (completely) certain regarding various aspects of architectural knowledge, including correctness, impact, importance, suitability, etc. As an example, a stakeholder may assume that "*the number of users (visitors) of the system would be around 1 million per day*". When the uncertainty of an AA is eliminated, the AA can be removed or transformed to other types of software artifacts (e.g., a design decision).

AA that are not well managed (and thus remain implicit AA or become invalid AA) can lead to a multitude of problems in software development [5]. As an example of such a problem, consider architectural misunderstanding: stakeholders may misunderstand an architectural design decision, because they are not aware of the AA behind this decision. Another example is undetected risks: one essential characteristic of assumptions is uncertainty, which may lead to risks in projects, especially if AA remain implicit.

Little empirical research has been conducted regarding the notion of AA as well as their management. In this paper, we conducted an exploratory case study with twenty-four architects to analyze AA and their management in industry. The results confirm certain findings from our previous survey on AA [5]: (1) neither the term nor the concept of AA is commonly used in industry, and stakeholders may have different understandings of the AA concept; (2) AA are not only important in architecting, but also of paramount importance in software development as they span the whole software development lifecycle; (3) there is a lack of approaches, tools, and guidelines for AA management, and there are certain challenges in managing AA. Furthermore, we got five new findings: (1) architects frequently make AA in their work; (2) the AA concept is subjective; (3) AA are context-dependent and have a dynamic nature (e.g., turning out to be invalid or vice versa during their lifecycle); (4) there is a connection between AA and certain types of software artifacts (e.g., requirements and design decisions); (5) twelve AA management activities and four benefits of managing AA were identified.

The rest of this paper is structured as follows: Sect. 2 describes related work on AA and their management. Section 3 introduces the case study design. Section 4 presents the results of the case study, while Sect. 5 discusses the findings. Section 6 describes the threats to the validity of the case study, and Sect. 7 concludes this work along with future research directions.

---

[1] AA in this paper is singular as well as plural based on the context in which it is used.

[2] http://www.oxforddictionaries.com/definition/english/assumption.

[3] http://www.merriam-webster.com/dictionary/assumption.

2 Related Work

Garlan et al. [11] treated AA as an important factor that causes architectural mismatch. The authors suggested that guidelines should be provided for documenting AA (e.g., how to integrate AA Documentation into architecture documentation). The authors further suggested several approaches (e.g., architecture views and description languages) and techniques (e.g., XML) to support AA Documentation.

Lago and van Vliet [10] distinguished AA from requirements and constraints as the reasons for architectural design decisions that are arbitrarily taken based on personal experience and knowledge. An assumption meta-model was proposed to document these assumptions in an explicit way. The authors classified AA into three types: (1) managerial assumptions, (2) organizational assumptions, and (3) technical assumptions. Roeller et al. [9] classified AA into four types: (1) implicit and undocumented (the architect is unaware of the assumption, or it concerns tacit knowledge), (2) explicit but undocumented (the architect takes a decision for a specific reason), (3) explicit and explicitly undocumented (the reasoning is hidden), (4) explicit and documented (this is the preferred, but often exceptional, situation). The authors also proposed an approach (RAAM – Recovering Architectural Assumption Method) for AA Recovery from five sources in development (e.g., source code and documentation).

Van Landuyt et al. [12] discussed a specific type of AA (i.e., early AA), which are made by requirements engineers in the early phases of development (e.g., requirements elicitation). The authors highlighted the necessity of the documentation of early AA. In their subsequent work, Van Landuyt and Joosen [13] introduced a metamodel and an instantiation strategy to document early AA based on quality attribute scenarios and use cases.

Ordibehesht [14] argued that implicit and invalid AA are the major cause that leads to system failures and poor performance. The author proposed an approach based on an architectural analysis and description language to document AA.

Mamun and Hansson [15] conducted a literature review on assumptions in software development. In their review, the authors identified problems (e.g., architectural mismatch), challenges (e.g., distinguishing assumptions from other software artifacts), and approaches (e.g., assumption description language) for assumptions management (e.g., Assumptions Documentation). In their following work, Mamun et al. [16] proposed to use Alloy language to document AA in software development.

Ostacchini and Wermelinger [17] proposed a lightweight approach to manage AA in agile development, and summarized four main tasks of AA management from existing literature: (1) recording new assumptions, (2) monitoring assumptions regularly, (3) searching for assumptions, and (4) recovering past assumptions. The authors used the taxonomy of AA proposed by Lago and van Vliet in [10].

In our previous work [18], we focused on AA and their documentation in agile development, and proposed a simplified conceptual model for AA with a lightweight approach for AA Documentation. Furthermore, we surveyed 112 practitioners to investigate the practice of AA in software development [5]. The results of the survey show that most AA are kept implicit due to the lack of documentation; the lack of specific approaches and tools is the major challenge (reason) of (not) identifying and documenting AA.

To the best of our knowledge, there are currently no exploratory case studies regarding AA and their management in software development from architects' perspective. The aforementioned studies mostly focus on proposing and evaluating approaches for AA management, while this study aims to explore how architects perceive AA as well as the existing activities, practices, tools, challenges, and benefits of AA management. Moreover, this work is a follow-up from our survey on AA [5]; we detail the comparison between the survey and this study in Sect. 3.2.

3 Case Study

We followed the guidelines proposed by Runeson and Höst [6] to design and report on this case study.

3.1 Goal and Research Questions

The goal of the case study, formulated using the Goal-Question-Metric approach [3], is to **analyze** AA and their management **for the purpose** of characterization **with respect to** understanding AA and activities, practices, tools, challenges, and benefits of AA management **from the point of view of** architects **in the context of** software development in industry. The research questions (RQs) of this study according to the goal are formulated as follows:

RQ1: How do architects perceive AA?

Stakeholders may perceive AA differently [5]. This RQ intends to explore how architects understand the concept of AA through definitions and examples, as well as characteristics of AA and potential relationships between AA and other software artifacts (e.g., requirements).

RQ2: What are the activities, practices, tools, challenges, and benefits of AA management?

As evidenced in our systematic mapping study on assumptions and their management in software development [4], assumptions management is comprised of a set of assumptions management activities (e.g., Assumptions Making) and supported by various practices and tools. Furthermore, AA management leads to certain benefits in software development but also has challenges. This RQ aims at helping researchers and practitioners to get a practical understanding of AA management in software development.

3.2 Case and Units of Analysis

Our case study explores a phenomenon (managing AA) in a real context, by asking each subject to select one non-trivial software project from their work and to manage AA in the context of the selected project. Note that we did not study the AA managed by the subjects, but their opinions on AA and their management. Therefore, we treat this study as a multiple and holistic case study [8]: each architect is both a case and a unit of analysis. Furthermore, this case study aims at exploring new insights of AA and their management as well as generating new ideas for further research, so it is an exploratory case study [6].

This case study follows up on our earlier work [5]: a survey with 112 practitioners on AA and their identification and documentation in software development. Compared to that survey, there are several key differences with the current study: (1) We only used questionnaire for data collection to answer the RQs in our survey, while this case study employs both interview and focus group for data collection (two different data sources help in improving the validity of the study) to answer the RQs; (2) The subjects in the survey were practitioners in software development, including various roles, such as project manager and designer, while the subjects of this study were architects; (3) The subjects in the survey were asked to fill in a questionnaire and give their opinions, while the subjects in this study received a tutorial on AA and their management and managed AA in their own projects as practice; (4) The scope of this study is broader, as it not only extends from AA Identification and Recording (i.e., the survey) to AA management in general (i.e., this study), but also included several new aspects, such as characteristics of AA and relationships between AA and other software artifacts (e.g., requirements).

3.3   Data Collection and Analysis

We conducted five workshops (half day per workshop, including a half-hour tutorial on AA and their management) in Beijing and Shenzhen, China and Gothenburg, Sweden with twenty-four architects from ten companies and different domains (e.g., Internet of Things and Automotive Industry) to collect data.

Three data collection methods were used in the case study: questionnaire, interview, and focus group. We asked each subject to fill in a questionnaire to collect their background information. We interviewed all the subjects (one by one, 30 min per subject) with specific questions related to the RQs. We conducted five focus groups (30 min per focus group per workshop) according to the RQs.

We used descriptive statistics to analyze quantitative answers (i.e., background information of the subjects), and Constant Comparison [7] for qualitative answers (i.e., generating concepts and categories from the collected data to answer the RQs). Constant Comparison (the core of the Grounded Theory approach) is a systematic approach used for qualitative analysis, and a continuous process for verifying the generated concepts and categories [7]. In this case study, Constant Comparison was iteratively performed, and the codes and their relationships were refined in each iteration. Table 1 shows the relationships among the data collection methods, data analysis methods, and RQs. Furthermore, we used MAXQDA[4] to analyze the qualitative data.

---

[4] http://www.maxqda.com/.

Table 1. Relationships among the data collection methods, data analysis methods, and RQs

Data collection method	Data analysis method	RQs
Questionnaire	Descriptive statistics	Background information
Interview	Constant comparison	RQ1, RQ2
Focus group	Constant comparison	RQ1, RQ2

4   Results

4.1   Subjects Experience and Projects Information

The experience of the subjects in software-intensive systems and architecting is generally classified in three levels as shown in Fig. 1. Most of the subjects (22 out of 24, 91.7%) have at least five years of experience in software-intensive systems, and 15 subjects (out of 24, 62.5%) have at least five years of experience in architecting. We also asked the subjects whether they had architecture-related training (excluding higher education). Four subjects (out of 24, 16.7%) claimed that they had such training experience.

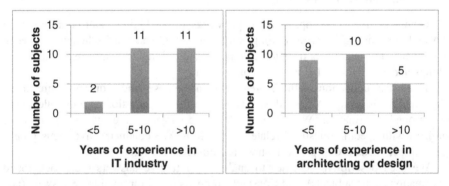

Fig. 1. Years of experience in software-intensive systems and architecting of the subjects

Furthermore, the twenty-four subjects managed AA in twenty-eight projects, i.e., there are four subjects that each of them had managed AA in two of their projects. The duration, team size, and lines of code of the projects are shown in Fig. 2. Note that two subjects did not provide us the lines of code of their projects (two projects) because the projects were in progress when we conducted the workshops.

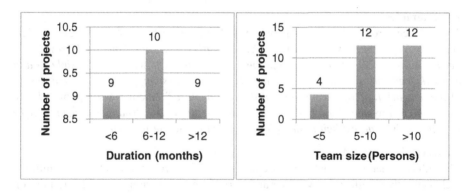

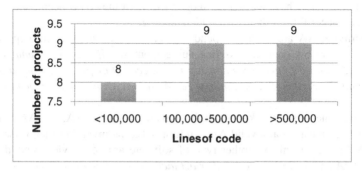

Fig. 2. Information of the projects used by the subjects in the case study

4.2   Results of RQ1 – Perception of AA

Term and Concept of AA
The results show that neither the term nor the concept of AA is commonly used in industry, although the subjects admitted that they frequently made AA in their work. As one subject put it: *"I had something in my thinking about architecture work that transformed into an assumption, but I missed that, and assumption is a very good word to use here."*

Moreover, the results support that stakeholders may have different understandings of the AA concept. One of the most intensive arguments between the subjects concerned the nature of AA. As one subject understood: *"When we develop systems, we have various flows. AA are like uncertain key points in these flows."* As another subject stated: *"If a statement is made based on personal experience without being able to prove that it is feasible or has no risks, it is an AA."*

Finally, the subjects agreed that AA are not only important in architecting, but also of paramount importance in software development, and the influence of AA is through the entire development process, instead of only during the architecting or design phase. As one subject explained: *"AA are made from requirements engineering. When architecting, we make new AA, and the existing AA would evolve. I think AA can influence the whole project lifecycle as well as product lifecycle."*

AA Examples

The subjects provided more than twenty AA examples based on their own under-standing. We present two examples: *"As we can't foresee the functional growth, we need to have a scalable network topology, which means it should be possible to add network segments without changing the architecture, assuming that the actual design of the network topology is not part of the architecture."* Another assumption: *"There would not be any need for a high speed bus inside the vehicle dynamics area until 2019 or later. This is an explicit assumption. We actually wrote it down."*

Characteristics of AA

The subjects mentioned that the AA concept is subjective (e.g., whether something is architecturally-significant or whether an information is an assumption). This is a reason that stakeholders may have a different understanding of the AA concept, and can make different AA according to their own understanding.

Furthermore, AA are context-dependent, i.e., they can be different depending on context (e.g., project context). As one subject put it: *"If I have assumption1 and assumption2, and they have a relationship in project 1. For project 2, they don't have any relationship. So the relationship between these two AA is context-dependent on the project."*

Moreover, the subjects talked about the dynamic nature of AA, i.e., AA can evolve over time. This means that a valid AA can turn out to be invalid or vice versa, as well as an AA can transform to another type of software artifact or vice versa during its lifecycle: *"AA may transform to another artifact, or something that is not an AA in the first place, but change to an AA. The transformation between AA and other artifacts should be bi-directional."*

Finally, the subjects agreed that relationships between two AA could be zero, one, or multiple. As one subject stated: *"In some way, two types of relationships (e.g., "is caused by" and "constrains") could coexist between two AA."*

AA and Other Software Artifacts

The subjects agreed that AA are not independent in software development; instead, there is a connection between AA and other software artifacts. As one subject men-tioned: *"I can see that a lot of things are based on assumptions. When we have a new project, we could start with some basic or important assumptions that we have, and base design patterns or requirements on those AA."*

The subjects listed several artifacts related to AA, including requirements, design decisions, design patterns, design models, components, and risks. As one subject sta-ted: *"Some requirements we have are actually AA, and we have strategies based on assumptions, so it could be good to acknowledge that."* As another subject put it: *"How does an AA evolve to a requirement? The dependencies between assumptions and things like that are the most important. We could connect AA to decisions, require-ments, and components."*

Summary of RQ1

We summarize the aforementioned results of RQ1: (1) Neither the term nor the concept of AA is commonly used in industry. (2) The subjects (architects) frequently made AA in their work. (3) Stakeholders may have different understandings of the AA concept.

(4) AA are important in both architecting and software development. (5) AA span the whole software development lifecycle. (6) The AA concept is subjective. (7) AA are context-dependent and have a dynamic nature. (8) There is a connection between AA and certain types of software artifacts.

4.3   Results of RQ2 – AA Management

AA Management Activities
By considering the assumptions management activities identified and summarized in our mapping study [4], we found that all the twelve assumptions management activities were mentioned by the subjects in the case study: AA Making, Description, Evaluation, Maintenance, Tracing, Monitoring, Communication, Understanding, Reuse, Recovery, Searching, and Organization. These AA management activities include both the activities the subjects used in their projects and the activities the subjects considered important or difficult. For example, the subjects agreed that making AA (including both identifying existing AA and making new AA) was hard for them. Furthermore, AA Making, Description, Evaluation, Maintenance, Tracing, and Monitoring were the most frequently discussed AA management activities by the subjects in the case study.

Practices and Tools Used for AA Management
The subjects did not employ any general AA management process or approaches in their work, but they used certain practices and tools for AA management activities. We listed all the practices and tools used by the subjects in Table 2. Note that the tools are listed without a mapping to the specific AA management activities because the subjects did not provide that information.

Challenges of AA Management
Furthermore, we identified a set of challenges regarding AA management in software development as shown in Table 3.

Benefits of AA Management
Finally, we identified a set of benefits of AA management in software development as shown in Table 4.

Summary of RQ2
We summarize the aforementioned results of RQ2: (1) Twelve AA management activities were identified. (2) No systematic approaches were used by the subjects for AA management. (3) Nine practices without guidelines were used by the subjects in five AA management activities. (4) All the tools used by the subjects for AA management are general in software development. (5) There are eight challenges and four benefits identified in managing AA.

Table 2. Practices and tools used for AA management

AA management activity	Practice	Tools
AA making	Making AA in requirements engineering	MS PowerPoint[a]; MS Visio[b]; MS Word[c]; MS Project[d]; Enterprise architect[e]; Rational Software Architect Designer[f]; SmartDraw[g]; Origin[h]; PowerDesigner[i]; ProcessOn[j]; internal tools
	Making AA in architecting	
	Making AA using brainstorming	
AA description	Describing AA in documents (e.g., design documents)	
	Describing AA in models (e.g., architecture models)	
AA evaluation	Evaluating AA in architecture evaluation	
	Evaluating AA in software testing	
AA maintenance	Involving customers and users in the discussions of maintaining AA	
AA communication	Face-to-face communication of AA	

[a]https://products.office.com/en/powerpoint
[b]https://products.office.com/en-us/visio/flowchart-software
[c]https://products.office.com/en-us/word
[d]https://products.office.com/en-us/project/project-and-portfolio-management-software
[e]http://www.sparxsystems.com/
[f]http://www-03.ibm.com/software/products/en/ratsadesigner
[g]https://www.smartdraw.com/
[h]http://www.originlab.com/
[i]http://www.powerdesigner.biz/EN/
[j]https://www.processon.com/

Table 3. Challenges of AA management

Challenge	Description
Understanding of AA	Neither the concept nor the term of AA was commonly used by the subjects. It is challenging to understand the AA concept and term: "*It was difficult to get started. You need to figure out getting to the mode of understanding, which was the trickiest part.*" Furthermore, stakeholders may have different understandings of the AA concept, which could cause inconsistency in AA management
AA management activities	One of the most important challenges is how to conduct individual AA management activities in software development, i.e., there is a lack of specific approaches for AA management. For example, considering AA Making and Description, one subject put it: "*We write a lot of things based on so many assumptions, but we don't document. The problem is actually how to catch the assumptions because we have so much in our heads.*"

(*continued*)

Table 3. (*continued*)

Challenge	Description
Tools	There is a lack of tools for AA management, which should be able to deal with different project context (e.g., an AA is valid in a project, but invalid in another project), support not only AA Description, but also other AA management activities (e.g., Making and Evaluation), have good quality of outputs, and support automation or semi-automation. As one subject mentioned: *"We have maybe 100 decisions and 400 requirements, and we have different projects, which have the same assumptions in different validation states, so the tool must handle these situations and be very scalable."*
Lack of data	There is a lack of data (e.g., empirical data) regarding AA and their management in existing projects, which makes conducting AA management activities (e.g., AA Reuse and Evaluation) difficult. As one subject put it: *"If you have data regarding AA from 10,000 projects, you can generate an AA model to analyze AA in future projects."*
Integration	AA are related to other software artifacts, such as requirements. Therefore, there is a challenge to integrate AA and their management with existing software development processes, approaches, tools, etc. An example given by one subject: *"In embedded systems, flowchart diagram is the most important, and AA management should be compatible with flowchart diagrams, when introducing AA in embedded systems."*
Project context	AA management depends on project context (e.g., resources, complexity, development processes employed, and application domain). Thus, an AA management approach may work in one project, but not work in another project. As one subject explained: *"For some projects AA management may grow to be a huge unwieldy thing that everyone is afraid of, and you need to maintain, because no one else touches that."*
Experience	AA management requires certain experience (project experience, architecting experience, etc.). One challenge is how to mitigate the gap between junior and experienced stakeholders regarding AA management. As one subject stated: *"Experienced architects understand AA management better than junior architects. Experienced architects can make more reasonable AA, while junior architects may not even know what AA they have or need to make. You can't just go out on the street and pick up the first guy, and say: you will be the architect!"*
Stakeholders	There is a lack of guidance regarding who should be involved in AA management. As one subject mentioned: *"AA are related to various aspects of software development, and AA management should be teamwork."*

Table 4. Benefits of AA management

Benefit	Description
Being aware of AA and related problems	The most intuitive benefit of managing AA is to make AA explicit, i.e., stakeholders become aware of the AA made in projects. This can further help stakeholders to be aware of and avoid potential problems (e.g., risks) caused by implicit or invalid AA. As one subject put it: "*It would definitely be good for us to acknowledge that we have assumptions in the first place and to work with them to some extent.*"
Improving traceability	AA are not independent in software development, but intertwined with various software artifacts, e.g., design decisions. Management of AA can help to trace AA to other artifacts. As one subject stated: "*The benefits of managing AA are that you can see what decisions have been made based on assumptions, and know why you made some decisions.*"
Facilitating maintenance and handover	AA are usually implicit, and intertwined with various software artifacts. Management of AA can make AA explicit, and prevent knowledge vaporization in software development, which can further facilitate maintenance and handover within projects. As one subject mentioned: "*AA management enriches software knowledge, which helps to maintain, for example, architecture or source code.*"
Reducing costs	Invalid AA may lead to problems such as inappropriate architecture design, and consequently increase costs (e.g., additional development effort) of a project. AA management aims at reducing invalid AA and thus reduces cost. As one subject explained: "*Invalid AA would make the system that is based on the architecture more expensive than it needs to be.*"

5 Discussion

5.1 Interpretation of RQs Results

Interpretation of the Results of RQ1

There is an obvious paradox: on the one hand, neither the term nor the concept of AA was commonly used in industry; on the other hand, the subjects frequently made AA in their work. One reason could be that the subjects were not aware of the AA when they made them. The most probable reason however is that AA were not treated as first class entities in software development. Instead, AA were considered as, for example, a type of constraint or rationale of other software artifacts (e.g., design decisions).

Stakeholders may have a different understanding of the AA concept. One reason could be that the AA concept is subjective, as the subjects mentioned. Furthermore, AA are context-dependent (e.g., project context). This indicates that, for example, an AA can be valid in one project but invalid in another project depending on the context. As mentioned by the subjects, one potential reason is that AA are related to various artifacts. For example, an AA can be caused or constrained by a requirement.

Therefore, if the requirement changes in another project, the AA may also change (e.g., from valid to invalid).

Moreover, AA have a dynamic nature, i.e., AA can evolve over time. This means that a valid AA can turn out to be invalid or vice versa, but also that an AA can transform to another type of software artifact or vice versa. A potential reason for the former (i.e., bi-directional changes between valid and invalid) is the context-dependent characteristic of AA. For the latter (i.e., bi-directional transformation between AA and other types of software artifacts), the reason could be that AA are inherently uncertain: once the uncertainty of an AA is eliminated, this AA transforms to another type of artifact; an artifact, such as a design decision, may also become uncertain and thus turn into an AA.

Finally, as stated by the subjects, AA are not only important in architecting, but also of paramount importance in software development; its lifecycle is throughout the whole software development lifecycle. One reason could be that AA are related to various software artifacts, such as requirements, design decisions, components, and risks. Another reason, as the subjects explained, is that AA management is teamwork, involving different stakeholders, instead of only architects.

Interpretation of the Results of RQ2

The results of RQ2 confirm the twelve assumptions management activities identified and summarized in our systematic mapping study [4]. Furthermore, AA Making, Description, Evaluation, Maintenance, Tracing, and Monitoring got the most attention by the subjects. One reason may be that the subjects considered these six activities as the primary AA management activities in software development; if AA management is employed in development, these activities are more likely to take place or get more attention than other activities.

In this study, we did not find any particular approaches the subjects used for AA management, which is consistent with the findings of our survey on AA [5]. Though the subjects suggested several practices for managing AA, these practices are general without any elaborated guidelines. We also found several tools for AA management used by the subjects. However, all of them are general software development tools, and thus do not specifically focus on AA management.

Furthermore, besides the lack of guidelines, approaches, tools, resources, etc. for AA management, which have also been discussed in our survey on AA [5], we found several other challenges of AA management in software development, including "Lack of data", "Integration", and "Project context" as elaborated in Table 3. For example, as mentioned by the subjects, there is a lack of data (e.g., empirical data) regarding AA and their management in existing projects. This is potentially because stakeholders do not make AA explicit and document them in a systematic way. The lack of existing data regarding AA from projects is also a reason that impedes conducting individual AA management activities in software development.

Finally, we identified four benefits of AA management in software development. However, we argue that these benefits are not for free, as they depend on certain conditions (e.g., related to specific AA management activities), and there is always a tradeoff between benefits and costs. For example, AA Tracing helps to improve traceability between AA and other software artifacts in software development, but the effort needed for establishing traces could be prohibitive.

5.2   Implications for Researchers

AA in Empirical Studies
The AA concept is subjective, and stakeholders may have different understandings of the AA concept. When conducting empirical studies regarding AA and their management, these nuances need to be taken into account during the study design. Especially when evaluating related approaches or tools for AA management in empirical studies, researchers need to make a decision: allowing their subjects to have their own understanding of AA or enforcing a consistent definition.

AA Management
On the one hand, AA are important in both architecting and software development. On the other hand, there are various challenges regarding AA and their management that need to be addressed in software development, as we identified in the case study. There is a clear need to develop, for example, dedicated approaches and tools, as well as well-designed practices and guidelines (e.g., when to manage AA or what AA should be managed in software development) for AA management.

Furthermore, the reasons that AA are usually not-well managed could be various: for example, the challenges listed in Table 3, or the return on investment is rather limited. We suggest that researchers collect evidence regarding the return on investment for AA management. Moreover, not-well managed AA can lead to a multitude problems in software development. There is a need for researchers to identify these problems from both literature and empirical studies. This could motivate spending extra effort on AA management.

Finally, since AA are intertwined with various types of software artifacts and their lifecycle spans the whole software development lifecycle, there is a possibility for further research regarding integrating AA management into existing software development approaches (e.g., decision-centric architecture evaluation approaches).

5.3   Implications for Practitioners

Treating AA as First Class Entities
AA are important in both architecting and software development, as they span the whole software development lifecycle. However, practitioners (e.g., architects) frequently make AA in their daily work, without always being aware what AA they made. We advocate treating AA as first class entities in software architecting as well as in software development, and integrating AA management with existing processes, approaches, tools, etc. in software development.

Understanding of AA
Understanding of AA (e.g., the AA concept) is usually an issue in AA management. We suggest that practitioners in a project should at least reach an agreement on, for example, what AA are, as well as how to manage them.

Teamwork
AA management is teamwork. Although, according to our systematic mapping study [4], in the context of software design, architects and designers are the major stakeholders in assumptions management, we encourage practitioners with different roles (e.g., project manager) being involved in managing AA. For example, practitioners can evaluate AA as a team, instead of only letting architects perform AA Evaluation.

Experience
AA management requires certain experience (including project experience and architecting experience). In general, experienced practitioners understand AA management deeper and perform it better than junior practitioners. We encourage discussions regarding AA and their management between practitioners with different levels of experience to alleviate this issue.

6 Threats to Validity

The threats to the validity of this case study are presented in this section according to the guidelines proposed by Runeson and Höst [6]. Note that internal validity is not discussed in this paper because this work does not study causality.

Construct validity
reflects to what extent the research questions and the studied operational measures are consistent [6]. A potential threat concerns whether the collected data can answer the RQs. To reduce this threat, we iteratively refined the RQs and the data collection procedures. To improve the validity of the case study we used both interviews and focus groups for the data collection.

External validity
concerns the generalization of the findings [6]. The subjects were architects from various companies and domains, and with different levels of working experience in software intensive-systems and architecting; we argue that the results are representative for practitioners with a similar background. However, the results may not be generalized to other contexts (e.g., project managers and programmers); replication of this case study is one way to reduce this threat.

Reliability
focuses on whether the study would yield the same results when other researchers replicate it [6]. We performed a pilot study to refine the case study design (e.g., the interview questions), and reduced the ambiguities in the execution of the case study. The protocol of the case study was reviewed by the researchers iteratively, and also by eight external reviewers, to mitigate the threat of bias in the design of the case study. The whole process of the case study was recorded through audio recording devices to reduce the threat of information vaporization. Furthermore, two authors conducted Constant Comparison through MAXQDA in parallel to reduce the threat of bias in the qualitative data analysis.

7 Conclusions and Future Work

As an important type of architectural knowledge, little empirical research has been conducted regarding AA and their management in software development. In this paper, we conducted an exploratory case study with twenty-four architects to analyze AA and their management in industry.

In this study, we confirmed certain findings from our previous survey on AA [5], including (1) neither the term nor the concept of AA is commonly used in industry, and stakeholders may have different understandings of the AA concept; (2) AA are not only important in architecting, but also of paramount importance in software development as they span the whole software development lifecycle; (3) there is a lack of approaches, tools, and guidelines for AA management, and there are certain challenges in managing AA. Furthermore, we had five new findings: (1) architects frequently make AA in their work; (2) the AA concept is subjective; (3) AA are context-dependent and have a dynamic nature (e.g., turning out to be invalid or vice versa during their lifecycle); (4) there is a connection between AA and certain types of software artifacts (e.g., requirements and design decisions); (5) twelve AA management activities and four benefits of managing AA were identified.

Our next steps are: (1) developing approaches for AA management, and particularly a general AA management process in software development; (2) developing practices and guidelines for AA management to address, for example, the identified challenges in the case study; and (3) developing a dedicated tool for AA management. Note that our intention is not to develop a standalone tool, but a tool integrated with existing software development tools (e.g., a plug-in of the existing tools).

Acknowledgements. This work is partially sponsored by the NSFC under Grant No. 61472286 and the Ubbo Emmius scholarship program by the University of Groningen. This work is also partially supported by the Vinnova FFI projects Next Generation Electronic Architecture and Next Generation Electronic Architecture step 2. We would like to thank the participants of the case study, and the architects who participated in the pilot study.

References

1. Haley, C.B., Laney, R.C., Moffett, J.D., Nuseibeh, B.: Using trust assumptions with security requirements. Requir. Eng. **11**(2), 138–151 (2006)
2. Lehman, M.M., Ramil, J.F.: Rules and tools for software evolution planning and management. Annal. Soft Eng. **11**(1), 15–44 (2001)
3. Basili, V., Caldiera, G., Rombach, D.: The Goal Question Metric Approach. In: Marciniak, J.J. (ed.) Encyclopedia of Software Engineering. Wiley, New York (1994)
4. Yang, C., Liang, P., Avgeriou, P.: Assumptions and their management in software development: A systematic mapping study (under review)
5. Yang, C., Liang, P., Avgeriou, P.: A survey on software architectural assumptions. J. Syst. Softw. **113**(3), 362–380 (2016)
6. Runeson, P., Höst, M.: Guidelines for conducting and reporting case study research in software engineering. Empir. Softw. Eng. **14**(2), 131–164 (2009)

7. Glaser, B.G., Strauss, A.L.: The Discovery of Grounded Theory: Strategies for Qualitative Research. Aldine Publishing, New York (1967)
8. Runeson, P., Host, M., Rainer, A., Regnell, B.: Case Study Research in Software Engineering: Guidelines and Examples. Wiley, New york (2012)
9. Roeller, R., Lago, P., van Vliet, H.: Recovering architectural assumptions. J. Syst. Softw. **79**(4), 552–573 (2006)
10. Lago, P., van Vliet, H.: Explicit assumptions enrich architectural models. In: Proceedings of the 27th International Conference on Software Engineering (ICSE), St Louis, Missouri, USA, pp. 206–214 (2005)
11. Garlan, D., Allen, R., Ockerbloom, J.: Architectural mismatch: Why reuse is still so hard. IEEE Softw. **26**(4), 66–69 (2009)
12. Van Landuyt, D., Truyen, E., Joosen, W.: Documenting early architectural assumptions in scenario-based requirements. In: Proceeding of the Joint Working IEEE/IFIP Conference on Software Architecture (WICSA) and European Conference on Software Architecture (ECSA), Helsinki, Finland, pp. 329–333 (2012)
13. Van Landuyt, D., Joosen, W.: Modularizing early architectural assumptions in scenario-based requirements. In: Proceedings of the 17th International Conference on Fundamental Approaches to Software Engineering (FASE), Grenoble, France, pp. 170–184 (2014)
14. Ordibehesht, H.: Explicating critical assumptions in software architectures using AADL. Master thesis, University of Gothenburg (2010)
15. Mamun, M.A.A., Hansson, J.: Review and challenges of assumptions in software development. In: Proceedings of the 2nd Analytic Virtual Integration of Cyber-Physical Systems Workshop (AVICPS), Vienna, Austria (2011)
16. Mamun, M.A.A., Tichy, M., Hansson, J.: Towards formalizing assumptions on architectural level: a proof-of-concept. Research report, University of Gothenburg (2012)
17. Ostacchini, I., Wermelinger, M.: Managing assumptions during agile development. In: Proceedings of the 2009 ICSE Workshop on Sharing and Reusing Architectural Knowledge (SHARK), Vancouver, BC, Canada, pp. 9–16 (2009)
18. Yang, C., Liang, P.: Identifying and recording software architectural assumptions in agile development. In: Proceedings of the 26th International Conference on Software Engineering and Knowledge Engineering (SEKE), Vancouver, Canada, pp. 308–313 (2014)

Microservices in a Small Development Organization

An Industrial Experience Report

Georg Buchgeher[1]([⊠]), Mario Winterer[1], Rainer Weinreich[2], Johannes Luger[3], Roland Wingelhofer[3], and Mario Aistleitner[3]

[1] Software Competence Center Hagenberg GmbH, Hagenberg im Mühlkreis, Austria
{georg.buchgeher,mario.winterer}@scch.at
[2] Johannes Kepler University Linz, Linz, Austria
rainer.weinreich@jku.at
[3] AMS Engineering GmbH, Hagenberg im Mühlkreis, Austria
{johannes.luger,roland.wingelhofer,mario.aistleitner}@stiwa.com

Abstract. Microservice architectures promise high flexibility and sustainability in system development. Multiple principles have emerged for the successful adoption of microservices, principles which impact not only the technical but also the organizational levels of a development organization. This paper reports our experiences introducing microservices in a company with a small development organization and a customer-solution-oriented business model. Our experiences show that the company can benefit from using microservices on a technical level but requires adaptations at the organizational level.

Keywords: Microservices · Microservice architecture · Small development organization · Microservice principles · Services · Service-oriented architecture

1 Introduction

Microservice architecture is an approach to software architecture in which a system comprises many small, independently developed and operated services. Microservices began to emerge a few years ago and have been successfully adopted by many large companies, like Google, Amazon, Netflix, and Spotify [7,11]. In these companies, development organizations with hundreds, even thousands of developers are working on microservice architectures. Microservices promise to overcome many drawbacks of monolithic applications, with a modular design, the ability to bring new features quickly into production, and improved sustainability through continuous system evolution. These same benefits also make microservice architecture interesting for small and medium-sized enterprises (SMEs) with only small development departments and different business models.

A. Lopes and R. de Lemos (Eds.): ECSA 2017, LNCS 10475, pp. 208–215, 2017.
DOI: 10.1007/978-3-319-65831-5_15

Multiple principles have emerged for the development of microservice architectures [9,10], guiding development at both the technical and the organizational levels of software development. Adopting microservices is not easy [3,5,8]. They are said to have a high learning curve and to introduce new complexities and challenges [3]. This raises the question if small companies or companies with different business models can also adopt a microservice architecture. Singleton [11] argues that microservices make no sense for teams of fewer than 60 people (with some exceptions). The literature is still lacking experience reports discussing the introduction of microservice architecture in such a context. Francesco et al. [4] identified eight existing experience reports on microservices, only one of which [1] describes the migration to a microservice architecture, but that report provides no information on the size of the development organization and and does not extensively discuss of the usefulness of microservice principles. In general, industry- and practitioner-oriented studies have not yet been a focus of microservice research [4].

In this paper, we report our experiences introducing microservice architecture at an Austrian company developing solutions for laboratory automation. The company has a small development organization with a customer-solution-oriented business model. We report whether and to what degree central principles of microservice architecture [9,10] could be adopted by the development organization, along with other experiences we had.

The remainder of this paper is organized as follows. Section 2 presents the industrial context for the work presented in this paper. Section 3 overviews the central principles of microservice development. Section 4 discusses these principles in the context of a small development organization. In Sect. 5, we discuss further lessons learned, and Sect. 6 presents a summary and some conclusions.

2 Context

AMS Engineering, part of the STIWA Group[1], is an Austrian company developing industrial automation solutions. AMS Engineering is organized into multiple business units, one of which is developing solutions for the automation of laboratories analyzing medical samples from hospitals and medical practices. AMS Engineering provides solutions for laboratories of different sizes, from small laboratories analyzing only a few hundred samples per day to big laboratories analyzing more than 50,000 samples daily on fully automated assembly lines.

AMS Engineering is in the process of replacing their system for laboratory automation, which is expected to reach its end of life in 2020. At the beginning of 2016, AMS Engineering held a requirements workshop with central system stakeholders to identify the central requirements for the next version of their laboratory automation solution. Some of the identified requirements were:

- *Scalability*: The new system must scale from very small to very large laboratories.

---

[1] http://www.stiwa.com/en/.

- *Flexibility of Provided Functionality*: Each laboratory requires different functionality, such as interaction with different kinds of hardware products and communication with different hospital information systems.
- *Fast Time-to-Market*: New functionality - requested by customers - needs to be brought into production as fast as possible.
- *Stepwise Migration*: The new system needs to be developed incrementally. Old and new systems must be operated in parallel until the old system is completely replaced.
- *Operation in Private Computing Centers*: Large laboratories want to operate the new system in their own computing centers (private cloud environment).

A microservice architecture promises to address these requirements for AMS Engineering to achieve future business goals. However, the development team had some reservations about whether a microservice architecture was the right way to go. Their main concerns were the limited experience and expertise of the development organization with service-based development and the impression that microservice architectures are mainly useful within large development organizations. The development organization at AMS Engineering currently comprises only eight developers, and their business model differs from other companies developing microservices. While such companies typically develop and operate their systems themselves, AMS Engineering is developing a system where customers operate customized solutions at over 100 different sites. This raised the questions of (Q1) whether a microservice architecture-based system could be developed by such a small development team and (Q2) whether the development of a microservice architecture in such a context would make sense from a cost/benefit perspective.

In order to answer these questions, AMS Engineering launched a pilot project for a adopting microservice architecture. As part of this pilot project, four services and a set infrastructure services for the laboratory automation solution were implemented as microservices. Over eight months, a spearhead team comprising three developers was working on this project. All project members were experienced software developers with multiple years of experience, though not in the context of service-based development.

3   Microservice Principles

Multiple principles have emerged from practice [9,10] for the development of microservice architectures, which are briefly described below.

Componentization via Services [9] (*Hide Internal Implementation Details* [10]): Microservice architectures componentize their software by means of independently deployable and evolvable services. Services provide technology-agnostic APIs (e.g., REST) to be used from different technology stacks.

Organized Around Business Capabilities [9] (*Model Around Business Concepts* [10]): Microservices structure an application into business capabilities (also business-bounded contexts) and not into technical layers like user interface, application logic, and persistence. This leads to cross-functional teams (also known as full-stack teams) with a full range of skills.

Products not Projects [9]: Development teams are not only responsible for developing but also for building, testing, deploying, and monitoring a microservice. This enables developers to get feedback about how their software behaves in production.

Smart Endpoints and Dumb Pipes [9]: Microservice architectures avoid the use of heavy-weight messaging infrastructures for message routing, choreography, data transformation and applying business rules. Instead they are as decoupled and cohesive as possible, following a request - process - response process. Communication is performed through HTTP or lightweight messaging.

Decentralized Governance [9] (*Decentralize All the Things* [10]): There is (almost) no centralized governance, maximizing the autonomy of microservices. Instead, the development team is responsible for all decisions regarding their services, including, the selection of implementation technologies and the frequency of releases. Decisions concerning more than one microservice can be made using a shared governance model, where decisions are made together by members of different teams.

Decentralized Data Management [9] (*Hide Internal Implementation Details* [10]): Each service manages its own data. This applies not only to data models but also to storage solutions, like databases.

Infrastructure Automation [9] (*Adapt a Culture of Automation* [10]): Microservices are developed using an automated continuous delivery pipeline that permits the frequent release of new service versions. Automated activities include automated testing and quality control, automated creation of deployable executables (e.g., Docker images), and even automated deployment into production zones.

Design for Failure [9] (*Isolate Failure* [10]): Single services may become unavailable; Thus, microservices must be able to tolerate the failure of services, and services failing must be restored automatically.

Evolutionary Design [9]: Microservices foster evolutionary design. Since they are independently deployable, services can evolve independently. Single services can also be replaced with a completely new implementation of a service, and services can be removed when no longer needed.

Independently Deployable [10]: Individual microservices can be deployed independently from the other services of a system, permitting the frequent release of services with new features or resolved bugs. Multiple versions of a microservice can co-exist in order to handle breaking API changes, giving service consumers time to switch to new service versions.

Highly Observable [10]: Microservice architectures require a comprehensive monitoring infrastructure that permits observation of the running system and all its constituent services and their interactions. Monitoring solutions need to support aggregating data from different services, but they also need to support drilling down to single services in order to investigate issues.

4   Applying Microservice Principles in a Small Development Organization

In the following, we discuss our experiences applying the microservice principles presented in the previous section at AMS Engineering.

Componentization via Services: An appropriate system modularization was defined and adhered to from the beginning of the project. An issue was calculating the memory resources required for the whole system, since different clients have laboratory infrastructures that range from dedicated private clouds for large laboratories to less powerful infrastructures for small laboratories. Public cloud infrastructures were excluded from consideration because of privacy issues when handling patient-related medical data.

Organized Around Business Capabilities: Business services were easily identified due to the small size of the development team and the product-line character of the existing system, with system features previously identified. AMS Engineering plans in the future to have small service teams with two developers per service, with the option to bring in developers with specialized skills on demand.

Products not Projects: A pure *DevOps* approach is not possible for AMS Engineering because of its customer-solution-oriented business model that differs from the product-oriented business model of other organizations that use microservices. The systems AMS develops are operated by AMS customers, not by AMS Engineering itself. Currently, AMS Engineering has over 100 customers with significantly different system features and configurations. It would be impossible for the development team to manage and monitor over 100 system installations. A dedicated quality-control team is responsible for installing and servicing the systems at customer sites. This team is also involved in the development process, for example, by reviewing the software/system architecture and test plans. There is a defined feedback process between system operators and developers. If AMS Engineering also operated the developed system, a *DevOps* approach would be feasible, even for a small development organization.

Smart Endpoints and Dumb Pipes: AMS has never used heavy-weight messaging infrastructure. AMS already uses an HTTP-based request-response interaction style, which is typical of many microservice architectures.

Decentralized Governance: Developers cannot freely select implementation technologies due to the small size of the development team and the resulting low bus factor that may lead to the loss of technology-specific knowledge. Also, the use of libraries has to follow a defined process for legal reasons related to the business. Developers can make their own technology decisions, as long as they are approved centrally. Frequent service releases are also limited, because customers do not want release cycles shorter than three months, which can again be attributed to the business model of AMS Engineering. However, service teams can perform frequent "internal" releases that are not shipped to customers immediately. It also remains to be seen how requirements regarding the release frequency at customer sites might change in the future if more frequent releases can be provided more easily by the development team of AMS Engineering.

Decentralized Data Management: While the existing system has one centralized data model, newly developed services will manage their own data. It is still unresolved whether this model can be pursued for all future services; that is, AMS Engineering will decide on a case-by-case basis whether or not services can be decoupled on the data level. However, it is their clear intention to decouple services on the data level as much as possible.

Infrastructure Automation: AMS Engineering is using an automated deployment pipeline for their services. Pushing new releases directly into production is not possible, because their clients operate the systems. Consumer-driven contract testing has been implemented as part of the deployment pipeline.

Design for Failure: Services using other services have been designed to deal with the temporary unavailability of the used services. Failing services are automatically detected and restarted by the infrastructure.

Evolutionary Design: Continuous evolvability is perceived as the main benefit by AMS Engineering, because this will save system evolution costs in the future. Currently, no long-term data are available regarding whether or not this will work as intended.

Independently Deployable: Developed services are all independently deployable, permitting not only their independent development and evolution but also offering customized solutions with different functionality for different clients.

Highly Observable: AMS Engineering has set up a dedicated monitoring infrastructure, where metrics for each service are collected and aggregated in a centralized monitoring service for the entire system.

5   Lessons Learned

The discussion of AMS' adherence to microservice principles in the previous section revealed that while technical principles could be applied very well, adherence to organizational principles was not always possible and adaptations were required. It can be further observed that the required adaptations at the organizational level mainly resulted from the business model of the developed system rather than from the small size of the development team. Thus, we conclude that, theoretically, the presented organizational principles could also be implemented by a small development team.

Deviations from the *Decentralized Governance* principle can also be observed in larger companies. For instance, Spotify [6], Soundcloud [2], and PegahTech Co. [1] also restrict decision-making around service teams' selection of implementation technologies. The fact that multiple companies break the principle of *Decentralized Governance* is an interesting point worth further investigation, especially considering the fact that microservices should be so small that they can be easily re-implemented (replaced) within a short period of time (about two weeks) [10].

We can also confirm that microservices currently have a high learning curve. Neither the concepts nor the principles were perceived as difficult, but their technical realization in learning and using dedicated frameworks and technologies was time-intensive and thus costly. Companies considering the adoption of microservices should be aware of the required effort, giving the development teams sufficient time to develop and master a microservice infrastructure.

Technology selection for the microservice infrastructure was considered to be complex as well, because of the large number of different implementation technologies from which to choose, and because a developer had to learn each technology. AMS Engineering did not have the time to evaluate all existing solutions and then choose the best one. Instead, they followed a more pragmatic approach to technology selection, selecting technologies that were frequently used in practice, meaning they were discussed on tech blogs and expert exchange sites like Stack Overflow[2] and had enough documentation available.

At the beginning, we observed skepticism about new technologies in the development team, especially when functionality that was previously developed in-house was planned to be replaced by third-party frameworks. For example, AMS engineering developed its own concept for tracing requests across service boundaries (via a correlation ID). First, AMS engineering wanted to keep this functionality, although the selected communication infrastructure provided the same functionality in an even more powerful way that could also be used by the monitoring infrastructure out of the box. Only after a prototype was developed showing the advantages of the built-in solution did the development team decide to remove the custom solution. This also shows how a microservices architecture requires a paradigm shift towards dependence on third-party functionality, one which a development team has to accept.

Experiences with microservices that are operated at customer sites are still lacking. Thus, it remains unclear how easily this can be achieved with regard to the knowledge required to operate microservices and the communication between the development organization and customers.

6   Conclusion

AMS Engineering has invested about 2,500 h in building up a dedicated microservice infrastructure. The development of the first business services took only about 100 h. This shows that adopting microservices requires a huge one-time, up-front investment before bringing the first services into production. At AMS Engineering, this was seen as an investment from which the organization will benefit in the future; that is, it was seen as likely that microservices will become relevant in other (larger) business units of the company, where the gained knowledge can be reused.

AMS Engineering is planning to increase the size of the development team in the future from eight to ten developers. They expect their future system to comprise about 100 services, leading to a services-per-developer ratio of 10 services per developer. The planned ratio of services per developer is much higher

---

[2] http://stackoverflow.com/.

than at large companies. For instance, Spotify has over 600 developers working on over 800 services [6], while Zalando has more than 1000 employees in technology working on 200 services [5]. It remains to be seen if this number of services will be manageable in the future, or if the size of the development team must be increased.

Our experiences show that a microservice architecture can be developed by a small development organization. In the context at AMS Engineering, a team of three developers built a microservice infrastructure and a first set of services. The software architect at AMS Engineering would have wished for a slightly larger team (5–6 people) so that individual developers could focus more on single technologies. After eight months of trial, AMS Engineering is confident that a microservice architecture is the right choice to adopt for their future system.

Acknowledgement. The research reported in this paper was supported by the Austrian Ministry for Transport, Innovation and Technology, the Federal Ministry of Science, Research and Economy, and the Province of Upper Austria in the frame of the COMET center SCCH.

References

1. Balalaie, A., Heydarnoori, A., Jamshidi, P.: Migrating to cloud-native architectures using microservices: an experience report. In: Celesti, A., Leitner, P. (eds.) ESOCC Workshops 2015. CCIS, vol. 567, pp. 201–215. Springer, Cham (2016). doi:10.1007/978-3-319-33313-7_15

2. Calçado, P.: Building products at soundcloud–part III: Microservices in scala and finagle (2014). https://developers.soundcloud.com/blog/building-products-at-soundcloud-part-3-microservices-in-scala-and-finagle. Accessed 10 April 2017

3. Dehghani, Z.: Real world microservices - lessons from the frontline (2014). https://www.youtube.com/watch?v=hsoovFbpAoE. Accessed 10 April 2017

4. Di Francesco, P., Malavolta, I., Lago, P.: Research on architecting microservices: Trends, focus, and potential for industrial adoption. In: Proceedings of the 1st International Conference on Software Architecture (ICSA) (2017)

5. Giamas, A.: From monolith to microservices, zalando's journey (2016). http://www.infoq.com/news/2016/02/Monolith-Microservices-Zalando. Accessed 10 April 2017

6. Goldsmith, K.: Microservices @ spotify (2015). https://www.youtube.com/watch?v=7LGPeBgNFuU. Accessed 10 April 2017

7. Gray, J.: A conversation with werner vogels. ACM Queue **4**(4), 14–22 (2006)

8. Killalea, T.: The hidden dividends of microservices. Commun. ACM **59**(8), 42–45 (2016)

9. Lewis, J., Fowler, M.: Microservices - a definition of this new architectural term (2014). http://martinfowler.com/articles/microservices.html. Accessed 10 April 2017

10. Newman, S.: Building Microservices. O'Reilly Media Inc., Sebastopol (2015)

11. Singleton, A.: The economics of microservices. IEEE Cloud Comput. **3**(5), 16–20 (2016)

Author Index

Printed in the United States
By Bookmasters